NEW MUSICAL
ENTREPRENEURS

by Paul Brindley

INSTITUTE FOR PUBLIC POLICY RESEARCH

IPPR

INSTITUTE FOR PUBLIC POLICY RESEARCH

30-32 Southampton St
London WC2E 7RA
Tel: 0171 470 6100
Fax: 0171 470 6111
postmaster@ippr.org.uk
www.ippr.org.uk
Registered charity 800065

The Institute for Public Policy Research is an independent charity whose purpose is to contribute to public understanding of social, economic and political questions through research, discussion and publication. It was established in 1988 by leading figures in the academic, business and trade-union communities to provide an alternative to the free market think tanks.

IPPR's research agenda reflects the challenges facing Britain and Europe. Current programmes cover the areas of economic and industrial policy, Europe, governmental reform, human rights, defence, social policy, the environment and media issues.

Besides its programme of research and publication, IPPR also provides a forum for political and trade union leaders, academic experts and those from business, finance, government and the media, to meet and discuss issues of common concern.

Production & design by **EMPHASIS**
ISBN 1 86030 103 7
© IPPR 2000

Contents

Acknowledgements

I should like to extend my appreciation and thanks to all those people who willingly gave their time, and often hospitality, to be interviewed during the course of this project. Special thanks are due to Nanette Rigg, Andrea Westall, Stuart Worthington, David Lane, Marek Rymaszewski, Peter Scaping, Harry Leckstein, Gavin Robertson, Alison Wenham, Pete Jenner, Pete Fulwell, John Enser, Matthew Taylor and Jenny Ramkalawon.

IPPR is particularly grateful to British Music Rights, the British Phonographic Industry (BPI), Andersen Consulting and BT Internet and Multimedia Services who kindly funded the research.

About the author

Paul Brindley has been a research fellow at the Institute for Public Policy Research since 1996. He has written mainly on local government issues. Previous publications include *The Greater London Authority: Principles and Organisational Structure*, IPPR, 1997.

Paul has also been an active musician, playing bass guitar with The Sundays since 1988.

Preface

New technologies are exerting a profound influence at work, in the democratic process, in our private lives and, of course, in our leisure. Though there is clearly a sense of inevitability about technological development, society is far from powerless to help shape the changes. But public policy makers, as much as the industries themselves, must understand the full implications of change if we are to ensure that Britain is able to take full advantage of the opportunities afforded by new technologies.

The music industry makes an especially intriguing case study, due to the substantial impact of the new models of distribution facilitated by new technologies. The online trade in digital music impacts upon the means of purchasing music, the distribution of the product, the physical nature of the product and in turn the fundamental economics of the business. Opinion is sharply divided over whether the opportunities will outweigh the threats.

This report, based on seminars and a series of over 50 interviews with key industry players, attempts to make sense of current trends and examines the steps that the industry and public policy need to take to ensure that the UK continues its excellent track record in one of our key creative industries.

Together with a study on barriers to growth for small music companies (*Agenda for Growth*, IPPR, 1999), IPPR's work has already played an influential role in shaping government policy towards the music industry.

Matthew Taylor
Director, IPPR
January 2000

Executive summary

An awful lot of the speculation is a load of 30-something people trying to envisage what an audience that might be five or six might be doing when they are in their teens.
Danny Van Emden, Head of New Media, Virgin Group

The report argues that the new models of music distribution facilitated by new technologies can be divided into three categories:

- the *hybrid retail* model – physical product ordered electronically and delivered via mail order

- the *digital download* model – digital audio file, ordered and delivered electronically and stored by the end user

- the *on-demand streaming* model – digital audio stream delivered electronically at the request of the end user but with no permanent, stored copy – the same principle as video-on-demand

Each of these models is likely to become more significant at different stages along the route to a fully networked environment when music will be available through a multitude of different platforms and playback devices. The ultimate end game is the seamless delivery of music – anywhere, anytime and through any media. All three models offer the consumer considerable benefits over the traditional distribution models. These can be summarised as follows:

Three models

Hybrid retail model – benefits common to all online ordering

- products are easier to find and purchase – click and buy → increased choice

- ease of price comparison exerts downward pressure → lower costs

- the online shops never close → spontaneity of ordering is facilitated

- retailers establish better knowledge of consumers and their buying habits → direct 'permission' marketing facilitated → further choice

Digital download model – additional benefits

- manufacturing and distribution costs virtually eliminated → even lower costs

- no more dependency upon the vagaries of the post → immediacy of delivery

- assuming greater interoperability between playback devices (for example TV, radio, PC) → greater flexibility of use

On-demand streaming model – additional benefits

- no ownership of content → facilitates access to a wider range of music

- more permanent relationship with the consumer → encourages development of subscription models

- greater choice and new types of services → provides for possibilities for a variety of new intermediary services in adding value to consumers' listening patterns

It is argued that the hybrid retail model is likely to be the dominant new form of distribution in the short term, with the digital download model remaining mainly a promotional tool until the current inconveniences for consumers can be overcome. In the fully networked environment, the on-demand streaming model could prove more popular due to the flexibility of use it offers to the consumer and to its increased potential in controlling online piracy.

Above all other considerations, the most significant impact of the new distribution models is that they will change the fundamental economics of the music industry. The new models present opportunities to circumvent the current limitations of minimum production levels, consolidation amongst music distributors and retail shelf space. Far from devaluing intellectual property, they should help rectify the current market failures that prevent much of today's musical intellectual property from being able to find its true market value.

As for the piracy threat that has largely dominated the media debate so far, the report argues that the dangers should not obscure the opportunities which new technologies represent for the industry. Indeed, online distribution via open, interconnected networks such as the World Wide Web should prove far easier to monitor than illicit CD manufacturing in the offline environment. In reality, very little piracy occurs on the web itself, but is more common in private forms of communication such as e-mail and online chat groups. Despite the fact that it is likely to prove more difficult to contain the growth of copying through these communications, the report argues that rights owners and content creators should be able to continue to generate revenues from a range of new business models, often based upon access rather than copying.

However, a distinction must be made between existing content and previously unreleased material, since it is clear that little can be done to protect the existing supply of digital music. The music industry itself is already labeling existing CDs, 'legacy' CDs. With over 11 billion unencrypted, unprotected sources in circulation at present, the industry has decided to concentrate its efforts upon protecting the future supply. The recent increased availability of new recordable CD formats, such as CD-R and CD-RW, makes the task of controlling traditional hard carrier commercial piracy even more difficult.

The implications for content creators, service provider intermediaries, policy makers and government can be summarised as follows:

Top ten policy recommendations for the music industry

1   *Maximise competitiveness and create value added services and products*

In the new environment it is likely to prove far more difficult to control the importation of intangible products or services from service providers based in other territories. A danger for the UK is that the digital music economy could become dominated by foreign-based service providers undercutting UK prices. Maximising competitiveness and adding value to services and products is the only viable response. E-commerce is shifting seller-driven models of business to buyer-driven models. In the new environment what the consumer wants, the consumer gets.

2   *Test out new business models as soon as possible*

The sooner music companies make their existing material available for digital delivery in new secure formats, the easier it will be both to prevent the growth of an illegal pirate market and to familiarise consumers with what is currently a rather complex, awkward and time-consuming process. It is impossible to predict with any certainty which delivery models are going to prove most popular from the consumer's perspective, so a variety of strategies should be market-tested. Innovation, experimentation and flexibility will be crucial in the new environment.

3   *Collaborate to reach consensus on simplifying licensing processes and procedures for users and agreeing the commercial framework for new delivery models – and set up a one-stop online shop for all music licensing and rights clearance*

The industry must simplify and clarify licensing processes and procedures and reach consensus on the commercial framework for digital delivery for the benefit of all users – whether consumers or other intermediaries. This will necessitate a far greater level of collaboration between various industry bodies, particularly the collection societies, than has been the case in the past.

The industry's immediate priority should be to establish a one-stop online shop for licensing and rights clearance to simplify processes and educate users, which could link to or be part of a wider single access point for all copyright industries. A concerted consensual industry approach could prove a significant spur to the competitiveness of the UK digital music economy.

4   *Develop the technical infrastructure to ensure the secure delivery and monitoring of digital content*

The technical infrastructure required to ensure the secure delivery and monitoring of digital content includes the need for robust rights management systems, common standards for identifying and monitoring digital content, shared databases and total interoperability between delivery formats, playback devices, operating systems and metadata (data about data – to identify products and rights owners for payment and monitoring purposes). At the same time, *de facto* industry standards should not be abused by dominant players as a means of excluding access to new technologies for smaller companies and individuals, and ultimately consumers.

5   *Establish an adequately resourced single pan-industry body – Music.UK – to further intra-industry collaboration, present a more unified voice to government and the media and ensure a voice for the UK's micro-businesses and small companies.*

A new, modernised version of the current National Music Council with a more forward-looking name, such as Music.UK, should be created to fulfill both a representative and a unifying role on behalf of the UK music industry. This should benefit from some government funding to prevent domination by overseas-based interests and to ensure that the UK's small businesses and micro-businesses are adequately represented. However, it must also have the support of the larger companies.

This body should take the lead with government and provide a forum for achieving consensus on pan-industry issues such as e-commerce and new technology issues, copyright, education and training, lobbying for funding and co-ordinating links with UK music-related websites.

This will require a degree of reorganisation within the industry to avoid creating another layer of representative bureaucracy.

6   *Establish more permanent relationships with the consumer*

The current relationship between the content distributor and the consumer generally ends with the purchase of a piece of plastic. In the online environment, the ability to establish more direct, personalised and permanent relationships with the consumer will be more important, both from the content creator's perspective and that of the intermediary. Content distributors will have to learn how to manage this relationship, to encourage loyalty in the consumer base in order to be able to market-test new products and services more effectively.

7   *Recognise the importance of being a service provider*

All intermediaries between the content creators and the consumers must recognise that their role is increasingly becoming one of service provision. The ability to bundle services in new ways or to become specialised in the provision of very specific dedicated services will be highly valued in the new environment. Intermediaries have to look for new ways of adding value either by redefining roles, devising new services in the future supply chain or establishing strategic partnerships with other types of service provider.

8   *Learn new skills*

Finding new ways to add value to services will require the acquisition of new, transferable skills to understand the technological and commercial demands appropriate to the new environment (see MusicRight). Intermediaries must be able to respond more quickly in an increasingly competitive marketplace. The proliferation of strategic partnership deals between current internet-based music companies and other players is testament to the demand for flexibility and constant innovation across all sectors of the industry in the burgeoning online market.

9   *Develop more dynamic pricing models and establish a value-based Chart (that does not exclude CD singles with website links)*

Pricing is one of the most important and controversial issues for the future online trade in music. Too high pricing could lead to growth in the illegitimate supply of music. Too low pricing could drive down the value of music to a point at which the business of investing in future creativity becomes unsustainable. The industry will have to learn how to price its products and services more in accordance with the changing demands of consumers. This implies that consumers will have to be persuaded to move away from the concept that the value of music is associated with the physical product towards an understanding that the value lies in the content – the music and lyrics. Old pricing models should not necessarily be used as a benchmark for new models, as the new market is likely to be far more dynamic.

In view of the growing importance of interactive elements on CDs, the Chart Information Network (CIN) should immediately remove the exclusion of CD singles that link to other websites when played in a computer's CD-ROM drive. CIN should also move to a placement system based upon the value of overall sales to discourage heavy discounting (of singles) and to accommodate the new forms of delivery.

10   *Develop greater transparency, flexibility and a 'partnership' approach in the relationship with content creators*

The use of digital tagging technologies (which automatically track and report back on usage to rights owners) should empower content creators by enabling DIY business models. Internet users are becoming increasingly used to having direct access to artists. Together with the increased competition in service provision and the more direct, non-exclusive relationships facilitated by the new means of distribution, there is likely to be a commercial imperative for intermediaries to become more open, accountable and flexible in their relationship with content creators. It seems likely in the future that the convergence of previously distinct retail models will encourage intermediaries to develop a relationship with content creators based more upon partnership and the licensing of rights.

Top ten policy recommendations for the Government

1   *Implement a revised and balanced framework for copyright legislation as soon as possible whilst encouraging self-regulation initiatives such as Rightswatch – legislation must also ensure adequate protection against software tools or devices that circumvent or tamper with copy protection and rights management information systems or facilitate piracy*

Government must ensure that the legislative framework for the emerging digital music market is revised as soon as possible to maintain protection for rights owners and other intermediaries in the online environment. This will help create greater security and stability for emerging business models in the online trade in music. The default position whereby all copying should be subject to the authorisation of rights owners should therefore be maintained in the new environment. Provided online intermediaries cooperate with rights owners in ensuring the removal of unauthorised material from their networks and protecting rights owners' material against abuse, they should be afforded a degree of protection against liability themselves.

More immediately, the Government should encourage self-regulation initiatives (such as the Rightswatch hotline warning system proposal) to help contain the online piracy threat, reach consensus on the details of developing procedures for the resolution of liability disputes and educate consumers and users alike.

Legislation must also provide adequate protection against software tools or devices that enable users to circumvent or tamper with copy protection mechanisms and rights management information systems. These are crucial to ensure that content creators and rights owners are paid for the use of their content. Equally, rights owners need to be protected against devices that facilitate or encourage piracy.

2   *Use competition law and regulation to ensure a level playing-field in the digital music economy*

Government should do all it can to help maintain a level-playing field for current players and new market entrants in the digital music economy. Competition law and regulation must be used if necessary to remove bottlenecks, encourage interoperability and the use of open standards (and open access to those standards) and keep a watchful eye on the emergence of new gatekeepers, whilst ensuring that the new musical entrepreneurs are not driven overseas by over-restrictive regulation.

Government and the industry should ensure that the Office of Fair Trading (OFT) and Office of Telecommunication Regulation (OFTEL) take account of the particular pressure points for the music industry in their review of competition and associated regulatory principles in emerging e-commerce markets. Government and the industry should jointly commission further research into this complex area.

International co-operation will be required if regulation is to be effective.

3   *Remove the broadcasting statutory licence for all on-demand and near-on-demand services which are similar in nature and effect and allow performers to collect broadcasting and public performance revenues directly from the users (broadcasters)*

The broadcasting statutory licence was introduced at a time when broadcasting was considered a non-competitive, distinct form of distribution from retail sales. In the new environment, certain forms of interactive broadcasting – such as on-demand services (when the listener chooses what they wish to listen to) and near-on-demand services (heavily-themed, genre-specific content) are likely to compete with and prove substitutional for retail sales. The statutory licence could provide users (broadcasters) with a potentially unfair advantage in the distribution of copyright owners' content. The UK should therefore withdraw the licence for those services that are likely to compete with traditional sales, to enable rights owners to exercise greater control over the pricing and distribution of their work.

In view of the fact that income from public performance and broadcasting is likely to become increasingly significant in the new environment and in the interest of bringing the UK into line with the rest of Europe, the Government should allow UK performers to collect revenues directly from the user.

4   *Encourage flat-rate internet access tariff packages*

A recent Government report on e-commerce recommended that 'telecommunications operators should be encouraged to offer a wider range of tariff structure options'. (PIU, 1999) The Government should go a step further and ensure the development of flat-rate internet access tariffs. Flat-rate tariffs are widely cited as the single most effective spur to encouraging e-commerce. The psychological effect of knowing that the meter is ticking will constitute a particular financial disincentive for entertainment-based e-commerce services in the long term.

5   *Ensure a rapid roll out of broadband access*

Online music-based services, like all other entertainment-based bandwidth intensive services, cannot develop until the current technological restrictions are overcome. The upgrading of BT's local network with ADSL (Asymmetric Digital Subscriber Loop) currently offers a viable solution. Whether regulation or competition provides the better means, the end for the Government should remain the same – to ensure the rollout of broadband access as soon as possible.

6   *Develop low-cost e-commerce transaction mechanisms*

New business models for the digital delivery of music will require the development of payment systems that permit low-cost transactions. It is not surprising that under 18 year olds are responsible for such a significant amount of online piracy, as they generally have less money and no access to legitimate payment systems such as credit cards. Both the Government and industry should therefore seek to encourage the development of systems that particularly facilitate low-cost transactions and which can be accessed by people of all ages.

7   *Use new technologies to help children learn about the value of copyright and include copyright theft as part of an 'education for information' programme within the citizenship curriculum – using more accessible language such as 'creative rights' rather than 'intellectual property rights'.*

The industry should be encouraged by government to create CD-ROM packages and software tools (in collaboration with other copyright-based creative industries) to be made available to every school in the country so that children can learn about the value of copyright through a creative interaction with the internet and music-based websites (by creating their own websites and e-zines). Respect for the value of copyright is more appropriately learned not taught, in a positive, active environment, not as a negative passive message.

In the information society, there is a need to equip children with the necessary skills to translate information into knowledge that empowers them to act (for example, information about health, education and issues of governance). 'Education for information' should therefore be included within the national citizenship curriculum. Within this framework children can learn about all issues of information management, such as copyright theft, privacy and confidentiality.

In order to maximise accessibility and understanding, it would be useful to employ less alienating language, for example referring to 'creative rights' rather than 'intellectual property rights' or even 'copyright'.

8   *Widen access to new technologies in music education and encourage the development of schemes that allow musicians to collaborate with other musicians via the internet or other networks*

Government should encourage the music industry to help develop educational packages that will widen access to creative music education in schools. Interactive CD-ROM packages and software tools are now so inexpensive and user-friendly that it should be possible to set a target for each child in the country to have the opportunity to create their own piece of music without any previous musical knowledge as part of the standard music education.

Government should also encourage the development of schemes that allow musicians to make use of new technologies to collaborate with other musicians via the internet or other networks. Government should encourage the music industry, via one of the new recommended bodies or the Musicians Union (which has a strong regional structure), to promote the concept and ensure local authorities, arts, cultural and community bodies are aware of where to bid for and how to access funding.

9   *Work with the relevant industry organisations to help establish an online resource site for music content creators – ArtistRight – and to help coordinate the provision of a comprehensive online music industry resource for all parts of the industry – MusicRight*

Given the expected proliferation in new services targeted at unsigned artists, government should encourage the relevant recording artists, composers and songwriters' trade associations, local music development organisations and Metier to work together to develop a single online national resource site for music content creators – ArtistRight. The site could provide unsigned writers and artists with basic information about the importance of rights and contractual issues in both the online and offline environment and help establish a code of conduct for the new internet-based service-providing companies, possibly in co-operation with TrustUK.

ArtistRight could link to, or form part of, a wider online music industry resource portal – MusicRight – in cooperation with other industry bodies. This initiative would provide online training and business advice services, link up musicians with other musicians and service providers, disseminate and provide links to all information on European, national and local government grants and schemes, signpost on to online or local expertise when necessary and act as a focal point for pooling together disparate industry support initiatives.

10 *Investigate barriers to take-up and nature of usage of Information and Communication Technologies (ICTs), such as web presence, for music-related micro-businesses and SMEs and encourage a better interaction between the music industry and the Regional Development Agencies (RDAs) and the new Small Business Service in order to ensure UK companies are capable of taking full advantage of the digital future*

Given the lack of current information and the likely importance of a web presence and online strategy for all music companies, the Government should commission a national survey of ICT take-up and usage by music-related SMEs and micro-businesses. This would reveal whether or not ICT take-up and usage is a problem, the nature of regional disparities and indicate the potential for developing strategies to increase take-up rates or improve the skills base, if necessary. Much of this support will take place at the regional and local levels, so it is important that the Government encourages a better interaction between the music industry and the new Regional Development Agencies (RDAs) (particularly through the new regional cultural consortiums) and the Small Business Service.

Introduction and overview

A change to a new type of music is something to beware of as a hazard of all our fortunes. For the modes of music are never distributed without unsettling of the most fundamental political and social conventions.

Plato – The Republic[1]

Music is a valuable cultural artifact with universal appeal, a powerful social force and a tool in the battle against social exclusion as well as a significant economic product and source of employment. Besides the industry's estimated £3.2 billion contribution to the domestic economy, it plays a significant role in contributing to the definition of national, local and group identities, and generates unquantifiable indirect employment in a host of related sectors such as tourism, broadcasting, advertising and new media.

But of most importance for the purposes of this study, music is a key content providing industry for the multimedia information society that is widely recognised to be of critical importance to future economic growth.

The global music industry is undergoing a period of transition, potentially more significant than any since the invention of the first wax cylinder sound recording device. New technologies are hitherto bringing unimagined possibilities for the ordering, delivery and consumption of music undermining the industry's traditional business models.

Traditionally the UK has been rightfully proud of the success of the musical entrepreneurs who have driven the industry – both the creative talent behind the music and the business entrepreneurs who have invested in that talent. But past success is no guarantee of future performance. The net overseas export figures for UK-based record companies have shown a significant decline over recent years. Despite many favourable conditions, Britain currently lags some way behind the US in the digital music economy with its higher levels of internet usage, larger online consumer base, higher levels of investment in internet-based music companies, updated copyright legislation and its position as the *de facto* base for the world's largest music companies.

Britain has previously woken up too late and found its traditional manufacturing base eaten away by more innovative foreign competition. The same should not be allowed to happen to one of its key creative industries. The aim should be to establish UK.com as the creative hub for the new musical entrepreneurs of the digital music economy.

If the sector is to maintain its success, the content creators (on whom the entire industry depends) and the vast array of individuals, micro, small and large companies who service the content creators and music consumers worldwide, require a better appreciation of their needs and demands within government. Crucially, intellectual property must be valued and treated with the same respect as physical property. Ownership of ideas is a prime asset or commodity of the knowledge-driven economy.

Encouragingly, the British music industry has received greater interest from the current government than at any time in the past. In 1997 the Government set up the Music Industry Forum think tank of leading industry figures, which provides a formal channel of communication with the industry, and the Creative Industries Task Force – a similar body representing a range of creative industries including music. But the sector has remained largely unstudied from a national policy perspective.

Research carried out at IPPR on barriers to growth for small businesses in the music industry revealed a number of key areas for further policy development (Westall and Cowling, 1999). But whilst the report noted a need to bring often overlooked issues to the attention of policy makers, it was also apparent that an overriding concern of all parts of the industry was to understand the implications arising from the impact of new technologies.

The fundamental dilemma lies in anticipating the impact of new distribution models that as yet are massively underdeveloped, with little proven track record for either technical or commercial viability. At the same time, the future financial expectations of new internet-based music companies are so high that the total market capitalisation of the new companies at over $100 billion already far exceeds the estimated total value of the entire global music industry at $40 billion.

This project builds upon IPPR's analysis and attempts to map out a possible evolutionary route, highlighting the major policy implications for both government and the industry. The primary focus of the research was on the market for recordings of musical works. Between May and September 1999, the research involved a policy seminar and a series of more than 50 interviews with key industry players and representatives from related sectors which addressed the following issues:

- the current state of the British music industry and the dynamics for growth within the sector

- the impact of new digital delivery systems for music upon the structure and business models of the industry

- how intellectual property rights and revenue streams will be affected by new patterns of production, distribution and consumption in music

- public policy responses to encourage, protect and reward innovation and enterprise within the digital music economy

Chapter 1 briefly outlines the current structure of the music industry, giving an overview of its value to the UK economy and the elements of the current value chain for recordings of musical works. Observations are made about the extent of industry consolidation that currently restricts access and growth within the music market for smaller music companies, and the four traditional delivery models for music are outlined. **Chapter 2** discusses the technologies driving the forces of change – digitisation, audio file compression technologies, telecommunications and the growth of the internet and digital broadcasting. It then outlines three new categories of delivery models facilitated by these technologies. In **Chapter 3**, the benefits and barriers to growth of these models are discussed from the consumer's perspective, by considering how each model becomes more significant at three different stages along the route towards a fully networked, converged world.

Chapter 4 considers the piracy threat and the technological solutions required to ensure an adequate rights management infrastructure for the new distribution models. **Chapter 5** then considers the nature of current business models before outlining the implications of increased competition for the new supply chain, for government in maintaining open access to the supply chain and for intermediaries and content creators. **Chapter 6** observes the legislative framework in more detail, focusing upon the impact of e-commerce and the new delivery models on copyright legislation. Finally, **Chapter 7** outlines further policy responses for both government and the industry, concentrating upon the importance of education, the issue of industry representation and the attitude and understanding of the music industry within government.

At the end of the report there is an appendix of music-related websites which have been chosen to give a snapshot of internet-based music activity at the end of 1999.

1. The music industry @ 1999

The major companies need to show that they are mounting a massive marketing campaign in order to convince the programmers at radio that a single is likely to do well and in order to reassure the retailers that it is worth their while stocking the product. The money from the large corporations is therefore a key driving force in the judgement of some of the most important current filters.

Pete Jenner, Artist Manager

Value of the UK music industry

The phrases 'music/record business', and 'music/record industry' are convenient shorthand terms for a whole series of individuals and companies with differing interests, united only by the fact that their ability to make a living depends upon music. Only within the last six years has there been any serious attempt to provide a detailed economic analysis of the music industry; calculating the overall value of the industry to the UK economy remains a complex task.

The two previous reports measuring the value of the domestic music market and the UK music industry's contribution to foreign earnings were recently updated in a combined survey organised by the National Music Council (NMC), an umbrella body representing all the constituent elements of the UK music industry (NMC, 1999). The report calculates the music industry's direct economic contribution to the UK economy as being £3.2 billion. It confirms the music industry's status as the UK's third highest gross export earner after whisky and Formula One (with net overseas earnings of £519 million in 1997-98), providing the equivalent of over 130,000 full-time jobs.

However, it is important to note that these statistics are likely to have under-represented the true figures. The report's authors were forced to exclude certain parts of the music economy, particularly small clubs and elements of the dance scene that proved too difficult to quantify accurately.

The UK music industry is rightly proud of the success of its domestic writers, recording artists and companies in overseas markets. UK-based acts have a world market share of the recorded music market of around 10-15 per cent, second only to the US, whilst the domestic industry generates an estimated £1.3 billion annually from overseas sales (NMC, 1999). But there is no room for complacency. When compared to previous statistics, the latest survey shows a general decline in the UK music industry's net overseas earnings from the relatively high figure of 1995. This is illustrated in Table 1.1.

Table 1.1 Net overseas earnings in UK music industry

Overseas earnings	1995	1996	1997	1998
UK-based record companies' net invisible earnings (£ millions)	317.7	280.0	262.5	207.7

Source: *A Sound Performance* National Music Council and KPMG, 1999

The decline in figures is due in part to the strength of sterling, but it also reflects the increasing competitiveness of indigenous repertoire in overseas markets over the last five years and a global trend towards flat CD sales. The message is clear – the continued success of the UK music industry's content creators and companies in overseas markets should not be taken for granted.

Structure of the UK music industry

The music industry has evolved a highly complex, fragmented series of organisations and agencies derived from the commercial exploitation of writers' and performers' rights.

Rights are vested by copyright law in the authors of original works (composers and lyricists), and the producers of the sound recording of the work (generally the record company). This confers upon the rights owners the ability to authorise and prohibit certain restricted acts, such as reproduction, distribution, public performance, broadcasting and adaptation.

In functional terms, the traditional value chain for the supply of music recordings from creator to consumer is summarised in Figure 1.1.

The most significant commercial exploiters are therefore the record companies and music publishers who agree commercial contracts directly with the content creators – the recording artists and the

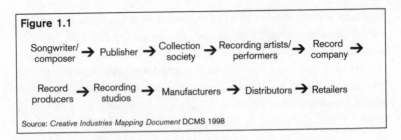

Figure 1.1

Songwriter/composer → Publisher → Collection society → Recording artists/performers → Record company →

Record producers → Recording studios → Manufacturers → Distributors → Retailers

Source: *Creative Industries Mapping Document* DCMS 1998

composers/lyricists respectively. Though record companies may contain both a recording and a publishing division, the two functions tend to operate currently as distinct units.

The key functions for a record company are: artist and repertoire (A&R) who find and develop talent, marketing and promotion, the production of the recording and the manufacture of the product.[2] Smaller record companies are more likely to outsource production, manufacturing and distribution and very often promotion.

Five global music companies – Universal Music Group, Sony, Warner Music Group, Bertelsmann Music Group (BMG) and EMI, dominate the market in recorded music. Together they account for nearly 75 per cent of the domestic recorded music market and 80 per cent of the global market. EMI is the only one of the five that is currently British-owned and has been the subject of much takeover speculation. One further takeover of a multinational could leave nearly half of global record sales in the hands of two major companies.[3]

However, one of the particular features of the British recorded music market is the success of its fertile, so-called 'independent' sector'.[4] These companies are renowned for nurturing much of the more innovative domestic talent upon which the entire industry thrives. In the 1990s, 40 per cent of all new British artists who achieved gold status in the UK (selling 100,000 albums) were recording with British independent companies. Together they employ approximately the same numbers as the big five music companies.

Industry consolidation

The broader growth concerns for smaller music companies are dealt with in another IPPR report (Westall and Cowling, 1999). But it is important to understand the significance of the main structural barrier to growth for smaller music companies in the market for recordings of musical works – consolidation. Consolidation arises from both the market dominance of larger music companies and from within the retail end of the supply chain.

The larger companies are able to derive significant competitive advantages from the following factors:

- extensive marketing and promotion budgets

- superior distribution channels

- increased bargaining strength with retail outlets

- ability to sustain higher investment losses due to possession of profitable back catalogues

- better access to foreign markets and foreign catalogues

The mass market has been driven by ever-soaring marketing costs and heavy discounting of stock, particularly singles, which have increasingly been used as promotional tools for the more profitable album format. The top selling 40 albums over the year account for almost one quarter of all domestic album sales (BPI, 1999). This is common to most territories in the world. In the US, out of 32,000 new records released in 1998, only 250 sold more than 10,000 copies.[5] Recent statistics for 1999 from the Chart Information Network (CIN) for UK singles and album chart entries revealed the lowest number of new releases debuting on the Top 75 since 1990.

But the most critical barrier to growth for small record companies lies in distribution and retail. Larger companies are able to negotiate more favourable terms with both distributors, who are probably owned by them, and the most important retail outlets who, even though they may be owned by the larger companies, tend to operate at arm's length.

Retail stores such as Woolworths and HMV exert a powerful influence upon Chart placings, with a total retail share of approximately 40 per cent of the domestic market. Since Woolworths only stock about nine out of the 150-200 new releases each week, their buyers' decisions hold the key to Top 20 Chart success for most records. In the album market the situation has become even more of a concern now that the large supermarket chains have entered the

---

The Charts

The future of national Charts in an increasingly international market place is uncertain. But, however they evolve, the Charts will have to be adapted to reflect the realities of the new environment. An obvious first move would be for the Chart Information Network (CIN) to remove the current exclusion of CD singles which, when played in the CD drive of a computer, can link to other websites.

For the Charts to discourage heavy discounting to influence chart position and to accommodate all forms of online sales in addition to traditional sales (at least in the UK), a more sensible solution is to base positions upon the total value of sales rather than the number of units sold.

---

market. The leading supermarkets have already established a double figures market share within two years, often stocking limited material. (See Table 1.2)

The global nature of the larger companies also enables them to access foreign markets and foreign catalogues more easily and sustain higher investment losses due to their possession of extensive and often profitable back catalogues. Some critics also allege that their global internal accounting and pricing systems enable them to shelter profits from taxation.

Consolidation is, of course, a matter of competition. Government and regulatory authorities should only be expected to intervene to prevent anti-competitive practices and to investigate concerns over concentration of ownership. But the impact of new technologies is such that there is now a widespread belief that the new distribution channels and the changing economics of distribution and retail should provide smaller companies and individuals with greater opportunities to bypass such industry consolidation. Indeed, both the larger and smaller companies should be able to expand the music market by offering more choice to more consumers.

But before examining the nature of change in the distribution channels, it is first necessary to outline the traditional delivery models.

Traditional delivery models

Traditionally, there have been two basic models by which music is delivered to the consumer (for audio only or as part of an audio-visual package): 'retail' (buying) and 'public performance' (listening).

Table 1.2 Source of UK purchases

Albums	1996	1997	1998
HMV	14%	19%	19%
Woolworths	18%	17%	18%
Our Price	13%	11%	10%
Virgin	8%	8%	9%
WH Smith	12%	9%	9%
Other record shops	9%	9%	8%
Asda	–	5%	7%
Record clubs	6%	5%	4%
Tesco	–	2%	4%
MVC	1%	2%	3%
John Menzies	3%	3%	2%
Mail order	4%	3%	2%
Andys Records	2%	2%	2%
Sainsbury	–	1%	1%
Market Stall	2%	1%	1%
Boots	2%	2%	1%
Safeway	–	–	1%
Other supermarkets	6%	1%	1%

Singles			
Woolworths	23%	25%	23%
HMV	16%	18%	21%
Our Price	15%	15%	13%
Virgin	8%	8%	11%
WH Smith	11%	9%	8%
Other record shops	11%	9%	7%
Asda	–	6%	6%
Andys Records	2%	2%	2%
John Menzies	3%	2%	2%
MVC	1%	1%	2%
Mail order	3%	1%	2%
Other supermarkets	5%	2%	2%
Market stall	2%	1%	1%

Source: BPI Statistical Handbook, 1999, from BPI music buyers' survey 1997-1999.

However, these can each be broken down into two sub-sets: 'retail' including both the 'high-street retail' model and the 'mail-order retail' model; and 'public performance' including the 'public performance of recorded works' model as well as the pure 'live performance' model.

High-street retail

The high-street retail model involves the manufacturing and distribution of a physical product (sound carrier) which is sold to the consumer through a high-street retail outlet. This model has operated since sound recordings were first mass-produced on shellac in the early part of the 20th century.

The model therefore generally requires the consumer to be active in that the consumer must seek out the product themselves from a variety of retail outlets. The vast majority of music is purchased as sound carriers from retail stores (see Table 1.2).

Mail-order retail

The mail-order retail model encompasses a range of ordering models including mail-order companies such as Readers Digest, record club membership (for example Britannia), newspaper offers, on pack promotions, and the internet. But delivery of the product is always through the post. The BPI music-buying survey revealed that 14 per cent of respondents had acquired music through the post in 1998. Interestingly, only 0.5 per cent bought music via the internet.

The most prevalent model is the record club, by which members subscribe to receive a certain minimum number of deliveries on a regular basis from a limited number of titles. The same survey revealed that six per cent of respondents were members of record clubs in 1998 with the highest membership amongst those aged 30-39 years, an important demographic group for increasing overall music sales and a key target market for e-commerce operations.

Public performance (recorded works)

The 'public performance (recorded works)' model encompasses an extensive range of delivery models, including radio, television, jukeboxes, restaurants, shops, hotels, pubs and clubs. The performance in public of recordings of musical works requires payment by the user to both the author of the composition and the owner of the recording. The raison d'être for these payments is that the recording is providing an economic benefit to the user (for example, music in a supermarket contributes to increasing sales).

This model involves neither physical product nor a distinct nor easily identifiable economic value, at least from the consumer's perspective. The value of the music is either covered by advertising revenues (the commercial radio model), bundled within a subscription to a package of broadcasting services (the public broadcasting licence, cable or digital TV package) or covered by a public performance licence (shops, restaurants, hotels and other public places). Such omnipresence of music has tended to obscure the real value, as consumers are tempted to believe that such music is 'free', if no direct economic transaction is involved.

Public performance (live model)

This is the simplest and most persistent model of all. Before technologies facilitated the mass production of recorded music, a live performance was the only way by which music could be delivered to the consumer.

Observations about the models

Generally speaking, these four categories have remained technologically distinct forms of delivery. The technological means of delivery is therefore the critical element in distinguishing between the old distribution models – a distinction that breaks down in the new environment.

Broadcasting and public performance revenues have become increasingly significant revenue streams for rights owners over recent years and most observers expect this trend to accelerate even more with the proliferation of new channels of communication in the future.

It is also instructive to note that under these models the economic value of sound carriers has largely become associated with the quality of the physical product. Record companies tend to charge a little more for compact discs than analogue cassettes or vinyl records since the sound quality is judged to be superior. It is therefore useful to consider the sound carrier in terms of its functional use, which is to fulfill the consumer's wish to buy the ability to listen to the music as and when they wish. In effect the consumer is purchasing a personal license to listen to the music in perpetuity, subject to the legal requirements (however unenforceable) which prevent the subsequent copying of the music.

The formats of sound carriers have been limited by record companies in order to continue the traditional model of offering the consumer two standardised choices which can be monitored through the weekly Charts – a single (with additional bonus tracks), and a full-length album version containing up to approximately 70 minutes of music. The same 70-minute limit in the case of CDs has recently been agreed for DVD-Audio (Digital Versatile Disc), an enhanced capacity optical disc format, in order to maintain similar delivery models. DVD would otherwise be able to contain over 700 minutes of CD-quality music on one disc.

These therefore are the characteristics of the current and past market for distributing music. In the next Chapter, we shall consider briefly the technologies that are driving changes in the distribution models, before setting out three broad categories for future delivery models facilitated by the new environment.

2. Good technologies

Either you're on the steamroller, or you're part of the road.
Stewart Brand on the digital economy *Feed Magazine*
October 1995

There can be few other industries run by people with less knowledge of how to operate even a computer.
Tony Wilson, Partner, music33.com

The key driver of change in the digital economy is technological convergence – the process by which previously distinct information delivery systems appear seamless from the end user's perspective. But it is necessary to appreciate the importance of the technologies that provide the motor for convergence. The process begins with digitisation, the technology that enables all information to assume the same format. Then we consider the technologies that facilitate the new digital distribution models – audio file compression, the internet and digital broadcasting, telecommunications and mobile telephony – before outlining three categories of delivery models facilitated by the new technologies.

Digitisation

Digitisation is most easily understood as the process of converting all information – text, audio, graphics and film – into a language that is understood by computers. Though the initial impact of digitisation was in the creation of music with the music samplers of the early 1980s, digitisation also dramatically improved the quality of the sound recording in both the recording process and in the reproductions from the master recording (though vinyl enthusiasts may disagree). Indeed, digital music arrived at a significant time for the global music industry, which was facing stagnating sales of vinyl records towards the end of the 1970s. Digital recordings could be reproduced any number of times without suffering any noticeable deterioration in sound quality. They become 'clones' rather than copies of the original master recording. This caused considerable initial concern within the industry, but has not surfaced as a major issue until relatively recently due to the fact that the principal digital sound carrier format, the CD, has for so long been used as a non-recordable audio format.[6]

The fact that music could be stored as digital information in a computer seemed of little commercial consequence initially when an average CD would still have occupied the entire memory of most computers and when digital broadcasting was still an aspiration. But developments in new audio file compression technologies, digital broadcasting and telecommunications technologies now mean that CD-quality music can be digitally delivered to the consumer through wires or the airwaves, obviating the need for any physical sound carrier. The rapid growth of the internet and the World Wide Web makes it increasingly easy for consumers to find music files, legitimate or illegitimate, simply by tapping in the name of the artist into search engines.

MPEG7

A new audio file standard, MPEG 7, is currently being developed that builds in more sophisticated monitoring and searching capabilities. All digital content (music and video) can be found through voice recognition technologies (for example, by simply humming part of a melody or remembering some of the lyrics of a song). This search technique should make MPEG7 the all-knowing salesperson with the ability for consumers to find the desired content on the basis of minimal information. Furthermore, it provides a powerful tool against unauthorised use, since the standard will automatically track each time a digital file is broadcast or sold.

Audio file compression

The most popular audio file compression technology, MP3, (Motion Picture Expert Group-1/Level 3) arose from an intergovernmental attempt to establish standards for interactive television. It has been seized upon by musicians, websites and hardware manufacturers as the burgeoning new form of distribution of music. MP3 utilises a compression technology whose fundamental benefit is the ability to reduce the capacity of required storage space to contain the necessary digital information without unduly affecting the quality of the sound. As an open standard the code is freely available for anyone to 'encode' music in the format. A BMI (Broadcast Music Incorporated – a US performing right society) study in March 1999, found that MP3 files account for a third of all audio files used on the web.[7] Some web watchers, like searchterms.com, cite MP3 as the most searched for term on the web, even more popular than sex.

The internet, digital broadcasting, telecommunications and convergence

The internet has become the fastest growing communications medium of all time. Its most impressive boast is the fact that it only took four years for the internet to reach 50 million users whereas television took thirteen and radio took eight. There are currently over 200 million users worldwide and Nua internet surveys expects that number to surpass 250 million by 2002 – with the vast majority of users in the US and Europe.

But the internet and the World Wide Web are only part of a trend towards global interconnected networks. The rapid growth of digital interactive television, combined with a highly competitive telecommunications market resulting from the deregulation of the 1980s, now offers the possibility for a wider range of options for the delivery of music, since new platforms can also deliver CD-quality music and video-on-demand to the end user. Though currently restricted by technological restraints, the television is seen by many observers as one of the most important future distribution platforms for all digital content.

However, the ultimate effect of convergence is to blur the distinctions between current delivery platforms. Consumers will soon be able to access digital content over a wide range of networks and through a variety of different consumer electronic devices. As bandwidth (the information capacity of networks) becomes less of a barrier and mobile telephony becomes nearly ubiquitous, music, like all other digital information, will be available anywhere, anytime and through any platform – PC, television, mobile phone, hi-fi, car stereo or even games consoles.[8]

The launch of UMTS (Universal Mobile Telecommunication Systems) in 2002 will radically alter the information-processing capacities of today's mobile phones. UMTS, part of the so-called third generation (3G) mobile phone technologies, will deliver pictures, graphics, video communications and other wide-band information as well as voice and data.[9]

In the fully-networked environment, the medium of delivery should appear seamless to the end user. Provided technology companies and the consumer electronics industries cooperate on interoperability, by utilising hard carrier formats such as CDs, DVDs, Super Audio CD and chip-based storage cards, music could then be compatible for playback by any number of different devices.[10] The digital mobile phones and palm top computers can themselves operate as digital players.[11]

The new delivery models

The technologies outlined above create the possibility for a whole variety of new forms of ordering, delivery and consumption of music. But it is helpful to outline three different categories of models, each of which currently exists and which together provide a useful guide to future delivery systems:

- the *hybrid retail* model – physical product ordered electronically and delivered via mail order

- the *digital download* model – digital audio file, ordered and delivered electronically and stored by the end user

- the *on-demand streaming* model – digital audio delivered online at the request of the end user but with no permanent, stored copy – the same principle as video-on-demand

Under the hybrid retail model, only the purchasing takes place electronically. The delivery and consumption both follow traditional patterns from the offline environment, since a physical sound carrier format, normally the CD, is delivered via the post, as in the current mail-order model, and played back on any optical disc player.

In the digital download model, the digital audio file is sent via cables or through the airwaves, downloaded and stored on the user's PC hard drive (set-top box or other device or storage card) to be played back through proprietary software players such as RealPlayer or Winamp. The players can be downloaded free of charge via the internet with the option of upgrading to higher capacity, more sophisticated players for a relatively small fee.[12] The model therefore involves both online purchasing and delivery. Though there is no visible product, the file is still 'owned' by the consumer in that a permanent copy is retained by the end user.

In the on-demand streaming model, the entire process – purchasing, delivery and consumption – takes place online. So-called 'streaming' technology means that audio files can be transmitted in small packages and played in real time by the same software players without the need to make or retain a permanent copy. This is the principal behind internet radio or webcasting, mimicking broadcast.

Internet/web radio

Some of the biggest names on the internet have recently been setting up or buying into internet/web radio services. Yahoo! have launched Yahoo! Radio, delivering 10 channels of genre-specific music with links to the artists through Yahoo!Music, a database of 50,000 performers and 125,000 albums. Programming is provided by Spinner.com which itself delivers more than 120 channels of audio. Yahoo!Radio has also bought Broadcast.com which distributes 410 radio stations and networks.

Lycos launched its Lycos Radio Network service in April 1999 with real disc jockeys to which it has since added 30 genre-specific music channels from Digital Music Express.

Spinner Networks, parent company of Spinner.com was itself acquired by AOL (America Online) in June, along with Nullsoft Inc, developer of the most popular MP3 downloading software, Winamp.

MTV, through its interactive division, MTVi, acquired Imagine Radio early in 1999 to signal its move into the new arena.

The US leads the world in internet radio services since most users do not have to pay for local telephone calls and/or internet provision.

'On-demand' streaming is different from webcasting (which is effectively radio via the internet) as it is an interactive process, enabling the consumer to choose the music they want to hear or access. It is in some ways a DIY radio service – the principle behind a remote digital jukebox for which the consumer pays a subscription for conditional access, or pays per play, like video-on-demand. Ownership is completely removed from the process, as the consumer retains no permanent copy. Access now becomes the key mode of control, not copying. There are

---

Radio Moi

Radio Moi is one of the few truly interactive radio stations on the internet. Based in Montreal, Radio Moi allows the listener to choose the music they wish to listen to or the option of pre-programmed music shows. The service also provides the listener with the opportunity to purchase the music. Radio Moi is the first interactive internet radio station to agree a licensing agreement with the Recording Industry Association of America (RIAA).

See www.radiomoi.com

already some significant key players emerging within the streaming media world, such as Microsoft, RealNetworks and Quicktime.

Crucially, all three of the above models give the consumer the potential to access a wider range of content than is the case under the traditional delivery models. All three models are also competing for the same consumers, highlighting the fact that there is less distinction between the technological means of delivery in the new environment.

Though all three forms of delivery are already facilitated by current technologies, the nature of technological change will begin to highlight the relative advantages of the different models at different stages. The next Chapter considers how technological progress will shape the three key stages in relation to the delivery models outlined above. The process is viewed from the consumer's perspective outlining the potential benefits and barriers to growth.

3. Three steps to consumer heaven? benefits and barriers to growth

When we live with the luxury of choice, we tend to delegate that choice to someone else, because the luxury becomes a burden after a time.
Jim Griffin, Director of internet music consultancy, OneHouse, and advocate of the on-demand streaming model[13]

The number one reason why a record is not sold is because the consumer didn't know it was available.
David Pakman, Senior Vice President Business Development, myplay.com[14]

The internet is the most radical global development this side of the printing press.
Marc Geiger, CEO, ArtistDirect[15]

In an age when the online world becomes increasingly important in shaping the relationship between business and the consumer, few dispute that new models will be led above all by the demands of the consumer. This is the lesson of the popularity of MP3 files. This time, the consumers have reached the technology before the multinational music corporations.

The wider process of customer adaptation to the new delivery systems will most likely lead to a pluralistic scenario with many different business models operating concurrently, fulfilling particular demands from the variety of segments of the music market. But the three models outlined previously prove helpful in mapping out a possible evolutionary route.

Stage one: the hybrid retail era

Stage one has already begun and can be characterised by the dominance of the hybrid retail sale as the principle form of delivery facilitated by new technologies. Industry analysts predict that this will continue to be the dominant online distribution model for a number of years. Both Jupiter Communications and MTI (Market Tracking International) estimate that digital downloading will only reach one per cent of the overall US sound carrier market by 2003 whereas hybrid retail sales are predicted to account for 13 per cent (according to Jupiter) and 12.5 per cent (according to MTI) of the overall US market.

Both the digital download and on-demand streaming models are currently severely limited by inconvenience of use for consumers due mainly to restrictions in bandwidth (the information capacity of networks) and a lack of interoperability between playback devices.

Notwithstanding the fact that downloading is currently tied to multimedia PCs, even with a 56K modem it can currently take up to three hours to download an average length CD album. US college sites with T-1 cable modem connections can download MP3 files of individual tracks in as little as ten seconds, but there is still a problem of storage even with higher capacity hard drives.

For those consumers who manage to negotiate successfully the downloading process, the current lack of interoperability between playback devices severely limits playback options. Recordings are only replayable on PCs or new portable players (such as the Rio player), as opposed to the hi-fi hardware consumers are more used to using. If users wish to make recordings in formats compatible to their existing and familiar hardware, they then need to buy and learn how to use new software and hardware (for example, CD Creator software and CD-R).

The same barriers also prohibit the immediate growth of on-demand streaming which is more likely to become a mainstream activity in the fully networked environment.

However, the hybrid retail model should help inspire greater consumer confidence in e-commerce generally, allowing consumers to familiarise themselves with the transaction process and accessing music in new ways. Even with this model, which is after all only a slight variant on the traditional retail mail-order model, new technologies should increase considerably the diversity of content and distribution channels for both consumers and content providers.

The hybrid retail model already offers consumers the added value common to all forms of electronic ordering (including both the digital download and the on-demand streaming models) arising from the fact that in the online world:

- products are easier to find and purchase – click and buy ➔ increased choice

- ease of price comparison exerts downward pressure ➔ lower costs

- the online shops never close ➔ spontaneity of ordering is facilitated

- retailers establish better knowledge of consumers and their buying habits ➔ direct 'permission' marketing facilitated ➔ further choice

Search engines make it increasingly easy for consumers to link up to e-commerce sites. Consumers can either go to an online retailer and type in the name of the band or they can simply search the web. Online retailers, like Amazon, use a string of vast warehouses of products, books and CDs in particular, to supply the local consumer from a wider range than would be possible from the traditional high-street store. By storing music on a server and 'burning' (or manufacturing) CDs on-demand, the concept of storage as a limitation to choice for the supplier becomes outmoded. This facilitates not only a greater diversity of overall content for the consumer, but also allows consumers to create their own customised CDs.[16]

Aside from the generic concerns of purchasing over an open network such as the internet (which are considered later in the Chapter), the transaction process in the hybrid sale is much more straightforward currently than a digital download – just click and buy.

Consumers are already benefiting from decreased costs as prices are driven down by a greater ease of comparison through price search engines (for example www.bestbuy.com.). Even senior industry figures are willing to admit publicly that the global reach of the internet will exert a general downward trend in prices.

> *I suspect that the internet is going to have the effect of levelling global prices. I suspect that within five years our prices, everyone's prices, will be within ten per cent either way of American prices...I suspect that this global levelling of prices is a natural process in any event.*
>
> Martin Mills, Chairman, Beggar's Banquet.[17]

The 24 hour-a-day online ordering option will clearly facilitate greater spontaneous purchasing opportunities for consumers, not just via the internet. So-called lean back technologies, such as the TV, (as opposed to lean forward technologies like the PC) make it increasingly easy for consumers to find the kind of products and services they desire without having to seek out the products actively. But as all media platforms become interactive, the consumer will be able to make purchases at any time and from any place.

New purchasing platforms – car and television

StarCD

A US mobile phone service called *CD already offers consumers the ability to purchase CDs of songs heard on the radio. The listener keys in the frequency of the radio station and the service uses sound recognition technology to link the song to music in its own database (see www.starcd.com).

RadioSat

A forthcoming innovation is IRC's (Interactive Radio Corporation) RadioSat. This is a satellite-based interactive radio service that allows consumers to order CDs heard in the car through a touch-screen. It is expected to launch in 2001 (see www.radiosat.com).

Open

A new interactive television shopping mall service, called Open, operated by British Interactive Broadcasting currently offers viewers the opportunity to order the Top 10 UK singles and albums via the television set through a mail order facility fulfilled by Woolworths. Open plan to extend this facility to a wider selection of titles soon.

Provided they comply with data protection and privacy legislation, with the consent of the purchaser, online music retailers are able to track an individual's consumption patterns (see RealNetworks below). By making use of detailed marketing databases, the content distributor is able to inform purchasers about other content in which they might be interested – *if you like that, why not try this*. This is the concept labeled 'permission' marketing by marketing guru, Seth Godin, Vice-President, Direct Marketing at Yahoo! (Godin, 1999). Online retailers can then further tailor their service through customised home pages built around the individual consumer's tastes.

Stage one, with the online trade dominated by hybrid sales, therefore offers consumers the benefits associated with most forms of online purchasing. The shopping experience familiarises consumers with electronic transactions, becoming more personalised, easier to navigate

---

RealNetworks

Two lawsuits were filed in the US in late 1999 against RealNetworks, the leading supplier of PC-based MP3 players, for its collection of information from users of its RealJukebox music management software without the users' consent. RealNetworks admitted using RealJukebox to collect data on users' listening habits and other personal information without seeking permission. However, they claimed that the data was only used to measure aggregate use of the software, not to track use by specific individuals and pledged to stop collecting the data until the company could provide clear consent mechanisms.

Clearly, the ability to track the users' listening habits (with the user's permission) would provide invaluable marketing information to content suppliers.

---

and with more choice compared to the physical store. The imperative for companies employing the hybrid retail model is to invest in increasing the speed of delivery to the consumer to be able to compete with digital downloading or on-demand streaming.

None of this seems great news for traditional high-street retailers. However, most analysts' reports and industry experts agree that current online retailing should facilitate incremental sales amongst music purchasers who are constrained by time or who simply feel alienated by the current retailing experience in bricks and mortar stores. Retail studies frequently reveal that whilst 80 per cent of bricks and mortar retail sales are chart product compared to 20 per cent from back catalogue, the percentages are reversed in the online environment. This indicates a strong element of incremental sales as the physical limits of shelf space prevent bricks and mortar shops from being able to stock too much back catalogue. It is also potentially good news for specialist and niche music companies whose content particularly suffers from this problem.

The extent to which traditional high-street sales may be cannibalised by these new forms of ordering music is a contentious issue. But new technologies will also enable them to compete with new market entrants, not simply with their own online services, but also through developments such as digital kiosks where the manufacturing of the CD takes place within the store itself.

Stage two: digital downloading – make or break?

Stage two makes certain assumptions – that broadband access levels have increased dramatically, piracy and rights management issues have largely been resolved and interoperability in playback devices is more commonplace. This stage should be only a few years away. At this point, the digital download model could offer three main additional benefits to the consumer:

● manufacturing and distribution costs virtually eliminated → even lower costs

● no more dependency upon the vagaries of the post → immediacy of delivery

● interoperability between playback devices (for example TV, radio, PC) → greater flexibility of use

The cost equation from the consumer's perspective is simple in that since manufacturing and distribution costs are virtually eliminated in digital distribution, the intangible product must be considerably cheaper. The question is, by how much? Some argue that the initial costs involved in setting up reliable online distribution systems and providing adequate levels of technical consumer support could remove much of the potential for savings. There is no simple calculation since the recording and marketing budgets can vary so much, but other informed estimates suggest the saving could be as much as a third of all costs. In any case, the digital download model (and the on-demand streaming model) should ultimately prove considerably cheaper than either traditional retail or the hybrid retail model. Webnoize editor, Ric Dube, recently predicted that the average price paid for a commercial downloadable song would be 57 cents in 2002 (Dube, 1999).

Given sufficient bandwidth capacity on networks and faster internet access, digital delivery should eventually be almost instantaneous. Once again this is much more attractive than the hybrid retail model since the online shop could now deliver immediately 24 hours a day, adding far more value to the spontaneous purchasing experience.

The digital download model is potentially more flexible than a hard carrier format in terms of consumption since a wider variety of both delivery and playback options are facilitated. These include time-out expirations (the file only plays a certain number of times before it switches itself off), super-distribution (the file can be distributed by the consumer to their friends who then have to pay to open it) and pay-per-play (incorporating the ability to reduce the price according to the number of plays). The possibilities for the rules governing access to the file are endless.

Most PC-based software audio file players such as RealPlayer or Winamp also facilitate the creation of customised playlists that can be created at the click of a mouse rather than having to wait for real-time recording.[18] These playlists can then be moved onto portable players or recorded upon optical disc players such as CD-R and CD-RW.

The growth in popularity of compilation albums and customised CDs in the UK and the rest of Europe, where the consumer selects a number of tracks from various sources to make up an album, indicates that this could prove a popular way of enhancing listening patterns. Multi-artist compilation albums have grown in popularity over recent years rising from 15.1 per cent of the UK market in 1989 to 26.5 per cent in 1997 (BPI, 1999). Consumer research from industry analysts Forrester indicates that multi-artist compilations would be the most popular option for MP3-formatted music (Hardie, 1999). Furthermore, surveys of listening habits indicate that most consumers only listen to a limited number of tracks on individual albums. Most CD players are not well suited to such listening patterns, as the user must normally change the CD in order to listen to tracks from another album.

Digital downloading particularly facilitates track-by-track purchasing, as it is much easier for distributors to allow consumers to cherry-pick from tracks stored on a server. The current prohibitive download times for album-length CDs may also mean that consumers get more used to the convenience of ordering on a track-by-track basis.

Digital downloading will be most beneficial to consumers provided they can be persuaded to get used to the idea of maintaining a digital jukebox of music which can be topped up by both hard carriers such as CDs and digital audio files, which could then be used to create instant playlists. Currently most software players enable users to 'extract' the digital music from the carrier to convert it into a digital audio file – a process known as 'ripping'. This technology facilitates piracy, since users can extract the content from any existing CDs any number of times. But it is also a helpful feature in order to grow the digital download market. Without the ability to convert CDs into digital audio files, consumers would lose the option to mix and match in creating new playlists from their CD and digital audio file collections.

Stage two and the digital download model therefore offers the consumer the same benefits associated with all online purchasing together with the additional benefits of even lower costs, immediacy of delivery and greater flexibility in use. It encourages the consumer to become accustomed to the idea of music as an intangible object – though a continued demand for tactile or associated products could be met either through accompanying graphics, printed lyrics or links to websites.

However, due to the current technological barriers, digital downloading may remain primarily a promotional tool in the short term. This begs the question as to whether digital downloading will eventually be widely adopted or if it might prove to be a staging post along the way to other delivery models.

Myplay.com

Myplay offers a service to relieve the pressures of storage space on PC hard drives. Users upload their digital music onto myplay's lockers which then enables the user to access their music collection from any place. Once internet tariffs move to flat-rate models, this could prove a popular way for people who are frequently on the move to retain permanent access to their music collection, without it having to occupy physical or even localised hard drive space. Myplay are building in further music-related services, products and links.

See www.myplay.com

Stage three: on-demand streaming model

This stage could be defined as the point at which the majority of consumers are able to access digital content anytime, anywhere and through any medium. The timing depends upon a number of different factors, but the question is no longer whether but when.

On-demand streaming can be characterised as a model based upon accessing rather than owning content. It is the most flexible of all the models as it could be used in a number of different ways, but it would particularly facilitate the following additional benefits:

- no ownership of content → facilitates access to a wider range of music

- more permanent relationship with the consumer → encourages development of subscription models

- greater choice and new types of services → provides for

possibilities for a variety of new intermediary services in adding
value to consumers' listening patterns

As consumers become more familiar with interactive technologies and
prices are driven down through increased competition, the highest value
for consumers could become the ability to hear music as and when they
want to.

This would enable consumers the possibility of accessing a far wider
selection of music or particular forms of content that could be paid for
in many different ways. Subscription is likely to be one of the most
popular options as consumers are already familiar with this concept in
audio-visual services. The subscription model could apply to individual
artists, record labels, musical genres, new releases, or even all recorded
music.

The on-demand streaming model could then open up a whole new
range of ways of adding value to listening patterns.

Online music services could be developed to offer innovative ways of
classifying music to make suggestions for playlists, or to offer tailor-
made packages of music from a wider selection of music. These could
either be combined with the downloading model by scanning the user's
existing files or through knowledge of the user's previous listening
habits. On-demand streaming music services are likely to prove a
popular alternative to radio or compilation CDs for consumers wishing
to purchase customised playlists designed for particular occasions.

The first stage in the process is interactive internet radio stations
that enable the user to begin to tailor the output according to their
specific tastes (see Radio Moi, page 17). But these should develop
further so that the unsophisticated time-poor music user of the future
could simply dial up trendymusic.com for a one-play only selection of
music to impress their dinner guests.

This kind of service encourages a much more permanent relationship
between the service provider and the consumer as the consumer comes
back to the same internet site or service provider each time they want to
hear the music. This encourages both loyalty and a sense of community
– highly desirable factors in the online trading environment.

Jim Griffen, of the internet consultancy OneHouse, sees this as the
key benefit of the on-demand streaming model. He views any kind of
physical medium, whether it be a CD or digital audio file in music or the

video tape for films and television, as a kind of 'buffer' between the supplier and the consumer, preventing a more direct relationship. Drawing an analogy with new Personal Television Devices (such as TiVO and Replay TV) which filter multiple channels to deliver viewing customised to individual viewing tastes, he believes the same demands will be made by consumers for the consumption of music – just-in-time delivery of content in a customised form.

Before offering some concluding thoughts as to which of these three models may prove dominant in the future, it is first necessary to consider the current and potential future barriers to growth.

Barriers to growth

The barriers to growth for the new delivery models in the electronic trade in music can be summarised under the following headings:

- Trust and security

- Access – Information and Communication Technologies (ICTs) take up and payment systems

- Cost

- Inconvenience

- Lack of interoperability

- Sound quality

Trust and Security

Surveys consistently reveal that the most significant concerns for consumers in all e-commerce transactions are trust and security. A Gallop survey of UK consumers in May 1999 revealed that only seven per cent of respondents felt secure in submitting credit card details over the internet. In the EU generally, Visa found in 1999 that only five per cent of consumers trusted e-commerce (PIU, 1999). Businesses, particularly SMEs, also express the same concerns about internet security.

The Performance and Innovation Unit (PIU) report produced a number of recommendations to help inspire greater confidence in e-commerce generally, including the development of PKI (Public Key

Infrastructure) standards, e-commerce hallmarks and smartcards. All of the report's recommendations have been accepted by the Government and there are encouraging signs that consumer confidence is growing. The establishment of the industry-led body, TrustUK, to create an e-hallmark for websites to guarantee standards of consumer protection is an important measure in attempting to encourage best practice from online service providers and instil greater confidence in consumers. However, the Government will have to promote trust and confidence in e-commerce far more actively if it is to achieve its stated aim of making the UK the best environment in the world for e-commerce by 2002.

Access – Information and Communication Technologies (ICTs) take up and payment mechanisms

The purchase of a multimedia PC is the most significant current financial barrier in engaging in e-commerce for most domestic users and even some SMEs. As for domestic users, the Office of Fair Trading (OFT) and the DTI are looking into the price of PCs as part of their enquiry into 'rip-off' Britain. The PIU report concludes that the e-Minister and e-envoy (the leading Minister and civil servant charged with promoting and coordinating e-commerce initiatives across government) will have key roles in encouraging initiatives to remove access barriers for particular groups, such as the elderly, the less well educated and lower socio-economic groups. Certainly, the Government has an important role to play in facilitating access to computers and the internet for excluded groups, not simply as a way of growing internet use and e-commerce but also in order to encourage greater democratic participation. However, PC prices are decreasing dramatically, to such an extent that some companies in the US are giving away computers for free in return for obligatory on-screen advertising.

The announcement of more than £1 billion of public money to boost community access to the internet, through community-based IT learning centres, the provision of computers for the least well-off families and tax incentives to invest in IT training is a welcome initiative.

More specifically, whether or not access to computers and use of information and communication technologies (ICTs) is a particular barrier to growth for music companies is difficult to say, as there is a lack of statistical information from which to base opinions. Certainly there is a general concern about the under capitalisation of small music companies which may affect their ability to embrace the new technologies to position themselves in the emerging digital music economy (Westall and Cowling, 1999). The Department for Culture, Media and Sport (DCMS) are currently investigating ways of improving access to finance for small music companies.

The most comprehensive UK study of the commercial take-up of ICTs throughout British industry, undertaken by Spectrum on behalf of the Department of Trade and Industry (DTI), indicates that the UK's small and micro-businesses (under 100 employees) lagged well behind the other benchmarked G7 countries. The study found that US businesses are almost three times as likely to have a website as their UK counterparts (Spectrum, 1999). It also revealed a strong regional variation with London, unsurprisingly, the most advanced region in the UK.

The only study undertaken so far of ICT take-up in the UK music industry was carried out in 1999 by the Liverpool Institute for the Performing Arts (Fulwell, 1999). Its principal conclusion was that 'there is a surprisingly high level of web presence but the quality of design is generally poor and the level of innovation and strategic use is low.' The report therefore advised that better training and business advice were required to improve the local skills base. The report also notes an increasing imperative for small music companies to have access to web space just as much as the physical work space. Schemes which help subsidise or provide space for small music companies should therefore be encouraged, particularly those which aggregate music content, companies or services (see www.liverpoolmusic.com).

In view of the increasing importance of factors such as web presence, it would be helpful to have more accurate information from a national survey, broadly based around music-related SMEs and micro-businesses. This could provide the Government with an indication of ICT take-up and usage in music-related companies, reveal the nature of regional disparities and indicate the potential for developing strategies to increase take-up rates and improve the skills base. This should either be linked to a more general survey of ICT take up and usage in the creative industries or form part of a wider survey of barriers to growth for music industry companies.

Key drivers in stimulating ICT take up should be the new Regional Development Agencies (RDAs) at the regional level and the Small Business Service at the local level. The Secretary of State for Trade and

Industry has already written to the Chairs of the RDAs, tasking them with developing regional targets for ICT take up. It is therefore important for the music industry (and other creative industries) to ensure that it links effectively into such bodies to ensure that the sector is not overlooked in the process of developing and implementing regional and local support strategies. The Government should help encourage this interaction which would be most effectively achieved through the new regional cultural consortiums. Anecdotal evidence from IPPR research suggests that even where there is a strong regional creative industry presence, there is often little reflection of the potential and value of the creative industries within the RDA's overall thinking.

The Government should also ensure that the needs of the music industry and other creative industries in accessing new technologies (particularly e-commerce) to grow their businesses are taken into account in the development of the new Small Business Service. There is a tendency for current policy to concentrate rather more upon the needs of traditional manufacturing and high-tech industries (see Westall and Cowling, 1999).

Payment systems

Another aspect of access which is of particular importance to e-commerce for the music industry is the need to develop payment systems that permit low-cost transactions, and which are accessible to all ages. These would help facilitate the development of a greater range of business models. Most importantly, e-cash or electronic purses would enable those without credit cards (including all under-18 year olds) to familiarise themselves with paying for content, rather than seeking out unauthorised 'free' material. One reason why so many of the younger generation are dealing in unauthorised MP3 files is that, in most cases, even if the authorised material were available, they would still be unable to make purchases without a credit card. The Government and the industry should therefore seek to encourage the development of systems which particularly facilitate low-cost transactions and which can be accessed by people of all ages.

Cost

The current lack of flat-rate tariffs is a clear financial disincentive to both the development and take-up of online entertainment-based services.

Consumers are unlikely to want to spend hours downloading entire albums and internet/web radio services cannot hope to compete with leading US-based providers whilst UK users are forced to pay an additional tariff for listening.

In the words of the PIU e-commerce report, 'the ability to access high quality electronic content at reasonable cost is a prerequisite to the UK competing effectively with its international rivals in e-commerce.' (PIU, 1999).

In the UK almost all home internet access is through metered local telephone calls to an Internet Service Provider.[19] Subscription-free ISPs in the UK, such as Freeserve, have proven particularly successful in increasing access to the internet. With this in mind, the PIU recommended that 'telecommunications operators should be encouraged to offer a wider range of tariff structure options.' (PIU, 1999) This may be a sensible short-term solution but the psychological effect of knowing that the meter is ticking will constitute a particular financial disincentive for entertainment-based e-commerce services in the long term. In the UK the average connection time to the internet is 17 minutes per day, almost a quarter of that in the US.[20] Provided subscription-free ISPs are given time to adapt their business models, the Government should go further and encourage the development of flat-rate internet access tariffs.

It is worth noting that new broadband services such as those currently being rolled out in mainland Europe by companies like Chello Broadband and @home are likely to encourage a move to flat-rate tariffs as this is the model offered by their permanently connected cable modem service (see www.chello.com and www.home.net).

Inconvenience

The restricted capacity (bandwidth) of current delivery networks is the major technological barrier that needs to be overcome in order to grow the new market. The telephone network is the most accessible delivery system and BT is currently rolling out ADSL (Asymmetrical Digital Subscriber Loop), an upgrade of the existing telecommunications network that allows multiple use of one telecom line. This is currently a viable option for delivering high-speed internet access to most users within a relatively short time span.

OFTEL, the Trade and Industry Select Committee and the PIU have all expressed doubts about the merits of allowing BT to roll out DSL technologies without any effective competition. OFTEL therefore recently announced its intention to open up BT's local loop monopoly to competition. Meanwhile, organisations such as the Campaign for Unmetered Telecommunications, (CUT), believe regulation would be more effective than competition in ensuring both a rapid roll out of ADSL and in encouraging flat-rate internet tariff packages. CUT point to the US where there is no competition in the local loop, but where flat-rate tariffs are available in almost 95 per cent of the country. Whether regulation or competition provides the better means, the end for the Government should remain the same – to ensure the roll out of broadband access as soon as possible.[21]

It is, however, worth noting that other broadband connections, such as cable modems, enable users to send as well as receive larger quantities of data such as live video, encouraging self-publishing as well as consumption. This is the model being adopted in Helsinki under the Arena 2000 project that is set to make the city the most wired (and unwired) city in the world.[22]

Another important aspect of inconvenience for current users is the consumer's attitude to new technologies. Consumers need to be persuaded that the technologies and devices are user-friendly and easy to operate. Developments in areas such as voice recognition technologies should go a long way to help make delivery systems and processes far easier to use in the future.

Lack of interoperability

In order for the digital music market to grow, there must be interoperability between both delivery formats and playback devices. The danger is that *de facto* standards could be used by new dominant players as a means of excluding smaller players from the new supply chain. The industry is currently attempting to agree standards for interoperability (and security) through the Secure Digital Music Initiative (SDMI) intra-industry forum.[23]

Government should monitor progress to encourage the powerful economic players to keep interoperability at the top of the agenda whilst ensuring fair and open access to any *de facto* industry standards. Regulation would have to be considered should standards be used anti-competitively or as a barrier to trade for smaller companies and individuals.

Sound quality

A final concern, again particularly for digital downloading, is the sound quality of compressed audio files compared to optical disc formats. One of the features of digital delivery systems is that, unlike almost all previous technological developments in sound carrier formats, there is currently no added value in sound quality. Despite the ambitious claims of enthusiasts, the current sound quality of MP3 audio files is more accurately described as near-CD rather than CD quality.

However, technology is improving all the time and given the pace of change, sound quality can be expected to improve in the near future. It therefore remains unclear to what extent sound quality will prove a significant barrier to growth for the digital download model.[24] Digitally downloaded files could be constantly upgraded to improved sound quality formats as part of the purchasing options, but the on-demand streaming model may offer a more attractive option since the upgrading could happen automatically.

> *Today's compression schemes have impressively delivered near-CD quality sound. The problem is that onerous downloads are the reality for mainstream consumers accessing the internet over dial-up connections. For households with only one phone line, this is especially unrealistic. A new file format that doubles or triples the compression and subsequently cuts the download time while maintaining the sound fidelity may well obviate the demand for MP3 simply because it is far more practical. While the idea of achieving near CD-quality sound with better sound compression is highly appealing, attaining CD-quality sound is the Holy Grail, particularly from a marketing perspective.*
>
> Mark Mooradian, Jupiter Communications, quoted in an
> article for CNET News 25/3/99

Conclusion

The greatest difficulty in predicting future consumer demand is anticipating cultural and social trends. The degree to which consumers are wedded to the idea of music as a physical product with its accompanying packaging and sense of ownership remains a topic of much heated debate within the industry. This is a particular concern for the on-demand streaming model, and a partial concern for the digital download model.

The qualities which today's older consumers frequently associate with music – the anticipation of buying a record, the tactile nature of handling it for the first time, the sense of ownership as it becomes part of the collection – could well become anathema to the music fans of the future. On the other hand, for some MP3 fans, the amount of music they possess, more than the content, is often more important as a source of pride.

Either way, it seems likely that the physical manifestation of ownership, such as displaying CDs on shelves, could become less relevant to children who are used to storing PC software and computer games within the device itself. Furthermore, if music is more readily available at cheaper prices and marketed as an ephemeral fashion-led product, then the issue of ownership could become less important for consumers.

Certainly there is a noticeable trend towards a faster, more individualistic culture of immediate gratification of the kind which could be most appropriately serviced by the on-demand streaming model that enables consumers to move quickly from one product to the next. Like music television (such as MTV), streaming models can continually bombard consumers with customised content through the permanent nature of the relationship.

Whichever models prove more dominant, it seems likely that a number of different models will exist concurrently to serve the particular demands of individual segments within a more fragmented marketplace, attracting new consumers and offering increased choice.

Finally, it is worth noting that even those who have set up businesses to distribute music online are unclear as to how internet music distribution will actually develop. As Matt Wishnow of insound.com has concluded 'We don't yet know whether many people will want to purchase whole downloadable albums.' (Wishnow, 1999).

One element which we have not so far considered but which could influence the development of the new distribution models is the topic that has dominated the media debate about new technologies so far – piracy. In the next Chapter we look at the nature of the piracy threat and the technological solutions necessary to ensure growth in online delivery models.

4. Piracy and technological solutions

There has been such hysteria about piracy because people are failing to face up to the real issues.

Tony Wilson, Partner, music33.com

Piracy is a cost of doing business. Students may want to swap vast quantities of files but most consumers won't.

A music industry lawyer

The piracy threat of the new environment may have dominated the headlines over the last couple of years, but the digital genie has been out of the bottle for far longer. There are over 11 billion unprotected hard carrier sources in circulation at present – in the form of CDs. For every CD currently in circulation contains unencrypted, unprotected digital music that can be extracted or copied and converted into computer sound files or recorded onto another disc, allowing perfect 'cloned' copies of the original sound recording. Indeed, the music industry is already labeling existing CDs, 'legacy' CDs, since they have accepted the reality that little can be done to prevent home copying of the current content. Combined with the ever-expanding reach and anonymity of the online environment, some observers have therefore been tempted to talk in apocalyptic terms about the inability of rights owners to control distribution and monitor use of their content in the future.

But it should not be forgotten that the piracy threat still comes mainly from the offline environment where the economic effects are likely to prove far more damaging for the foreseeable future. The International Federation of Phonographic Industries (IFPI), the international trade association for record companies, estimates that one in three CDs currently in circulation in the world are illegal copies. According to the IFPI, global sales of pirate CDs rose by 18 per cent in 1998 to 400 million units. There are now over 20 territories in the world where over 50 per cent of the market is supplied by illegal sources. The problem has been exacerbated by the excess manufacturing capacity of CD plants, particularly in Asia and eastern Europe. Pressure should therefore continue to be exerted upon countries to adopt a rigorous approach to piracy, particularly those countries seeking membership of the European Union.

The recent increase in sales of CD-Rs (recordable CDs) in western Europe, particularly in France, Germany and Holland, is seen as one of the main reasons for a decline in the legitimate market. In France, where CD-R piracy forms about 12 per cent of the market, the music industry has launched a high-profile educational campaign with the campaign slogan 'It's Not Cool to Burn'. Meanwhile consumer research in Germany estimates that over half of all CD-Rs sold are used for the unauthorised copying of music – 30 million out of a total of an estimated 60 million CD-Rs in 1999.[25] In the US, the number of illegal counterfeit and pirate CD-Rs seized in raids in the first half of 1999 rose 552 per cent on the figures for 1998.[26]

Though CD-R market penetration is currently limited in the UK, with players now retailing under £400 and discs costing only £2 each, a greater impact can be expected over the next few years.[27]

CD-RWs, a rewritable version of CD-R, which allows for multiple recordings, just like a cassette, present a further challenge, particularly as CD-RW drives are now offered as standard features of some multimedia PC packages.

The industry's only hope to contain the piracy threat from these technologies is to be able to set universal standards that will imprint identity codes into each of the copies made from a single machine (the Recording Identifier Device). But this will only enable rights owners to trace the origin of large quantities of copies made from the same machine, and would be unlikely to discourage home copying.

The problem is not helped by the fact that companies who are also rights owners are manufacturing devices which clearly facilitate home copying, and are promoting them in ways that could be deemed to be encouraging copying (for example Sony minidisk). Therefore, containing widescale commercial piracy in CD-R and CD-RWs is the most that rights owners are likely to be able to achieve.

New technologies exacerbate the hard carrier piracy threat through their ability to enhance storage capacity and facilitate distribution. Compression techniques, such as MP3, enable vast quantities of music to be stored on a single CD.[28] The BPI anti-piracy unit has noted a recent rise in the presence of such digital audio file CDs, particularly at computer fairs. Once digital audio file players become more commonplace, this problem is likely to worsen. Also, the internet presents more opportunities for commercial pirates to distribute their material through new avenues such as online auction sites. However, it is encouraging that under pressure from copyright owners, one of the leading online auction companies, e-bay, has recently banned CD-R sales from its site, unless the seller is also the copyright owner.

On the other hand, online piracy is described, even by the International Federation of Phonographic Industries (IFPI), as manageable.[29] In fact very little piracy occurs on the World Wide Web itself. According to results from a recent Webnoize survey, just 2.9 per cent of US College students use the web as their main source of MP3 files.[30]

One reason why the web is not a common source for pirated music is the ability of the industry to monitor use of illegal material through new technologies, such as 'bots'. Bots, like the E-Z seeker developed by the American Society of Composers, Authors and Publishers (ASCAP), are spider-like computer programs that scan the web's hyper-linked network for illegal MP3 files. Technology therefore facilitates the ability of rights owners as well as casual pirates to seek out unauthorised material.

Computer-literate users, like the US college students, prefer the internet's other means of data transfer for the distribution of their MP3 files: e-mail, File Transfer Protocol (FTP) archives and ICQ or similar online chat platforms. These essentially private forms of communication constitute a long-term threat to the music industry in that they represent the digital age's more sophisticated version of home taping. The online pirate no longer needs a factory of copying machines, but has the ability to distribute limitless amounts of unauthorised content at the click of a button and for a minimal cost. The introduction of technical measures to restrict the amount of copies from a single source will help to contain this threat, but the threat is exacerbated by the kind of sophisticated software and technology tools which are constantly being developed to facilitate the user's ability to find and 'share' MP3 files, such as Napster and Y2MP3 (see below). Rights owners face difficult legal battles controlling the spread of such popular tools but ultimately they must have a degree of protection against devices that clearly facilitate or encourage piracy, even when the device may have other legitimate purposes.

The challenge for the music industry is to develop more attractive authorised sources of content to persuade the majority of consumers not to be bothered seeking out cheaper, unauthorised alternatives.

Napster

Napster is a free Windows-based software application that enables the user to become part of a virtual MP3 swapping community. Whilst chatting online, the user is able to scan the hard drives of other users, in effect enabling all users to set themselves up as servers of mainly unauthorised material.

The Recording Industry Association of America (RIAA) is suing Napster for contributory copyright infringement by materially contributing to, and actively encouraging, copyright infringement.

Some US colleges complain that the popularity of MP3 file swapping is straining their computer networks. According to Northwestern University in Illinois, traffic to Napster's servers represents between 20 and 30 per cent of the school's total internet traffic.

See www.napster.com and www.riaa.com.

Y2MP3 Server

The Y2MP3 Jukebox is a storage and server unit for MP3 files that can be managed with a web interface by any number of users. The server enables large groups of people to listen to MP3s, and place requests and download files through the web interface. The device is being marketed primarily at US college dormitories and offices. For areas larger than an office, an optional low-power FM transmitter can be used to broadcast the unit's signal to radios.

The device is planned to launch in January 2000.

See www.y2brand.com.

See also www.swapstation.com and www.mediasharing.com

But in order to ensure the growth of a legitimate market in digital delivery systems, rights owners firstly need to be able to rely upon two key technological elements – protection systems and a rights management infrastructure. Both of which will need to be extremely flexible in order to deal with the variety of business models facilitated by the distribution models outlined in the previous chapter.

Protection systems

Various technological protection measures, many of which have yet to be invented or perfected, will be needed to protect online content from unauthorised access, transfer and use in the digital environment, but the most popular current methods are encryption and watermarking.

Encryption (or Secure Envelope Technologies) normally involves scrambling and descrambling the bitstream with keys. It is the strongest form of protection in that, without a key, users cannot access the contents of a file. Its advantages are that it affords a higher level of protection against unauthorised access and can be used flexibly to facilitate new distribution techniques such as super distribution (passing the file on to a friend who pays to open it). Its disadvantages are that the most effective encryption techniques tend to distort audio quality and that it relies heavily upon closed, compliant proprietary systems which could alienate users.

Watermarking places an inaudible audio signal into a sound file that permits its tracing back to the original purchaser. Its advantages over encryption are that it is more robust since the digital signature is harder to remove than encryption packages. Watermarking's main drawback is that it is harder to police since it can only be used as a mechanism for monitoring use as it does not by itself prevent access to content.

How effective these protection measures will be is a matter of considerable debate. Software experts are generally confident that any security system (particularly encryption) will be broken before it can even reach the market place. Certainly, breaking any industry approved security system will represent a particular badge of honour for hardcore computer hackers.

But again, such activities are likely to be confined to particular groups of users in private groups away from the mainstream World Wide Web. Continual research and development into upgrading protection systems (as has been the case with set-top box smartcards for television subscription services) should be able to prevent hackers from causing more permanent damage.

The main hopes of the music industry to set standards and encourage greater awareness of rights owners' concerns in the manufacture of software and hardware devices for the digital delivery and consumption of music is the Secure Digital Music Initiative.

Secure Digital Music Initiative (SDMI)

In some ways the SDMI represents the most constructive move in the larger music companies' newly found willingness to embrace new technologies. It provides a forum in which the various industries involved in the digital delivery of music can reach consensus and agree common standards. Announced in December 1998, participants include record companies and music rights owners, telecommunications companies, hardware and software manufacturers and technology companies.[31] The SDMI's mission is 'to enable consumers to conveniently access music in all forms, artists and recording companies to protect their intellectual property and technology and music companies to build successful businesses in their chosen areas.'[32] Part of the SDMI's remit therefore is to provide a stamp of approval for devices and systems that make use of approved protection technologies, such as encryption and watermarking.

The significance of the SDMI is that it serves a wider function by acting as an umbrella body to coordinate developments with software and hardware manufacturers and technology companies. Rights owners can therefore encourage greater interoperability between systems and agree mutually beneficial approaches to future technological developments, avoiding costly and lengthy legal battles. Certainly the SDMI provides a forum outside the courtroom in which to attempt to resolve such problems.

Doubts remain over the ability of the SDMI to meet its demanding timetable. Other criticism of the SDMI centres upon the fear that it may lead to the creation of new monopolies or cartels. Governments and regulatory bodies will have to monitor the SDMI process carefully to ensure that it does not lead to anti-competitive or monopolistic behaviour.

By persuading the major consumer electronics manufacturers to meet commonly agreed standards, the music industry eventually hopes to be able to encourage the manufacture of devices that encourage consumers to seek out only legitimate content. For example, the current industry strategy for digital downloading (formulated by the SDMI) is to convince consumers to upgrade to second generation portable audio file players that will only accept legitimate new content.[33] Informed sources suggest that rights owners aim to contain piracy by building in copy-protection mechanisms into all future digital content which will facilitate two copies for home use only, but prevent any further copying. Thus, consumers will effectively buy the right to keep three permanent copies of a single track or album.

This will present two important challenges for the music industry. Firstly, the industry has to be able to convince consumers that such usage restrictions are compatible with the potential flexibility of the digital download model outlined earlier. Secondly, the industry will have to prevent consumers topping up their digital content from other cheaper or 'free' sources, such as digital radio.

As for government, it must ensure that copyright legislation provides adequate protection to rights owners against software tools or devices that tamper with or circumvent technical protection measures (or rights management information systems). Many music industry insiders see this as the most crucial legislative concern in the battle against piracy.

Rights management and licensing infrastructure

The complexity of the task of constructing a backbone infrastructure to handle rights management in the distribution of music, multimedia and other digital content should not be underestimated. Though new technologies should theoretically make the new distribution processes far more efficient, the current infrastructure is far from developed and is still being developed very slowly. The problem appears to have been exacerbated by the fragmented nature of the industry and a lack of communication between sectors (and between companies within sectors). For years, the music industry has developed catalogue numbers unique to individual countries, reflecting the territorial basis of the industry. Furthermore, broadcasters, including the BBC, have developed monitoring systems independently, such that there has been no common interface between the systems. Meanwhile other industries, such as book publishing, have developed commonly agreed international standards such as the International Standard Book Number (ISBN). Only in recent years has there been any concerted attempt to co-ordinate the development of shared databases and commonly agreed tagging codes.

International Standards Initiatives

CISAC, the international authors' association has been working to implement a universal virtual database covering all recorded or registered works known as the Common Information System (CIS). This has been built upon by the work of the International Music Joint Venture (IMJV) between MCPS/PRS, (UK collection societies), ASCAP (US collection society), and Buma/Sterma (Dutch Collection Society) – an initiative which aims to reduce costs and improve efficiency in the maintenance of common databases and by sharing 'back-office' facilities. Almost 50 per cent of the world's music should now be registered in one place.

The European-funded IMPRIMATUR project has provided an umbrella for a whole series of projects and trials to develop and test framework models for intellectual property rights (IPR) management issues arising from electronic trading. A fundamental component of this is the development of universally recognised metadata (data about data) to facilitate the identification of digital objects in multimedia products, sometimes called digital tagging. The much-praised <indecs> project (Interoperability of Data in E-Commerce Systems) was set up with European funding under the INFO2000 programme for this reason.

See www.imprimatur.alcs.co.uk and www.indecs.org.

The industry must therefore simplify processes and procedures for all users – whether consumers or other intermediaries. This means establishing clear signposting and promotion of licensing procedures, streamlining back office operations and improving the interface between databases. This will necessitate a far greater level of collaboration between various industry bodies, particularly the collection societies, than has been the case in the past. This should be both a national and international process. Simplifying and clarifying rights management and licensing processes for all users could prove a significant spur to the competitiveness of the UK digital music economy.

The Creative Industries Task Force is currently investigating the possibility of helping create a single access point through which potential licensees for all copyright industries could find out where to get information about licences. This initiative should be encouraged as a means of both simplifying processes and educating potential users. Meanwhile the music industry should establish a one-stop online shop for licensing and rights clearance for music users for the same purposes. This could either link to or be part of the single access portal for all copyright industries.

Government should also ensure that projects that seek to provide the necessary backbone infrastructure for e-commerce and the growth of the information society continue to receive the necessary funding. The more government can help drive the speed of development and reduce bureaucracy, the better.

A more difficult question is to what extent government should intervene to create incentives to encourage the adoption of new tagging technologies by other users, such as broadcasters. It is widely recognised that the cost of moving to a system of fully digitally tagged music will require significant investment by service providers as well as rights owners. Though not necessarily a barrier to growth in itself, direct reporting may help spur the growth of new DIY business models, particularly for smaller companies and individuals. For example, digital tagging should make it possible for any individual to distribute and make material available for use by broadcasters and other distributors without the need for any intermediary, such as a record company or collection society. It is already possible to monitor directly usage of content over open networks, like the World Wide Web.[34] Innovations like MPEG7 may help simplify the challenge (see page 14).

But the Government is understandably reluctant to place too many regulatory restrictions upon new service providers in order to grow the market. At this stage government should monitor the take up of digital tagging technologies by new service providers and consider the introduction of financial incentives and timetables to speed take up only if the pace of adoption proves unduly slow. Government should also help drive standardisation in digital tagging and monitoring in systems, data and metadata.

Conclusion

Hard carrier piracy, (for example CD-Rs and CD-RWs) is likely to continue to pose the greatest commercial threat to the music industry for the foreseeable future. The only realistic response for the industry is therefore to attempt to contain the threat from the larger commercial pirate operations. Technical restrictions to restrict copying for future content are likely to prove the only effective deterrent.

Meanwhile, there are reasons to believe that the online piracy threat can be contained, just as with home taping in the 1970s. The Webnoize survey mentioned earlier also showed that the legal use of MP3 files among US college students increased eightfold to 13.5 per cent of all usage between December 1998 and April 1999, indicating that internet users would switch to downloading and paying for legitimate content once it became available.[35]

The fact that online piracy is currently described by the IFPI as manageable should not detract from its potential long-term threat. Clearly, widescale online piracy could harm the entire business of investing in creativity. However, the online threat could be more effectively contained by particular models of distribution. For, whilst there are still concerns over the industry's ability to control piracy via digital downloading, the on-demand streaming model and the growth of wireless delivery present less of a concern since no permanent copy is retained by the end user. Access should prove far easier to control than copying. It is therefore possible that the relatively greater ease by which piracy can be contained via on-demand streaming could help spur growth in this kind of delivery model.

Whatever happens, whilst piracy is unlikely ever to be defeated all together, it is also equally unlikely to prevent rights owners from finding new ways of generating revenue from legitimate business models. But in order to facilitate the development of adequate protection measures, both government and industry should help support the development of common standards and maintain a dialogue with broadcasters, software and hardware manufacturers and all other companies involved in the new delivery models. Collaboration, again, is key to developing a secure digital music economy.

Finally, it is worth noting a measure that is seen by some observers as the only way of providing compensation for rights owners for uncontrollable acts of piracy – the blank carrier levy.

Blank carrier levy

A blank carrier levy has been introduced in all European territories except the UK, Ireland and Luxembourg. Some, though by no means all, rights owners have lobbied for the introduction of such a levy in the UK. However, there are significant drawbacks. Above all, the introduction of a levy sends an implicit signal that unauthorised copying is being recognised and accepted as a legitimate activity. The levy could be interpreted as an informal copying licence. In Germany where there is a blank carrier levy, it is permitted to promote home taping (or copying) in advertisements for certain devices.

Furthermore, the levy is a blunt mechanism that can neither reimburse rights owners accurately nor recognise legitimate uses from the consumer's perspective. In the long term, the growth of access-based models, such as the on-demand streaming model, could make the entire case for a blank carrier levy redundant. In the meantime, it should be resisted in any case.

5. Brave new world: implications for government, intermediaries and content creators

Music publishers have a head start over record companies in the new environment as they have had to adapt their business models in the past and have been dealing with a weightless product for years.

Mark Isherwood, Consultant, Rightspro Ltd

We are not taking the stance that we know for certain what the business model of the future is. There will be a transition phase and there will be a few models out there and we don't claim to be able to anticipate their relative success. The pure digital file market is relatively untested other than examples of an illegal market.

Fergal Gara, New Media Director, EMI Records UK

The power of promotional platforms will be all important in the future.

James Roberts, Consultant, Informed Sources

Aside from a few leaders who manage to sell brand-name content widely and cheaply, the most promising businesses in the Net world will be services and processes. They will include selecting, classifying, rating, interpreting, and customizing content for specific customer needs.

Esther Dyson (1994)

In this Chapter we shall make some brief observations about current business models, before considering how the new models are likely to lead to far greater competition in the new supply chain. We shall then consider the implications for government in maintaining open access within the supply chain, before outlining how intermediaries and content creators should take advantage of the new opportunities.

Current business models

Currently, new music-related business models on the internet comprise mainly online hybrid sales retailers (such as Amazon and CDnow), independent record companies offering digital downloads (such as Atomic Pop and Rykodisc), Internet Radio services (such as spinner.com) and new service providers for unsigned bands (such as MP3.com or UK-based peoplesound.com). But all such internet-based services are establishing themselves as trusted intermediaries, generating traffic from music consumers with the ability to move into related areas of business or establish strategic partnerships when appropriate.

In terms of the supply of recorded music, it is the business models of the new intermediaries, like MP3.com and peoplesound, which are of most interest. The number of internet-based companies targeted at providing services for unsigned artists is proliferating in the US and is likely to grow rapidly in the UK too, presenting both potential benefits and pitfalls for content creators.[36]

The new business models stem from the twin forces that are driving change in the new supply chain – disintermediation and reintermediation. As we saw earlier, the impact of new digital distribution technologies on the traditional supply chain is to eradicate nearly all manufacturing and distribution costs. But the functional impact is to open up the distribution process to increased competition from a host of new service providers. Intermediaries therefore have to look for new ways of adding value in the chain – either through cutting out layers of middlemen (disintermediation) or redefining functional roles in new ways (reintermediation). This is a common feature of the impact of the internet. Airlines are able to sell tickets directly to customers, bypassing travel agents, whilst new entrants such as lastminute.com provide a new service by aggregating a variety of special offer late deals. In music, MP3.com and peoplesound are good examples of 'reintermediating' companies since they combine elements of both the traditional retail and record company functions, carrying out A&R, marketing and promotion as well as distribution and retail.

But even the most popular new entrants, such as MP3.com, still have to prove themselves profitable. The concern lies in whether such companies can sustain the current hype and financial interest and attract high quality content. Advertising accounted for 85 per cent of

---

Peoplesound.com

Artists send peoplesound their finished product and grant them a non-exclusive world-wide distribution licence for which peoplesound pay an initial fee of £100. Artists are then given a page on peoplesound's website, and are free to choose the price at which their content is sold from a given range. They are then entitled to 50 per cent of royalties on CD sales (subject to certain deductions) and a share of any compilation CDs sold. Much of the music is available free of charge, a point stressed in advertising for the site.

Peoplesound employ eight full-time A&R staff with a network of freelancers around the country. The portal went live in October 1999 with over 1,000 bands. In an interview for the project, founder Ernesto Schmitt described peoplesound as 'an interim record company'.

See www.peoplesound.com.

MP3.com's revenues for the first three months of 1999 and sales from compact discs only just topped $100,000 in the same quarter, from a roster of over 25,000 artists.[37]

As the authors of a recent City University Business School report into the international music industry concluded, traditional record companies will be exposed to far greater competition from all sides in the new environment: network operators (telecommunications companies and IT firms), financial institutions (venture capitalists and investment banks specialising in securitisation deals) and from within the music industry itself (publishers, managers) (CUBS, 1999).[38] The entire supply chain should therefore be opened up to increased competition.

Most analysts (outside record companies) argue that the only essential roles for record companies in the future will be A&R and marketing and promotion. But even these roles can already be hived off to specialists. Independent promotion is a popular option and most major record companies employ freelance A&R executives on an informal basis.

Implications for government

Open access and competition in the supply chain

In theory, such increased competition in service provision should lead to more choice for both content creators and consumers. But there is a danger of bottlenecks emerging in the new supply chain – such as imposing excessive tariffs for the use of *de facto* technological standards (for example watermarking, encryption or audio file players), or abuse of dominant position within the chain to drive down the profits of competitors.

Another worrying trend is the ability of US companies to apply for patents based not simply upon specific proprietary technologies, but on the business models themselves. Since 1993 a variety of patents have been awarded to US companies for the delivery, management and playback of music files over networks. Though many companies are reluctant to be seen to be enforcing compliance with patents, there is a concern that licensing demands for technologies and business models could present barriers to growth for new market entrants.

US Patents

Sightsound.com

Sightsound.com possess patents which cover a method for transferring digital-video and digital-audio signals over networks in return for payments (free downloads are not covered). The company has already issued provisional licensing letters to four companies, including MP3.com, asking for a 1 per cent royalty rate of the total price charged to customers per transaction for the download of music, audio or video recordings.

Intertrust

Intertrust holds 13 US patents and more than 30 applications pending, its most significant interest lying in digital rights management systems.

Open Market

Open Market possess patents covering technology that allows for secure, online credit card transactions, as well as the use of 'electronic shopping carts' that are popular at many online commerce sites.

Amazon.com

Amazon.com recently succeeded in a preliminary ruling in the US against online retailer rivals Barnes and Noble for the use of their patented '1-Click' technology which serves as an express checkout system that encourages users to make repeat purchases. The technology stores the billing and shipping information so that returning shoppers do not have to re-type their details.

An overarching fear for the music industry is that the value of music and the subsequent incentive to invest in creativity will be eroded by the superior bargaining power of new 'gatekeeper' intermediaries, who can effectively control access to new technologies or the new promotional platforms.

Regulation and competition law should therefore be used if necessary to help level the playing field for content distributors and service providers as well as content creators by monitoring anti-competitive practices.

Furthermore, when intermediaries are providing the same service, they should also be subject to the same regulatory environment. As broadcasters, telecommunications companies and other new entrants become involved in the same business of delivering content through cables or the airwaves, they should be subject to the same regulatory conditions.[39] Government must therefore guard against putting too great a burden upon any element of the delivery infrastructure.

The Government has indicated that it intends to move towards a single regulator for telecommunications, IT and media markets, which is the only sensible solution in view of the convergence of the sectors. Industry has called for an evolutionary approach but it may be necessary to speed up the process given the current pace of change. However, it should be noted that the international nature of the music industry and the internet will complicate attempts at national regulation. Such concerns will require a large degree of international co-operation.

Equally, there is a fine balance between hands-off regulation and ensuring fair and open access to new delivery systems. Over-burdensome regulation could drive some new musical entrepreneurs to other territories where compliance is less complicated. Technology must be harnessed as a liberating force, not a barrier to trade. Government should therefore ensure that the Office of Fair Trading (OFT) and Office of Telecommunication Regulation (OFTEL) take account of the particular pressure points for the music industry in their review of competition and associated regulatory principles in emerging e-commerce markets. Given the potential complexities of these issues, government and the industry should consider commissioning further research into this area.

Meanwhile, the most pressing current concern is the need to ensure a level playing field in the delivery of on-demand and similar near-on-demand services.

Statutory licence for broadcasting and cable transmission

The Government has recently consulted upon whether or not to amend the statutory licence which allows broadcasters and cable programme service operators who are unable to agree terms and conditions for the use of sound recordings in their output with collective licensing bodies to commence operations. Under the terms of the licence the operator is able to make use of the entire repertoire of collective licensing bodies, until the Copyright Tribunal has determined a reasonable rate.

The licence was originally introduced in 1990 to check the potential monopolistic bargaining position of the collection societies. However, at that time, new forms of distribution such as the on-demand streaming model (which would currently fall within the terms of the statutory licence) seemed relatively distant. Since, as we have seen, such a model could eventually substitute for traditional retail sales of music, the fear of current rights owners is that the application of the licence would create unfair competition in the distribution of their content and reduce the potential return on investment. In effect, broadcasters could set up an interactive music service which would be competing with other retail outlets and make use of a vast range of music without paying a penny until the Copyright Tribunal is able to decide an appropriate tariff. Furthermore, operators who have not taken advantage of the statutory licence (so-called consensual licensees) have complained that they can be commercially disadvantaged compared to companies who use the licence purposely to avoid agreeing a fair rate. A perverse incentive has thus been created for unscrupulous companies to use the statutory licence as a means of delaying or avoiding payment all together.

There is therefore clearly a strong case for removing all 'on-demand' transmissions from the scope of the statutory licence.

The case of so-called near-on-demand services is more complex since, though the user is unable to choose the time of transmission, the content is usually heavily themed and genre specific and delivered through numerous channels. The question is to what extent these services may compete with traditional forms of sales. Some services, like the infamous Japanese Star Digio 100 service, have clearly aped on-demand operators by pre-publishing schedules, thus making it easier for users to make copies.[40]

The US offers service operators a so-called compulsory licence, a similar mechanism to the statutory licence, which is subject to a range of requirements designed to prevent near-on-demand operators from employing similar tactics.[41] Similar requirements could also be employed in the UK. It should not prove too difficult to identify those services which have been put together in such a way that they are clearly not intended for general entertainment but for people to be able to pick out and copy material for later use. Government should therefore also exclude those near-on-demand services that are clearly intended to be similar in nature and effect to on-demand services.

An additional concern, for performers at least, is that the UK is the only country within the European Union to interpret the performers' entitlement to equitable remuneration from public performance and broadcasting, introduced by the adoption of the European Rental and Lending Directive into UK law in 1996, as being against the copyright owner rather than the user (normally the broadcaster). This has meant that performers must collect revenues via the record company's collection society, PPL (Phonographic Performance Limited). Some observers have pointed out that this creates a perverse incentive for record companies to keep accurate and up-to-date information on performers, since any revenue which is deemed to be unattributable (due to a lack of information) is kept by PPL and returned to the record companies.

In view of the fact that income from public performance and broadcasting is likely to become increasingly significant in the new environment and in the interest of bringing the UK into line with the rest of Europe, the Government should allow performers to collect revenues directly from the user. Under this arrangement, any unattributable income which was originally intended for the performers could at least be used by the performers' collection societies for their benefit.

Implications for intermediaries

Test out new business models as soon as possible

One of the reasons why so many internet-based music companies are targeting unsigned acts is simply due to the fact that the larger repertoire owners have so far been unwilling to release material in the new formats. Consequently, the battleground has centred upon the search for new content. But the release of premium content in the new formats is essential both to the growth of the legitimate digital delivery market and the suppression of the illegitimate market.

All the major companies are finally digitising their existing catalogues and entering into deals to begin testing out new business models. But given the relatively unproven nature of the models, rights owners must begin testing out new purchasing and distribution alternatives as soon as possible to find out which prove most popular with consumers.

Examples of major companies' online strategies

Universal have partnered with InterTrust Technologies whose DigiBox software provides copyright protection, supports SDMI standards and allows for 'tell-a-friend' distribution. Meanwhile Universal and BMG are working together with AT&T and InterTrust to develop EMD (Electronic Media Distribution) which is an open technology designed to provide online customers with a method of securely downloading music from the internet in various digital formats, along with graphics, video content, lyrics and website links. Universal and BMG are also collaborating on GetMusic.com, an online retail service, which sells music from all record companies but only promotes music from Universal and BMG.

EMI have announced a series of moves including a deal with musicmaker.com (involving a 40 per cent equity stake) making over 100,000 songs provisionally available for inclusion on custom CD compilations, a strategic alliance with Liquid Audio to digitise the back catalogue, a deal with Digital-On–Demand for in-store kiosk distribution, another licensing deal in return for equity with Launch Media, making thousands of videos available for worldwide distribution and an agreement to make 5,000 music videos available in the Microsoft Windows Media Format for on-demand web programming.

Sony and Time Warner's acquisition of CDnow means that they will be able to use the internet-based company as a key part of their e-commerce strategy. Sony have also announced deals with Microsoft to make material available for distribution through their new Windows Media 4.0 format and Digital-On Demand, for in-store kiosk distribution. Windows Media 4.0 technologies will be an integral part of the forthcoming Windows 2000 PC operating system which is likely to lead to much bigger growth in the digital music market. Sony, like EMI, also have a similar licensing and equity deal for music videos with Launch Media.

Establish a more permanent relationship with the consumer

As we have seen, the current relationship between the content supplier and the consumer generally ends with the purchase of a piece of plastic. A key advantage of the online world is therefore the ability to establish more direct, personalised and permanent relationships between content distributors and consumers. Content distributors and service providers will have to learn how to manage this relationship and encourage loyalty in the consumer base, in order to be able to market-test new products and services more effectively. All three new distribution models facilitate this kind of relationship, though the on-demand streaming and subscription based-models are likely to create the most permanent relationships.

Learn new skills

Rights owners are keenly aware of the challenge of learning the different skills involved in managing a more direct relationship with consumers. As Fergal Gara, New Media Director at EMI Records UK concluded 'Managing and having some expertise in the retail relationship with the end consumer is a new thing to record companies. It's another skill and one you need to master. We (EMI) are choosing to stick at what we're good at.' [42]

Record companies are wary of provoking unnecessary tension in their relationship with the traditional high-street retailers, as they are still likely to be the most significant outlet for music distribution for some years to come. The recent threat by HMV Europe to refuse to support the release of records that are first made available on the internet is evidence of the validity of their concerns. [43]

In the long term, however, the acquisition of new skills will be a vital tool in increasing flexibility in responses to compete in the new market place. Companies will need to understand both the new technologies for digital delivery and the commercial demands of the new environment (such as online marketing and how to make maximum use of information databases). As the different market sectors converge, transferable skills will become prized commodities. The proliferation of strategic partnership deals between online music companies and other players is testament to the demand for flexibility and constant innovation.

Marketing – niche opportunities

Marketing power in the mass market is unlikely to diminish in the online world, given the expected proliferation of new channels of communication. Positioning on an online retail portal or the home page of a popular search engine requires the same marketing muscle as securing the best displays in bricks and mortar retail outlets. New promotional platforms such as Yahoo! and AOL are already making deals with content suppliers to gain a foothold as a key portal to music-related sites.

In ten years it's going to be as easy to make a recording and post it on the net as it is to talk on a telephone today, but having a phone on your desk doesn't mean that anyone interesting is actually going to call you. Ubiquity does not imply demand.

Al Teller, Founder, Atomic Pop[44]

FirstLook.com

MusicNow has launched a website called FirstLook.com that promotes new music, which is prioritised based on the amount of money labels, artists and retailers are willing to pay. The site makes its 'chart placement for sale' approach known to site visitors and pays $0.01 per click each time a visitor clicks to hear the song.[45]

However, small companies, as well as the content creators themselves, should be able to take advantage of the opportunities afforded by new technologies to target niche markets more effectively. The brand names of both niche market artists and niche suppliers of music will be vital tools in enabling content creators and suppliers to market-test and sample new material in more cost-effective ways.

Musicindie.com

The trade organisation for independent record companies, the Association of Independent Music (AIM), has created a major initiative for its members (who represent nearly 30 per cent of the physical market) to trade together through a collective Internet Service Provider.

Musicindie is designed to be complementary to its members' individual online strategies, whilst offering the smaller companies a low cost opportunity to get onto the internet. The site is expected to be ready in late January/early February.

See www.musicindie.com.

Importance of service provision role

The interconnectedness and searching capabilities of the online world will create particular opportunities for new intermediary services that manage the massive increase in information and content. This particularly applies to the digital distribution of music. The immediate imperative is to establish first-mover advantage by building a brand-name for those services and processes. The long-term aim is then to build up trust and establish a relationship with the consumers as the reliable source of particular services or products. All intermediaries between the content creators and the consumers must therefore recognise that their role is essentially becoming one of service provision – as the link, filter or added value service between the content creator and the consumer.

Develop more dynamic pricing models

> *You won't see the pricing for downloading or streaming get settled before all the content becomes available. The crucial part is getting the pricing right since record companies like anyone else on the internet have to provide consumers with a value proposition. It's like asking consumers to pay the same price for bottled water as they pay for running water. It's going to have to be somewhere between CD price and free.*
>
> Marc Geiger, CEO, ArtistDirect[46]

Clearly, pricing will be one of the most important issues for the online trade in music. Pricing legitimate models too high could spur further growth in the illegitimate supply of music. Whilst pricing models too low could drive down the value of music to a point at which the entire business of investing in future creativity becomes unsustainable.

Many industry insiders privately concede that the physical market has so far largely failed to achieve dynamic pricing, basing prices upon formats rather than content. But pricing will inevitably become much more dynamic in the new environment, particularly given an increase in the supply of content. A recent independent consumer survey in the US showed that consumers would be willing to pay on average $1.45 for a typical song, and $2.46 for a favourite song.[47] By accepting that little can be done to protect the existing supply of unprotected CDs, the industry is already placing a higher premium upon new content.

The defensiveness of retailers in attempting to enforce a level playing field for release dates amongst content distributors further underlines the increasing value of controlling windows of access to premium content.[48] But the music industry may need to become more like the film industry in this regard with its different windows for release in different formats in cinemas, on video cassette, on pay-per-view channels and on terrestrial television.

The entire music industry therefore has to learn how to price products and services more in accordance with the changing demands of consumers. Any move towards subscription-based models based upon conditional access over the years ahead will involve a delicate balancing act between the interests of rights owners and traditional retailers and the need to convince consumers to appreciate that the real value of music lies in the content, not the physical product. There is clearly a concern that the more music is used as a high-value marketing tool and loss leader for other products, the more consumers will become used to the idea that music is essentially a 'free' commodity.

This is important for the digital download model but is particularly crucial to the on-demand streaming model as consumers will have to be persuaded of the value to them of a service that so clearly imitates radio – traditionally seen as a free service. Service providers will have to educate consumers to understand the economics of the new business models.

The value of music

The main value of music copyright lies in the public perception. Some of these new models are in danger of driving down the value of music if they encourage giving away music for free. Young people increasingly are used to consuming music like wallpaper as the background to their daily lives wherever they are.

Guy Fletcher, Co-Chairman, British Academy of Composers
and Songwriters

It is extremely worrying that on the internet there is a philosophy that everything is free. The fact that people might begin to think that music should also be free is doubly worrying.

Crispin Evans, Senior Vice President of International
Business and Legal Affairs, Universal Music Publishing
International Ltd

The desire to maintain the value of music in the new environment should not detract from the flexibility of new business models, some of which will generate revenues from sources other than the content itself, such as advertising. An increasing availability of new music will inevitably drive down prices. As with other content-based industries, such as publishing and film, intermediaries and content creators must adapt to find new ways of generating revenues from the new models. Old models should not necessarily be used as a benchmark for new models.

Far from devaluing intellectual property, the new distribution models should help rectify the current market failures that prevent much of today's intellectual property from finding its true worth. The new models present opportunities to circumvent the current limitations of minimum production levels, consolidation amongst music distributors and retail shelf space. The key for content creators who are concerned about their ability to access income under the new models is to ensure that they are able to secure a share of revenue from other sources, such as advertising (see below).But the value of intellectual property can only be upheld if society learns to treat it with the same respect it affords physical property (see page 76).

Transparency, flexibility and partnership in the intermediary/content creator relationship

Content creators and their representatives have voiced considerable concerns about a lack of transparency in their traditional relationships with record company intermediaries. Criticism has particularly centred upon the tendency of larger companies to make it difficult to assess the true value of a recording contract given the range of royalty deductions and the obstacles to auditing into foreign territories.[49] Of particular concern will be whether record companies will try to extend packaging deductions into the new environment.

But internet users are becoming used to the idea of having direct access to artists, albeit mainly unsigned or independent bands, via internet music companies such as MP3.com and through well known online brands. Increased competition in service provision, the more direct, open and non-exclusive relationships facilitated by the internet, and the use of digital tagging technologies which automatically report back to rights owners, should all encourage intermediaries to adopt a different approach to their relationship with content creators. It therefore seems likely that the new environment will encourage greater transparency and flexibility with intermediaries becoming both more open and accountable for their actions towards content creators and flexible in contract terms.

Some observers, most notably artist managers, express the hope that the old employer/employee model of the record company/artist relationship (whereby the record company pays to own the recording outright but agrees 'bonus' royalty payments with the artist) will become more similar to the 'partnership' model of the publisher/writer (or composer) relationship (based upon the licensing of rights rather than outright ownership). It seems likely that the convergence of the previously distinct retail models will encourage all intermediaries to adopt more of a partnership approach to their relationship with content creators, based upon the licensing of rights.

Although this is primarily an equity issue, a lack of transparency, flexibility and partnership could become a competitive issue for those intermediaries who refuse to adapt to the characteristics of the new environment.

Implications for content creators

Increased demand and Artists Direct

There is likely to be a significant increase in the global demand for musical content, due to the proliferation of the new communication channels, the importance of content as a commercial tool to attract online traffic and the consequences of the World Wide Web becoming an audio-visual (as opposed to a mainly visual) medium. Aside from the obvious rise of internet-based music companies targeting unsigned bands, another early sign of the growth of the new opportunities for music providers is the rise in numbers of new media composers, who specialise in developing music for computer games and websites.[50]

But the most widely trumpeted benefit is the empowerment which direct distribution could bestow upon the content creator. The principal content creator beneficiaries will inevitably be those writers and recording artists who have already established a strong brand name and taken care to maintain some control over their work – the kind of artists who are also able to enter into securitisation deals, such as David Bowie, Iron Maiden or Rod Stewart.[51]

Established artists can build upon the principle of fan clubs to set up subscription-based services to improve information flows with fans to encourage a loyal consumer base. As research undertaken by the Recording Industry Association of America (RIAA) has indicated, over 70 per cent of regular US music buyers are unaware when their favourite artists have released a new album.[52] The interactivity of these services also enables artists to market-test new material before releasing product to the wider market.

Some established artists have already secured the digital distribution rights to their back catalogue through renegotiations with record companies. Others have defied record companies offering free downloads as a promotional tool – most notably, Chuck D and Public Enemy. Certainly, in the long term, content creators should gain a greater degree of control through shorter durations of contracts, higher royalties and greater control over the master recordings. Content creators should then be able to outsource services on more flexible terms such as a fixed-fee or limited-royalty basis.

Kristen Hersh DIY Business Model

The website for Kristen Hersh, singer songwriter and ex-Throwing Muses, is listed by Netscape as one of the Top 50,000 most visited sites on the web, receiving approximately 20,000 hits daily. Billy O'Connell, Kristen's manager, described the motivation to develop the site partly as a reaction to his discovery that the local independent record shop in her home town of Providence did not stock her latest album. The site offers a subscription-based service giving fans the chance to download one work in progress each month from the website for an annual fee of $14.95. The songs are distributed in MP3 files since O'Connell maintains that proprietary formats with copying restrictions would alienate Kristen's fans. He is happy to relate that friends of fans have voluntarily sent in cheques, having received 'free' copies of the material.

See www.throwingmusic.com.

But artist empowerment should reach beyond the upper echelons of success. Niche market artists with less substantial yet loyal followings are already benefiting from the ability to establish a more direct relationship with their fan base.

One of the most exciting aspects of new distribution outlets such as the internet is the economic viability of deriving a reasonable income from extremely modest sales. The Chicago Tribune recently highlighted the case of Kim Baker, a little known guitarist from

Northern California, who sells about 200 CDs per month via the internet, enough to make music a viable employment option. With far lower overheads from digital distribution, the business becomes far more profitable.

Closer to home, Kate Rusby, a folk singer-songwriter from Yorkshire, has sold over 60,000 copies of her last two self-funded albums since May 1997 from her own family-run record company, Pure Records.[53] Whilst not providing the source for all sales, the internet has proven an invaluable marketing and purchasing tool to facilitate her self-funded DIY cottage industry approach.

But the increased competition in services and new routes to market brings challenges too.

Artist recording contracts and revenues

For contracted artists, problems may arise over the way that existing contracts interpret new technologies. Artists may argue that proceeds from digital distribution should fall within the category of ancillary income, in which they would generally be able to participate on a 50/50 basis. But when a similar situation arose at the time of the development of the CD market, record companies threatened not to release recordings in the new format unless artists agreed to a reduced royalty and a substantial packaging deduction. Faced with the potential loss of income, artists conceded and such agreements became commonplace. A similar dispute could arise over hybrid sales or compilation albums that could be deemed to fall within the category of mail-order or third-party exploitation, therefore attracting half-rate or substantially reduced royalties. But the more the new forms of distribution become significant, rather than ancillary, sources of income, the less justification there will be to treat them as exceptions to the basic royalty deal.

Faced with greater choice and with a greater emphasis upon service provision, artists are likely to demand more flexibility, shorter terms and higher royalties in their contracts. At the same time, given the range of possible business models, they are likely to be confronted by a bewildering array of possible deals. One area that is likely to prove particularly significant for unsigned content creators is the ability to derive revenues from other sources such as advertising or sponsorship. Given the proliferation of new content and services, advertising is likely to become an increasingly significant source of revenue.

The ownership of websites and marketing databases is likely to become another potential battleground. For uncontracted content creators, the potential problems stem from the complexities of negotiating their way around the new environment. Even a basic DIY e-commerce operation such as setting up a website can present a complex range of legal, regulatory and administrative issues such as hosting agreements, website maintenance contracts, ownership of copyright in the website, compliance with regulations in foreign jurisdictions, the importance of international trademark legislation, compliance with data protection and hypertext links liabilities. The most experienced industry practitioners may still need to acquire the new skills required to deal with these issues. In the music industry such skills are traditionally acquired on the job on an informal basis.

Given the likely proliferation of new service providers to help fulfill these functions for unsigned artists, there is a need to establish a better means of disseminating information on rights issues for content creators and monitoring the quality and competence of service providers.

But what can government do? Recording contracts and deals with service providers are, after all, private commercial agreements that can not be prescribed in advance. The strength of either side's negotiating position will largely dictate the terms and conditions. The primary responsibility therefore must rest with the content creators themselves to secure adequate legal advice before signing any agreement.

> *Question:* How do you go about paying people who are not members of MCPS or PRS?
> *Answer:* It's kind of up to people themselves really.

> Exchange from 'In The City' Conference, 1999 panel discussion. Answer from a representative of a new internet-based music company.

But government can be a useful catalyst in encouraging greater coordination within the industry to ensure that all content creators have sufficient access to good quality advice about the value and importance of their rights before they enter into commercial deals and in encouraging best practice in the operations of the new service providers.

This means helping rationalise the responses of the host of trade associations representing the interests of content creators, local music and creative industry development agencies and Metier (the National Training Organisation), who could all play important roles in educating members and aspiring musicians about the potential pitfalls of the new environment.[54] The aim should be to disseminate information about basic rights issues to the widest possible constituency of content creators; those who are neither members of trade associations or who can not afford to seek adequate independent legal advice. At the same time, it is recognised that an adequate incentive should be maintained for content creators to join appropriate trade bodies in order to access higher-level advice.

ArtistRight and MusicRight

Government should therefore encourage the relevant recording artists and songwriters' trade associations, local music development organisations and Metier to work together to develop a single online national resource site for artists – ArtistRight. The site could provide unsigned artists and writers with basic information about the importance of rights and contractual issues in both the online and offline environment and help establish a code of conduct for the new internet-based service-providing companies. The former would include the need to promote the content creators' abilities to derive revenues from new sources such as advertising. The latter service could be carried out in co-operation with TrustUK. A seal of approval from such bodies would at least indicate that the service provider meets certain minimum requirements.

ArtistRight could link to, or form a part of, a wider online music industry resource portal – MusicRight – in co-operation with other industry bodies. This initiative would provide online training and business advice services, link up musicians with other musicians and service providers, link to all information on government schemes, signpost on to online or local expertise when necessary and act as a focal point for pooling together disparate support initiatives.[55] For instance, MusicRight could link up local music initiatives such as the Merseyside Music Development Agency's plan to bring together music from local unsigned bands into a music portal with other similar local or regional ventures.

Both initiatives should benefit from some seedcorn funding from Government, but they should be clearly branded by the industry and aim to become financially self-sustaining as far as possible. However, the Government should seek to ensure that both organisations pay particular attention to the needs of individuals and micro-businesses without becoming dominated by the agenda of larger industry players.

Commercial framework for digital delivery

Since the commercial (as well as the legal and regulatory) framework for interpreting digital delivery systems has yet to be agreed, there is a concern as to what extent the arguments of different industry bodies will affect the growth of the digital music economy. This goes to the heart of the challenges of the new environment – how to classify the new forms of digital delivery systems and how to ensure that revenues are appropriately divided. Both content distributors and content creators could argue that inequitable remuneration may eventually prove a barrier to future growth.

These issues will, of course, largely be decided by the terms of the commercial deals between the content creators and intermediary service providers. But significant revenue streams will be affected by the interpretation of which rights are being exploited and the licensing rates agreed between rights owners and commercial intermediaries. For instance, the revenue which composers/lyricists receive from streaming and digital downloads will depend firstly upon agreeing whether both mechanical reproductions and a performance right are involved and then upon the ability of the collective licensing bodies to agree rates with users.[56]

Also there is the question of which applicable law should apply. For instance, UK and European rights owners understandably argue against the principle of paying royalties on the basis of the country of location the server, since that would often tend to be the US where lower rates will generally apply.

As panelists at the recent Webnoize 99 conference observed, the lack of a unified structure and approach to online mechanical rights is seen as a confusion and potential barrier to growth to the European digital music market. Reza Kad, Executive Vice-President of digital music distributor, Dx3, commented 'The consumers are ready, the labels are ready, the bandwidth is there. There must be education and there are problems to solve. Europe has not found a structure to [sort out] mechanical rights.'[57]

Again, there is a danger that the traditionally fragmented nature of the industry will lead to protracted arguments. Since significant revenue streams are affected, industry bodies will naturally advance arguments in support of the interests of their members. But despite the fact that these discussions carry extremely significant financial implications for all concerned, government should encourage rights owners not to lose sight of the need to reach consensus. Developing a mutually agreed framework for digital delivery systems should prove both a spur to the competitiveness of the UK digital music economy and to future business models. Meanwhile the Government should encourage openness in the commercial discussions and help ensure that the voices of the less well-represented interest groups are also heard in the discussions. This is particularly important for recording artists who, being represented by a number of different bodies, lack a single, unified voice.

It is equally essential for the wider legal framework concerning the online delivery of digital content to be updated and revised in line with the demands of the new environment. We consider this framework in the following Chapter.

6. The legislative framework: copyright and e-commerce

*Opportunities for new forms of supplying music are being used
as an excuse to undermine copyright.*
> David Lester, Director, Legal Affairs, MCPS/PRS

*The rights owning community should be wary of being greedy
or even being perceived to be being greedy, or else there could
be quite a backlash. The fear of excessive rights protection is
that you drive entrepreneurs elsewhere.*
> Andy Heath, Managing Director, Momentum Music

*There will inevitably be a gap between where the rights holders
draw the line and where the telecommunications companies
want it to be drawn, so business needs to find ways of resolving
issues by working together to deal with infringements.*
> Mark Isherwood, Consultant, Rightspro Ltd

In this Chapter we consider the impact of the new distribution models
on the legislative framework, concentrating upon the particular
implications for copyright legislation.

Together with trademark and patent legislation, copyright law is one
of the principal legislative tools by which rights owners are able to
protect their economic interests in the commercial exploitation of their
work. Copyright is essentially a balance designed to protect the interests
of content creators and users. It is premised on the idea that only the
copyright owner has the authority to make a copy.

However, copying is a fundamental part of the online digital
distribution process, in that it is necessary within networks in order to
speed up the delivery process (for example, copies made as a result of
caching and browsing).[58] On the other hand, models based upon access
rather than copying may well proliferate in the future. It may therefore
be more useful to consider a different basis of rights protection in the
fully networked environment.

Under the on-demand streaming model, both copying and ownership
(possession of a permanent physical copy) become an irrelevance. It is

'access' rather than copying which is the primary act that should be controlled. John Enser and Simon Olswang outlined this idea in a previous IPPR publication (in Collins, ed 1996). But current legislation has to be able to deal with an entire variety of models. As Enser has himself stated, the practical considerations involved in attempting to harmonise current copyright legislation provide sufficient enough a barrier to such a dramatic move.[59] However, the concept of an access right could nonetheless prove a useful model to consider in the future.

The immediate problem is how to build a harmonised legislative framework when no two countries in the world, let alone Europe, have identical copyright regimes. Copyright and related rights laws and their implementation are territorially based and are likely to remain so for the foreseeable future. Copyright can carry very different cultural and economic significance in some countries. Indeed the absence of copyright can be in itself an economic asset. As Mark Haftke, from Bird and Bird commented 'It seems to me no more likely that you can achieve a comprehensive global approach to copyright protection for intellectual property than you will achieve in relation to physical property.'[60]

However, there have been a whole series of international agreements and treaties to attempt to coordinate systems of rights protection and enforcement. Beginning with the Berne Convention of 1886, the most recent and significant international attempt to harmonise rights legislation for the digital environment was taken under the auspices of the World Intellectual Property Organisation (WIPO) at a diplomatic conference in Geneva in December 1996.[61] Two treaties were agreed, the WIPO Copyright Treaty and the WIPO Performances and Phonograms Treaty. For rights owners and users alike they represent the best effort yet to deal with the new technological environment, particularly through the establishment of two new broader rights – the communication to the public right for authors and the right of making available for performers and producers.

Despite leaving details of implementation open to interpretation by individual states, the WIPO treaties form a useful basis for the incorporation of harmonised definitions into the legislation of signatory states – in the US Digital Millennium Copyright Act (DMCA) of 1998 and from the UK's perspective, in the draft European Copyright Directive.[62]

However, there is still much to be clarified. Of particular concern is the fact that the WIPO treaties deal largely with digital downloading and are less clear on how to protect rights owners' interests in on-demand streaming and subscription services.

Debates in the UK and Europe have largely focussed upon two other significant issues which the WIPO treaties purposely left unclear – how to deal with temporary copies arising from acts such as caching or browsing which are seen as essential to the effective everyday operation of the internet and the issue of the extent of liability and monitoring responsibilities of online intermediaries for unauthorised content.

To simplify complex arguments, the online service provider intermediaries (for example the ISPs (Internet Service Providers) – *not* the rights owners) generally argue that copies which are technically necessary as part of the process of transmitting material over open networks such as the internet should be defined as exceptions to the reproduction right. They are also concerned that they should not be deemed responsible for unauthorised material passing through or being stored on their networks, given the vast amount of information involved – an issue more specifically addressed in the European E-Commerce Directive.

Meanwhile rights owners worry that copying exceptions drawn too widely and not subject to authorisation could provide a loophole for future abuse. Most argue that legal certainty would be better achieved if acts such as caching were covered by an exemption for liability under the E-Commerce Directive rather than through copying exceptions. Rights owners also maintain that the online intermediaries need to be incentivised to ensure adequate monitoring of their networks, arguably through an allocation of the liability risk. Both sides reason that a failure to recognise their needs could prove a barrier to trade for smaller companies who will not be able to afford the necessary indemnity insurance.

Such positions are not entirely irreconcilable. Clearly, for the moment, the act of copying should remain the primary act that needs to be controlled. The default position whereby all copying should be subject to the authorisation of rights owners should therefore be maintained in the new environment. However, there must be some exceptions to a blanket ban to allow for fair dealing and activities that are essential to the efficient operation of interconnected networks such as the internet.

Furthermore, both sides concede that there have to be some limits to the extent to which online intermediaries should be held responsible for unauthorised material passing through or stored on their networks.[63] Even if all copies were subject to authorisation from the rights owners, provided network operators or service providers take necessary steps to co-operate with rights owners in removing unauthorised material from their networks and protecting material stored on their networks against abuse, they should still be exempt from liability in certain circumstances under the terms of the E-Commerce Directive.

The remaining questions then are how to define the copying exceptions as tightly as possible to avoid potential abuse and how to ensure that the online service provider intermediaries are adequately incentivised to co-operate in the removal of unauthorised material whilst being protected against wrongful removal.

The important point to bear in mind in defining the exceptions is to avoid using descriptions that are tied too closely to current technologies in order to guard against any unanticipated loopholes, now and in the future. Such has been the lesson of the inadequacies of existing technology-specific legislation.

Meanwhile, there are optimistic signs of progress on the monitoring of illegal material through self-regulation initiatives such as those operated by the Internet Watch Foundation (IWF) and the Business Software Alliance (BSA). A similar proposal for the music industry, Rightswatch, based largely upon the IWF model, is currently being developed by both rights owners and telecommunications companies. The aim is to employ a hotline warning system and a process for a 'notice and take down' procedure similar to that instituted in the US Digital Millennium Copyright Act (DMCA). Both the IWF and the BSA's hotline warning systems have proven extremely effective in ensuring the removal of pornographic and unauthorised material from service providers' servers.

Though details will still need to be clarified in legislation, the self-regulation model is a useful tool both as a necessary interim measure in the absence of an adequate legal framework and as a practical means of encouraging rights owners and online intermediaries to work together to sort out the details of the mechanisms required to resolve disputes in the future. It could also serve as a useful means of educating users about the nature of infringing activities, without having to resort to heavy-handed tactics. It is, however, vital for its long-term credibility that all music industry rights owners are represented in such initiatives.[62]

The validity of a copyright infringement claim against piracy of information should be much more easily established than defamation. But there may still be cases where there is an element of risk during the time between the allocation of the notification and the granting of an injunction. Allocating this risk to the service providers would certainly incentivise online intermediaries to monitor their systems effectively, though the rights owners are better placed to make such judgments since they are responsible for developing the rights management systems. A shared risk mechanism may be a fairer though more complex solution. However this is settled, online intermediaries should not run the risk of becoming censors of the internet, stifling its attraction as a celebrated medium of free speech.

An additional problem is that the longer the debates over the legislation continue, the more likely it is that legislation will already be outdated by the time it appears in the member states' statute books. The European Copyright Directive was first issued as a Green Paper in 1995 and was accepted in draft form by the European Commission in December 1997. Since then it has undergone a whole series of amendments as it has passed between the Commission and the Parliament. It currently awaits approval by the Council of Ministers. At the time of writing, progress seemed much more encouraging on the E-Commerce Directive.

Evidently, such significant pieces of legislation need to be debated and considered carefully, touching as they do upon the interests of so many powerful industries, but technology moves at a far quicker pace than legislation. Ideally legislation should be able to be amended and updated on a regular basis, but this would hinder legal certainty. However, reaching agreement on the issues of copyright exceptions and the extent of liability of online intermediaries must not in themselves become barriers to trade. Whatever the drawbacks of the US Digital Millennium Copyright Act, it enables greater stability and security in the commercial strategic planning process. A potentially greater commercial threat to rights owners and service providers alike is to fall too far behind the US in the provision of information society services.

Finally it is worth noting that, as the choice of terms to describe the new roles has indicated, there is likely to be less distinction between categories of service providers in the new environment. Increasingly, rights owners, distributors and network service providers will all become varying kinds of service providing intermediaries. It is therefore arguable that the current differences of opinion will have less relevance in a fully converged world.

International implications

The global reach of open, interconnected networks such as the internet creates enormous problems for deciding the circumstances for which individual jurisdictions, legal and fiscal, should apply. These matters will be settled largely through international trade agreements, particularly through the World Trading Organisation (WTO), and to some extent through the trading practices of multinational companies.

The foundation of territoriality upon which the international legislative framework operates is clearly set to become far less stable in the new environment, even if marketing and promotion are likely to continue to operate on a territorial basis for the foreseeable future. As for copyright there are a whole host of areas where the question of applicable law is uncertain. For instance, where does an infringement of copyright take place? – in the country where the website host server is located, in the country where the user downloads the product, or in the country where the author posted the work? And where should the copyright owner pursue infringement?

The complexity of such issues lies outside the scope of this study. Suffice to say that it is only through international agreements through organisations like WIPO and the World Trade Organisation that the necessary harmonisation that is the key to legal clarity to help grow the new services can be found.

Taxation is just as complex. It is certainly likely to prove far more difficult to control the importation of intangible products or services from service providers based in other territories. Even with current hybrid sales, UK customs and excise may or may not charge duty upon imports. The territorial basis of taxation conflicts with the global nature of the new environment. Whilst taxation of internet transactions should seek to maintain the same principles as the offline environment, it should also guard against stifling the growth of new business opportunities.

Leaks in the system cannot and should not be plugged by protective legislation. The only effective answer to increased international competition is for UK-based service suppliers to become more competitive. In the new buyer-driven environment, what the consumer wants, the consumer gets.

7. Further policy responses

> *The question is not will people want music but will they pay for it. Unless we give children in primary schools an inherent understanding and appreciation of music, they will grow up without any sense of the worth of music – of the value of music to them and to society. If people do not value music, they will not pay for it no matter what medium is used to provide it to them.*
>
> Nanette Rigg, Director, Blencathra Productions Ltd and
> ex-Director General, British Music Rights

> *We have spent too much time looking at the things that are different between us rather than seeking common positions for mutual gain.*
>
> A trade association director on fragmentation within the
> music industry

In this Chapter, we consider further policy responses for both government and the industry, looking particularly at the role of education, the issue of industry representation and the attitude and understanding of the industry within Government.

Education

Fostering respect for copyright

The internet culture of 'free' content sharing is clearly a potential disincentive to future investment in all copyright industries. There is considerable concern that a significant proportion of the younger generation in places like California, where internet use and MP3 file sharing are far more commonplace, is growing up to believe that music is essentially a 'free' commodity. The question for the Government is how it can help foster greater respect for the value of intellectual property and copyright works.

The Creative Industries Task Force is working with the Government to investigate ways of tackling this issue. The PIU report recommended that the Government give intellectual property a higher profile in public understanding. But this must be achieved without sending a message that may be considered too negative, patronising or protectionist, at a time when the Government is seeking to promote the take-up of new technologies. Indeed, for the music industry itself, the imperative must be to avoid a rerun of the 'Home taping is killing music' campaign of the 1970s, which in hindsight now appears as an overreaction.[65]

Any campaign targeted at educating consumers to respect the value of copyright should not single out a particular copyright industry, must be careful not to send too negative a message and should be artist-led. However, such a campaign should be managed very carefully. It should not fall into the trap of lecturing or talking down to consumers.

A more effective strategy would be for the Government and the industry to target their efforts at the younger generation, who are, after all, tomorrow's consumers. The Government should therefore encourage the music industry to work with other entertainment industries to develop attractive CD-ROM packages for schools based on the use of music and multimedia products on the internet. This could be used both as an entertaining way of encouraging children to build up their skills in using the internet (through projects such as making their own websites and e-zines) whilst enabling them to learn to respect intellectual property through understanding what is and is not allowed.[66]

The clearest expression of this idea came from Danny Van Emden, Head of New Media at Virgin Group, when discussing the amount of e-mail enquiries which Virgin receives from younger fans who are seeking guidance as to what is permitted in constructing fans' websites. As she put it, 'At this age you can capture their imaginations without seeming like spoilsports.'[67] The advantage of this approach is that an educational message can be bundled into a bigger package, offering a more positive approach whilst building skills and inspiring experimentation. In all cases, respect for the value of copyright is more appropriately learned not taught, in a positive, active environment, not as a negative passive message.

From a wider perspective, children will increasingly need 'education for information' in the knowledge-driven economy. This is not simply a matter of understanding copyright but a recognition of the multiple demands of an information-rich society. There is a need to equip children with the necessary skills to translate information into knowledge that empowers them to act (for example information about health, education and issues of governance). 'Education for information' should therefore be included within the national citizenship curriculum. Within this framework children could learn about all issues of information management, such as copyright theft, privacy and confidentiality. The concept of copyright theft could then be related to contexts of more immediate relevance to them. How would they feel if someone copied their homework on which they had spent a long time working? If children think it is unacceptable to steal a cd from a shop, why should stealing music via the internet be considered acceptable?

This could be piloted in some schools in order to discover more about current views of intellectual property and copyright and to find out how to approach the subject in the most constructive way.

Furthermore, in order to maximise accessibility and understanding, it would be advisable to employ more user-friendly language such as 'creative rights' rather than 'intellectual property rights' or 'copyright'. Such terms may alienate a younger audience as they could be considered as the language of lawyers and officialdom. 'Creative rights' would be an appropriate term to use when discussing rights in the context of all creative industries.

Creating music

> *The net offers advanced technological societies a tantalizing pathway back to the pre-industrial democracy of art. In time, software will allow amateurs to make studio-quality recordings on a modest budget that will shock, delight and comfort audiences beyond their living room stages.*
>
> Stephen Brull *Business Week*[68]

Music tuition in schools is clearly one of the most vital tools in helping maintain the UK's excellent track record in producing innovative musical talent. The extra funding for music teaching announced by the DCMS and DfEE in January 1999 was a welcome move. But new technologies can be harnessed in schools to enable all children, including those without any formal musical training, to learn to interact with music and take part in the creative process. Today, musicians can create a piece of music without even being able to read, write or play a note of music. New interactive musical packages are being developed, aimed primarily at the musically illiterate, to enable them to make their own compositions simply by interacting with samples of music from a computer keyboard.

Shift Control

Audiorom produce an enhanced CD-ROM called 'Shift Control' that retails at under £20 and can be used with even fairly low specification PCs and Macs to produce music by interacting with samples of music. The product has won an Interactive BAFTA design award and a Milia D'Or award for Interactive media at Cannes.

See www.audiorom.com.

Through the use of innovative CD-ROM packages or software tools, it should be possible to set a target for every single child in the country to have the chance of creating their own piece of music, regardless of ability.

Government should also encourage the development of schemes that allow musicians to make use of new technologies to collaborate with other musicians via the internet or other networks. There are plenty of potential funding opportunities at both the national and European level for such schemes. Government should therefore encourage the industry, via one of the new recommended bodies or the Musicians Union (which has a strong regional structure), to promote the concept and ensure that local authorities, arts, cultural and community centres are aware of where to bid for and how to access such funding.

Industry representation

The fragmented structure of the music industry and its related trade organisations and interest groups has derived from the complex structure of rights involved in creating a musical work. But the lack of coordination and a united voice is increasingly seen as a reason why the music industry has been less successful than other comparable creative industries, most notably film, in representing its interests to government authorities, as well as a potential barrier to growth to new business models. This is as much a problem at the European level as it is nationally. The European Music Office is supposed to represent the European music industry in Brussels and yet neither the record companies' trade association, the International Federation of Phonographic Industries (IFPI) nor the UK collection societies, the Mechanical Copyright Protection Society (MCPS) and the Performing Right Society (PRS), are members.

At the national level, now that the Music Industry Forum has been established in consultation with the industry, there is at least a formal structure through which the industry is able to bring issues of concern to the Government's attention. However, it would still be helpful to establish a single united body to formally represent the official voice of the UK music industry to both government and the outside world and to provide a forum to achieve consensus on pan-industry issues such as e-commerce and new technology issues, copyright, education and training, lobbying for funding and co-ordinating links with UK music-related websites.

The National Music Council currently serves a similar function but with a limited remit, given its lack of funding and staffing.[69] A new, modernised version with a more forward-looking name, such as Music.UK, should therefore be created to fulfill a wider role as outlined above. It should benefit from some government funding to prevent domination by overseas-based interests and to ensure that the UK's small businesses and micro-businesses are adequately represented. However, it must have the support of the larger music companies or there is a danger that the organisation will be judged as an irrelevance by the mainstream industry.

This will require a large degree of reorganisation within the industry to avoid creating yet another layer of representative bureaucracy, but the rewards of collaborating to achieve a more united voice for the industry should outweigh the short-term political concerns of individual sectors within the industry.

Attitude and understanding of the music industry within government

A single unified industry voice would go some way to improving the understanding within government of the problems and needs of the various elements which make up the industry. The fact that the DCMS has the responsibility of promoting the interests of the music industry should inevitably lead to greater account being taken of the industry's concerns in policy development, but many of the problems lie in misunderstandings about the industry in other Departments. IPPR's work on barriers to growth for small music companies revealed a number of such examples in the Treasury, the Inland Revenue and the Department of Trade and Industry (Westall and Cowling, 1999). This is largely due to the industry failing to represent a broad enough agenda with government in the past.

With a view to the future, the aim must be to convince officials within other Departments that the music industry is not simply a rich cousin of the economy that can stand on its two feet without the need for any help from government (the principal message that government has heard from the industry for some years).

To help the digital economy to grow, the music industry needs to be taken seriously, both economically and culturally, consulted upon relevant policy development, and encouraged to take better advantage of all relevant support schemes. The *sine qua non* is to ensure that information is disseminated more effectively throughout the industry to ensure that all elements of the industry are kept informed of policy developments and available support schemes. There are encouraging signs that this is now happening but more could be done.

In general the industry requires no special treatment nor massive hand-outs of public money. But policy must take more account of the needs of all sectors of the music economy in future if the Government is to help create a climate in which the new musical entrepreneurs can continue the successes of those of the past.

Endnotes

1   As quoted in (Burnett, 1996) p44.

2   In view of the increasing importance of new forms of distribution EMI Records recently announced its intention to pull out of the manufacture of CDs as part of their core business.

3   In December 1998 Canadian conglomerate Seagram, which owned Universal Records, purchased PolyGram from Phillips for $10.6 billion to become the market leader with a world market share of approximately 23 per cent.

4   'Independent' is commonly defined as a company that owns and controls 50 percent or more of its equity. Independents encompass a range of companies from owner-managed micro-businesses to SMEs to large international companies.

5   Information from project interview.

6   The recordable formats, CD-R and CD-RW, are now becoming increasingly commonplace. CD-R is a once only recordable format whereas CD-RW is rewritable, meaning it can be recorded over repeatedly, like a cassette. (See Chapter Four)

7   See www.bmi.com

8   The new games consoles which link directly to the internet, such as the Sega Dreamcast, open up a vast potential for new marketing opportunities and for the development of multimedia products.

9   UMTS builds on and extends the capability of today's mobile technologies (like digital cellular and cordless) by providing increased capacity, data capability and a far greater range of services using an innovative radio access scheme and an enhanced, evolving core network.

10   Super Audio CD, developed by Sony and Philips is a rival to the DVD Audio format supported mainly by Matsushita, Pioneer and Toshiba. Super Audio CD, another enhanced CD format, can be played on existing CD players unlike DVD Audio.

11   Hewlett Packard's latest palm size PC includes a built-in MP3 player.

12   Currently, approximately $30.00

13   From a recorded interview with Webnoize. Available from Webnoize Inside at www.webnoize.com

14   Ibid.

15   From project interview.

16   For customised CDs, see www.cdnow.com, www.cdiy.com, www.musicmaker.com and www.cductive.com.

17   From evidence to the Trade and Industry's Select Committee Report into Trademarks, fakes and consumers, 1999, p39.

18   Consumers who are familiarised with manipulating digital audio files can already make use of free online services such as the leading audio information source CDDB, which links the user to a vast database that is able to recognise and provide immediate track listings for thousands of albums, thus saving much laborious data inputting. See www.cddb.com.

19   Some companies like 08004u offer an unmetered internet access service using an 0800 access number. Greatxscape.com are also offering unmetered internet access in the evenings and at weekends, if you sign your BT line over to a BT reseller. Furthermore BT themselves have recently announced a series of unmetered tariffs for libraries, colleges and Citizen Advice Bureaux.

20   Cited in the Financial Times, 26/10/99.

21   It should be noted that other forms of internet access such as cable modems and particularly the so-called 3rd generation mobile telephony technologies (which facilitate downloading), will also help drive access to entertainment-based products and services whilst exerting a downward pressure upon the cost of access.

22   See www.helsinkiarena2000.fi

23   See Chapter Four for description of the SDMI.

24   Other compression technologies, such as AT&T's a2b, use superior compression techniques to MP3, though MP3 can produce better sound quality using higher sampling rates. Many observers note that the best way for the music industry to encourage the growth of a legitimate digital audio file market is to adopt a new file format which is superior in sound quality to MP3. Experts also suggest that it is not necessarily the compression techniques that always make the difference in sound quality but also the quality of machine on which the content is compressed.

25   From project interview with IFPI representative.

26   Statistics from the RIAA, reported in FT Music and Copyright, 6 October, 1999.

27   The British Phonographic Industry (BPI) has expressed particular concern about sales of illegal CD-R compilations. Its anti-piracy unit

seized £300,000 worth of illegal bootleg CDs in one raid in 1999 in north London.

28 A particularly popular bootleg MP3 CD is the entire Beatles collection on one CD.

29 From Project interview.

30 Details can be found at www.webnoize.com.

31 Members include America Online, Microsoft, RealNetworks, Liquid Audio, a2b, Lucent Technologies, Diamond Multimedia, Toshiba and Matsushita as well as the big five music companies.

32 From SDMI's mission statement at www.sdmi.org

33 The SDMI readily admit that nothing can be done to prevent the manufacture of current players, such as the Rio Player, which accept both legitimate and illegitimate content.

34 British company MediaTag recently launched digital tagging technologies for this purpose. See Appendix and www.mediatag.com.

35 See Page 39.

36 Most of the websites for unsigned bands are US-based, though more are now launching in the UK. See Appendix for illustrative list of music-related sites.

37 By the end of September 1999, the roster had risen to over 31,000 artists.

38 It is instructive to note that the market capitalisation of Microsoft at $270 billion (as at September 1999) is itself over six times the estimated value of the entire global music industry.

39 Currently, broadcasters are subject to taste and decency regulation and BT is not; whereas BT is subject to Oftel regulations on pricing and broadcasters are not.

40 Star Digio is a 100 channel service which began publishing detailed play lists down to the second, thus greatly facilitating home recording.

41 US requirements include the fact that during any three-hour period there cannot be more than two consecutive selections from any one album, more than three non-consecutive selections from any one album or more than three consecutive selections from the same artist.

42 From project interview.

43 Reported in Musicweek, 2/10/99.

44 Quoted in Plugged In, 20/7/1999, www.MP3.com/news.

45 From a regulatory perspective, it is interesting to note that such a service ultimately has no higher authority to answer to, whereas broadcast radio in the US, as elsewhere, is subject to a regulatory body (the Federal Communications Commission) who would clearly view this activity as an illegal scheme.

46 From project interview.

47 Survey referred to by Wayne Parker, president of amplified.com at Webnoize 99, in Retailers, Digital Providers Differ on Sales Strategies, 16/11/99, www.webnoize.com.

48 See Page 55.

49 Under existing contracts many recording artists have no right to audit their record company's books for sales in foreign territories.

50 New Media composers are currently in the process of developing an informal e-mail network into an association to represent their interests and to improve their working terms and conditions. For further information contact Paul Weir – paulw@earcom.net.

51 It should of course also be possible for all artists to sell shares on the basis of future earnings without any kind of proven track record. An instructive example for the music industry comes from the case of a 24 year old actress in London, Caroline Ilana. She offered shares based upon her future income from acting which were bought by Andrew Lloyd-Webber, Bob Hoskins and Emma Thompson amongst others. Such a model could also be adopted by more entrepreneurial musicians.

52 From project interview.

53 See www.purerecords.demon.co.uk

54 It should be noted, however, that Metier, as a non sector-specific body, has yet to gain sufficient credibility within the mainstream music industry.

55 See also Westall and Cowling, 1999. For a discussion of electronic performance support systems, see www.epss.com.

56 This is currently the subject of a row following the MCPS's decision to set a new minimum flat-rate mechanical royalty rate of £0.10 for a digital download.

57 From Webnoize 99 panel discussion, International Online Music Looks to Catch Up to US, 18/11/99, www.webnoize.com.

58 Caching is the storage mechanism which speeds up the use of the internet. Caching will not always involve a permanent copy as a temporary copy of a web page can be stored in the PC's cache memory whilst browsing the web.

59   From IPPR seminar.

60   From project interview.

61   The World Intellectual Property Organisation (WIPO) is an intergovernmental organisation with headquarters in Geneva, Switzerland. It is one of the 16 specialised agencies of the United Nations system of organisations. WIPO is responsible for the promotion of the protection of intellectual property throughout the world through co-operation among States, and for the administration of various multilateral treaties dealing with the legal and administrative aspects of intellectual property.

62   The European Copyright Directive's stated aim is to implement the main provisions of the WIPO treaties and to bring about a coherent and favourable environment for creativity and investment in the framework of the internal market.

63   It is commonly accepted that different levels of liability should apply to the different levels of responsibility of the online intermediaries.

64   Currently UK sound recording rights owners are not part of the Rightswatch initiative.

65   Despite the industry's fears of cassettes cannibalising sales, vinyl records sales continued to rise by 20 per cent annually. For a discussion of this campaign see Wallis and Malm, 1984.

66   According to the DTI, 90 per cent of the UK's secondary schools and 68 per cent of primary schools are already connected to the internet (as at September, 1999). The Government has promised to ensure all schools are connected by 2002.

67   From project interview.

68   Quoted in Leckstein,1999.

69   The NMC's role mainly involves commissioning cross-industry research studies and lobbying on cross-industry issues such as music education. The staff comprises one part-time administrator. By October 1999 it was reaching the end of an internal review process.

Bibliography

BPI (1999) BPI Statistical Handbook: BPI

British Invisibles (1995) *Overseas earnings of the music industry* British Invisibles

Burnett, R (1996) *The Global Jukebox: the international music industry* London: Routledge

Collins, R (ed) (1996) Access Right or Copyright? By Enser, J, and Olswang, S, in *Converging Media? Converging Regulation?* IPPR

CUBS (City University Business School) (1999) *Globalisation, Technology and Creativity: Current trends in the Music Industry*

Dube, R (9/11/1999) *Can Micropayments Make a Macrodifference?* www.webnoize.com

Dyson, E (December 1994) 'What happens to intellectual property when it gets on the internet?' in *Intellectual Value* Esther Dyson's Monthly Report

Fulwell, P (1999) *MusicCity 2.0 – Developing The Digital Music Economy* Liverpool Institute for Performing Arts

Godin, S (1999) *Permission Marketing: Turning strangers into Friends and Friends into Customers* Simon and Schuster

Hardie, M (1999) *Virtual Music Rocks* Forrester Research

Kern, P (1999) *Music In The Digital Economy* European Music Office

Leckstein, H (1999) *Is the music industry missing the point? The commercial future of streaming music* (Contact: harryleckstein @eunite.co.uk)

PIU (Performance and Innovation Unit) (1999) *e-commerce@its.best.uk* Cabinet Office. (See www.cabinet-office.gov.uk/innovation)

NMC (National Music Council) (1999) *A Sound Performance – The economic value of music to the United Kingdom* National Music Council and KPMG.

NMC (National Music Council) (1996) *The Value of Music* National Music Council

Spectrum Strategy Consultants (1999) *Moving into the Information Age, A Sectoral Benchmarking Study* DTI (See www.isi.gov.uk/isi/isi/bench/1999)

Wallis, R and Malm, K (1984) *Big Sounds from small peoples: the music industry in small countries* Constable

Westall, A and Cowling, M (1999) *Agenda for Growth* IPPR

Wishnow, M (13/9/1999) *Choose Non-exclusivity: Message to the Indie Music Community* www.webnoize.com.

Appendix: Useful music-related sites

www.akoluthic.net
A music portal which offers digital music distribution, webzines and internet access, consultancy and implementation.

www.amp3.com
AMP3.com boasts that it is the only digital music delivery system to pay its artists a royalty each time their music is downloaded – currently $.05. But they claim artists should be able to earn up to as much as a dollar with additional sponsorships. Pay per downloads are enabled by attaching 5-second jingle advertisements to each AMP3.com song.

www.artistdirect.com
An online company established by industry guru Marc Geiger, acting as a combination of a booking agency, record label and new media division. Acts as a significant web retail presence for big names such as The Rolling Stones and Robbie Williams. It recently acquired $15 million in private funding from a combination of finance providers.

www.atomicpop.com
Atomic Pop describes itself as a music-driven, lifestyle web platform, specialising in hip-hop music. Most notably this was the company that distributed the first digitally downloadable album from an established artist, Public Enemy, whose lead singer Chuck D is considered as one of the leading lights in the internet revolution.

www.bands-online.com
A pay-to-play website service for unsigned bands.

www.bigmouth.co.uk
Information site for tours and live concerts.

www.broadcast.com
One of the leading providers of internet radio recently bought by Yahoo.com with a comprehensive search site for radio, CD jukebox and audio books.

www.cddb.com
The world's largest online database of audio CD information with over 400,000 album titles and over 4.5 million tracks.

www.crunch.co.uk
Online music label distributing UK independent music, specialising in dance music.

www.dejamuse.com
Online business consultancy for performance groups, artists, producers and musicians.

www.dustygroove.com
Online retailer specialising in vinyl rarities.

www.electricartists.com
One of the leading internet music consulting companies.

www.emusic.com
Online music retailer offering a wide selection of tracks, mainly from US independent record companies for direct downloading. Single tracks priced at 99 cents.

www.eunite.co.uk
Manchester-based start-up focused on convergent media and intranet streaming with venture capital from 3I and Deloitte and Touche offering services from consultancy to development and implementation.

www.firsttuesday.com
First Tuesday is a collection of resources for the internet entrepreneur in Europe that started out as an e-mail group which encouraged casual get-togethers for UK web entrepreneurs and venture capitalists. It has been the source of much venture capital for internet-based music start-ups and holds regular meetings for people in New Media across Europe.

www.garageband.com
Garageband is an online music community which offers users the chance to review material from unsigned acts. The site carries forward a

chart based upon listeners' views and offers the prospect of a $250,000 recording contracts for the most popular bands. George Martin, ex-Beatles producer, is chair of the advisory board.

www.getsigned.com
Free hosting and downloading service for unsigned bands.

www.indieaudio.com
A 24-hour-per-day radio station established by Canadian-based Global Media offering wall-to-wall independent music.

www.insound.com
An online music retailer, specialising in independent music, which was set up as a central space for like-minded music fans to communicate and shop without the distraction and clutter that accompanies a mainstream music retailer.

www.kashmirklub.com
Website for the innovative London-based Kashmir Klub which regularly webcasts its live concerts Tuesday to Friday.

www.knitmedia.com
Internet webcasts from cult New York venue, the Knitting Factory, run by Michael Dorf, can be heard at this site.

www.madasafish.com
The Internet Service Provider aimed at the music and games infatuated net generation.

www.mediatag.com
Originally a development group within the Central Research Laboratories of Thorn EMI at Hayes, UK, MediaTag was set up as a separate company in 1998 to provide practical, technology independent solutions, using advanced audio and video watermarking and internet and broadcast monitoring. MediaTag is now an industry leader in using technology to protect audio and visual intellectual property. It recently launched a new digital tagging and monitoring service.

www.mmda.org.uk
The website for the Merseyside Music Development Agency set up with mainly European funding to spur growth in the music industry within the Merseyside region. Provides business support, training, advice and signposting to local music companies.

www.mudhut.couk
A UK-based music community site, originally established as a record company, offering a 50-50 split with new bands and free site membership.

www.music.acu.edu/www/iawm/home.html
An information resource site for women in music, containing more than 300 archival resources.

www.musician.com
Music resource site for musicians including search, chat, interviews etc.

www.musicindie.com
Website for the independent record company trade organisation, AIM (Association of Independent Music). Currently in the process of launching a new portal for accessing music from all member companies.

www.musicmatch.com
Free hosting and downloading service for unsigned bands.

www.music.stayfree.co.uk
A Leicester-based organisation offering a range of services to bands, musicians and recording artists including free web space.

www.musicunsigned.com
Website for unsigned bands claiming to offer a more rigorous filtering mechanism with only 30-40 artists who have to pay for the service.

www.muze.com
Began as a provider of music information, and pioneered computer-driven technology for in-store listening. Over recent years their data has been adopted by more than 90 per cent of online music retailers including CDnow and Amazon.

www.onehouse.com
OneHouse is an internet consultancy that is dedicated to the digital delivery of art, with an emphasis on the transition from the analog marketplace to the digital market space, founded by Jim Griffen.

www.peoplesound.com
A UK-based online music service which aims to be the premier European-based navigation tool for genre music searching.

www.resrocket.net
Rocket Network develop software and services that facilitate professional audio collaboration over the internet. This technology was used to record 1999's War Child single – a re-working of Bob Marley's 'Them Belly Full (But We Hungry)' – over the internet using the Rocket Network *in only one hour*.

www.riffage.com
Website for unsigned bands for which artists receive 85 per cent of all sales. Guests can download for free a period of time.

www.shopguide.co.uk
Shopping portal that compares retail prices to give consumers the best deal.

www.shoutitoutloud.com
This site claims to be the UK's first online music label offering free music from unsigned bands.

www.sightsound.com
A US company which holds two patents on the download sale of audio and video recordings over the internet. They offer artists a 70 per cent receipt of sales and payment for every customer download.

www.songlink.com
Provides a linking service for songwriters and publishers based mainly upon placing songs with established artists. Active since 1993.

www.sonicnet.com
An online music network offering music news, live artist events, programmed music channel and a fully searchable music and artist-driven database.

www.soundsbig.com
An online music company which aims to build a participation-driven community to connect music fans and artists, by partnering with artists, music labels, publishers and web portals.

www.spinner.com
A website offering an internet radio service which provides 120 channels of music. Recently bought by AOL. By the end of the year AOL's millions of subscribers should be able to listen to and transmit a variety of music forms at their whim.

www.stargig.com
A website service for unsigned bands which now has a 50 per cent stake in the Band Register which possesses a database of 250,000 worldwide unsigned acts.

www.taxi.com
Intermediary service for artists and writers looking for record companies and vice versa. Writers and artists are charged for the service.

www.theorchard.com
The Orchard offers every artist with finished product, worldwide, non-exclusive distribution. They guarantee that product is sold at all the major online record stores. They charge a one-time fee of $40 per release to join and charge a 30 per cent distribution fee.

www.tunes.com
Chicago-based website that publishes thousands of songs from unsigned artists and independent record labels.

www.tranz-send.com
This San Francisco-based company has developed a system for delivering DVD-quality films, TV programmes or software over the Net

as compressed files that can only be used according to terms established by the copyright owner. Films are encrypted in such a way that the player can run through them once, with a five-minute window for rewinding. In effect, the film erases itself as it plays.

www.vitaminic.co.uk
Vitaminic is a website dedicated to digital music with thousands of MP3 files from bands from all over the world.

LUCKY GIRL GOODBYE

LUCKY GIRL

GOODBYE

Renate Greenshields

First published in December 1988
Reprinted February 1989
Renate Greenshields
Westhay Farm, Hawkchurch,
Axminster, Devon
in association with
The S.P.A. Ltd

© Renate Greenshields
ISBN 1 85421 027 0 (Hardback)
1 85421 034 3 (Paperback)

Typeset by Printit-Now,
Upton-upon Severn
and printed and bound in Great Britain by
Billing & Sons, Worcester, England

For my husband, Tom,
my children,
Anne, Jane, Tim, George and Maria,
and my brother,
Georg-Wilhelm.

About *RENATE GREENSHIELDS*

Renate Greenshields was so often asked, 'What was it like?', not only by her own children but by people from all walks of life, that she decided to sit down and write her story.

Now married to the British Officer who captured her heart at the end of the war, she lives in a beautiful old farmhouse on the Devon/Dorset border and is deeply involved with the work of her husband, who is a successful sculptor.

Renate also runs a summer language school for German students. One of her two sons runs the family farm, the other casts his father's sculptures. Two of Renate's daughters, one of whom is a sculptor, live in London and the third lives at home.

About *LUCKY GIRL GOODBYE*...

Renate Greenshields was born in the north of Germany, and the first part of her book describes a happy childhood in a small town near Hanover where her father was a Lutheran pastor. She describes in detail life in a pre-war Germany that no longer exists.

When Renate was ten, life changed dramatically. She had to join the Hitler Youth. War came and with it the end of happy days. The large vicarage was ideal for helping some Jews to escape. The house was under constant surveillance and the family experienced extreme tension.

Renate was harrassed for being a parson's daughter and found herself confused when her favourite teacher became her father's worst Nazi enemy.

When the war was over the British Town Commandant and Renate fell in love. This provoked a very mixed reaction from her father's parishioners.

In 1946 Renate left for England in the first "War Bride's" boat when she was just eighteen.

CHAPTER 1

It would not be a good idea to go back after all these long years and look at the place where I spent my childhood — my happy unforgettable childhood — and my youth, some of it happy, some sad.

I should love to see the old timber-framed house once again, but I know that would spoil my memory of its dear and welcoming, slightly wrinkled face. I am told that it has had a facelift, that its kind eyes — the windows — which told the truthful age of the house, have been replaced with modern ones. Instead of the pinkish yellow and slightly crumbling plaster, which at the same time was rather appealing, it stands dressed in a coat of brilliant white.

* * *

I was born in the early hours of 20th September 1928. When my father received the news on a golden September morning, he jumped onto his bike and cycled to the nearest station to catch the train to Osnabrueck. When he entered the Maternity Hospital he heard several babies crying, but one voice was especially loud and forceful. When he remarked upon it, he was told by the nurse, "That is our little Parson's daughter."

Mother recovered slowly after my birth. My Godmother, who lived in the same village, moved in and looked after us. I was christened on my father's birthday in his study by my paternal grandfather, as mother was still too weak to walk the short distance to the Church. My father was at that time the rector of a small Westphalian village and my grandfather, semi-retired at the age of seventy, still looked after his own parish near Gottingen. I was given six names: Renate Frida Emma Margarete Arnoldine Ethelinde.

The name Renate was not well known in Germany, and father explained the meaning of it to me when I was old enough to understand. It came from the Latin word *natare,* which means "to be born", but the *Re* was the important part of the name, meaning "again". So I was called born again.

The Winter of 1930 was a very severe one. The Parsonage became almost uninhabitable. In spite of all the love and care, I developed double pneumonia and for weeks was dangerously ill. My parents decided that the sea air would do my lungs good and a large party consisting of my parents, my brother, maternal grandmother and my Godmother set off to Langeoog, one of the North Sea islands, for six long weeks in the early summer.

Numerous photographs showed the happy party in large wicker chairs, whose backs ended in a roof above so as to provide shelter from both sun and wind. Or they showed me, plump and happy in a small basin of water, or my brother standing forlorn in the sand dunes looking out to sea. The funniest ones were of my parents in striped swimming costumes reaching as far as the knees and with little short sleeves. The only way to get to these islands then was by a horse-drawn carriage at low tide when the sea went out for miles.

The holiday was a great success and everybody returned home well. And my lungs have never given me any trouble again.

In the following Autumn my brother had a severe accident. It happened on a warm sunny October afternoon while my parents were having tea in the garden. I was sitting in my pram beside them and my brother was playing ball somewhere in the garden. Suddenly they heard the screeching of brakes. My brother had opened the gate and run into the road to retrieve the ball. A car hit him and dragged him along several metres. He suffered severe concussion, and for another winter my mother had to look after a sick child. Under her constant care and love and through her efficiency, he recovered completely.

After two more years father decided to move to a larger town for two reasons; firstly, he did not want his children to leave

8

home for school, as he never forgot the misery he suffered when he had to leave home at the early age of eight to go to a school twenty kilometres away. Secondly, his voice gave him trouble. The church was an enormous Gothic building with a chancel five metres high, the acoustics being bad and after every sermon his voice went. Thereafter, he found it difficult to speak loudly, and later, when I was old enough, it became my task to mix a raw egg with some milk and put it on the Vestry table before his sermon, to "lubricate" his throat.

He decided to move to Lehrte, near Hannover, where he stayed for twenty-seven years until his retirement. My parents left the little Westphalian village of Buer with heavy hearts. Several times a year father was asked back to preach on special occasions.

CHAPTER 2

The verdict of many who saw Lehrte was: the best thing about it is the station. Why? It is so boring but there is always a train to take you home. Or: the best thing to do in Lehrte is not to leave the station just to change trains.

It was not a pretty place, but I loved it. I loved its ugly watertower; the vulgar, ultra-modern clinker-built town hall; the church, built in 1870, a building devoid of any beauty, at least from the outside; the busy, exciting station and the many railway crossings which cut the little town into numerous sections and were a nuisance to drivers and pedestrians. Sometimes a queue of cars waited in front of the closed barrier, tooting impatiently. This made the guard in his tower-like house open the window: deliberately leaning out of it, he lit his pipe and, with the stateliness of an emperor, watched the growing crowd from above.

All sorts of trains passed through this little town; it was in fact a very important railway junction. There were endless goods trains, slow and fast passenger trains, a new electric train consisting of one coach only, and lastly the *Fliegende Hollaender* (The Flying Dutchman) on its way through from Brussels to Berlin. It was the fastest train in Europe. Once my aunt travelled on it. She had rung the night before from Brussels and I had promised that I would be at the station to wave. Proudly I told my friends, collected a gang of them and, in good time before the train was due, we stood at the station. Finally the signals annouced its approach. Excitedly, I fumbled for my handkerchief, but before I had even got it out of my pocket, the brown and white larvae-like train had shot past, leaving a small group of children huddled against the fence, frightened by the pressure of its speed. All we could see were two red lights disappearing into the distance.

Lehrte was divided into two parts, the village and the town. We lived in the village. About thirty farms lay closely beside each other and flanked the village street on both sides; only a few lay tucked away in some off-shoot of the main street. The centre of it was the village green, called the Lindenberg, with six large old lime trees. A long time ago the village green had been in a different place, in front of the oldest farmhouse, which had since crumbled away. But the old oak, also the oldest in the village, still stood, gnarled and decayed, determined to survive its rivals, the younger limes.

Not far from the village green stood the old 12th-century church, a building of rough pink and grey sandstone with its lead spire perched on a squat whitewashed tower, pointing towards the sky like a witch's hat with a cockerel as a weather-vane. The church stood slightly above the road, surrounded by a thorn hedge which hid the ancient tombstones and the rusted iron crosses of the churchyard.

The Old Church

12

Almost opposite was the Rectory into which we moved in 1932. The house lay back from the main street of the village, flanked by two old barns and guarded by tall acacias, a weeping willow in the middle of the lawn, and an enormous old oak tree. A long path of stone slabs led to the heavy front door with its brass handle and lock, fit for any stately home. A double and a single gate of wrought iron gave entry to the yard and house. The Rectory was a typical timber-framed cobb house of the 17th century. It looked like a friendly face, which even remained friendly in rainy weather, as the old bricks never seemed to change to the sad and dreary colour some houses take on when the rain wets their walls. Its many windows, thirty-two of them, made the house very light inside, and when the sun was shining, they twinkled in happy reflection.

It could be said that this Rectory was not exactly modern or even convenient for a housewife, but it did have running water and a bathroom and, of course, electricity. With the years, Mother insisted on various changes, but not nearly enough of them were effected before the War broke out, when everything came to a standstill. Most of the numerous plans for alterations never left the drawing board.

Large tiled stoves heated the rooms. Coal and logs had to be carried from the outhouses across the yard, and, as most of our living-rooms were on the first floor, many buckets of coal had to be taken upstairs. The lower and the upper hall were icy in the winter and no stove could even begin to heat them. We got into the habit of running across them in the winter months, to get to the warmth of the rooms and kitchen as quickly as possible. The lower hall had stone tiles and the upper one had wide, old wooden planks, which were highly polished and dusted every day. I once saw Mother going halfway down the stairs and when she was at eye level with the floor, she looked through the bannisters to see if there was any dust left on the boards. There was. The maid was fetched immediately and the last speck of dust removed.

In the summer we had our meals upstairs. I always felt rather uncomfortable because a large picture, easily ten foot in length in a heavy black frame, showing in most horrifying detail the

"Destruction of Jerusalem", dominated the hall. I tried to avoid looking at it when passing it. But sitting at the table the nicest food was somehow made less tasty by suddenly coming eye to eye with the gory happenings in the picture. I tried sitting with my back to it, but the mere knowledge of the "things" behind, jumped on to my shoulders like an *alpdruck* (nightmare).

I far preferred the winter months when we had our meals in the cosy little room downstairs, which was also our nursery.

Numerous doors with decorative brass handles and locks, each different, so that every door had its own particular sound when opened or shut, led from the upper hall into various rooms: six bedrooms, a bathroom, father's study, the large drawing-room with its four windows facing south and overlooking the garden, and mother's salon, called the "Green room" because everything in it was green. The velvet sofa and its matching green armchairs, the bow-legged mahogany chairs around the mahogany table had green velvet seats, even the carpet was green. Here mother sat at her desk writing letters. She preferred to give her tea-parties in this room rather than in the large drawing-room next door.

In the summer, blinds were drawn half-way to protect the furniture from the sun, but the open windows let in enough air to allow the white muslin curtains to play flirtingly with the light breeze.

In the autumn, we hardly had to lean out of the window to pick a juicy bunch of grapes which grew all over the south wall of the house. In the winter all the windows were tightly shut and each one was paired with another set brought down from the attic. Thick velvet curtains, held in place by heavy brass rings, replaced the playful muslin curtains which now, gathered tightly with a wide band, hung sad and lifeless all through the winter months.

Towards the end of February, pots with crocuses, tulips and hyacinths, still in their infancy, were put between the windows and gradually, through the next two months, came into flower. On a particularly warm, sunny and spring-promising day, the windows were opened. Drops of melted snow hung from the

14

gutters above, sparkling with rainbow colours in the sun and dripping steadily onto the snow below, just missing the window-sill. It was not until the end of April that the double windows were finally unhooked and taken back to the attic, the velvet curtains removed and folded, then packed into the camphor chest, and, at last, the white muslin curtains were released from their tight grip to play once again in the breeze.

Father's study was on the north side of the house, facing the courtyard. It was a dark room. The wall-paper had been originally of a light colour, but Father's constant smoking of pipes and cigars had made it brown. Brown also were his desk, chairs and table, as were the cushions and blankets on the sofa. Most of the books which stood shelf upon shelf along the walls were of brown leather with golden lettering; the shelves reached almost as high as the ceiling, but leaving enough room for large old Bibles lying on their sides. These were old family Bibles. One of the most precious possessions was an old Koran, a beautifully-bound small book.

At least twenty pipes of different shapes and sizes hung neatly arranged in a stand on the old smoking-table in the corner. On the shelf below stood cigar boxes, piled on top of each other, of "Handles Gold" and "Havanas". The little drawer above, with its decorative brass knob, took care of the pipe cleaners and matches.

Two things in that room concerned me most. One I feared, the other I loved. The one I dreaded was a long ruler of red lacquer, slightly faded, its varnish cracking. It stood, leaning against the wall, on the smoking-table, and the only time it was used was on my brother's and my own behinds. Father hated using it and only reached for it in extreme cases of naughtiness. It was used on my own behind far more than on my brother's, who bent over as told and took his punishment stoically, without uttering a sound. I fought back like a wild cat, biting and hitting out, trying to snatch the ruler out of my father's hand. This infuriated him so much that my punishment always ended up far more severe than originally intended.

The thing that delighted me was a wooden money-box on the

15

desk, about a foot long. It showed a black boy kneeling down in prayer on a grassy hilltop. As soon as a piece of money fell through the slot in front of him, he nodded his curly head in thanks, and resumed praying.

One picture in the study fascinated me. It showed Daniel in the Lions' Den, in a ray of sunlight looking up towards the window, with the lions standing behind him, one licking his feet like a faithful dog.

The attic was huge and covered the whole of the house. Two ordinary-sized windows at each end and numerous small ones on the tiled roof gave ample light during the day. It was a lovely place to be in but, when the daylight began to fade, I was scared to go up by myself. Whenever I had to fetch something from the loft in the evenings for my mother I went to extremes to find somebody to come with me. Mostly I ended up by bribing my brother that I would not tell that he was reading in bed when lights should be out. Reluctantly he would come with me as far as the attic door, where he would sit down on the upper step of the short but very steep staircase.

The switch for the electric light was outside the attic, and what I was really afraid of was that somebody could switch it off while I was inside. A horrid cousin had once done just that and I had nearly died of fright. My brother would never do that; I could rely on him.

Everything that appeared harmless and friendly during the day took on a threatening shape when the light became dim. The bunches of beans in the pods hanging up to dry looked like heads of Red Indians, and the rows and rows of corn cobs for the chickens looked like daggers.

The atmosphere was completely different during the day. It was a cheerful and exciting place in which lingered a sweet and mysterious aroma, coming mainly from the drying herbs, which hung in small bunches from the beams – camomile and peppermint for colds and tummy-aches, garlic and onions, and, most of all, from the apples. The floor space was vast and, although numerous bits of furniture were stored there, it was not in the least cluttered. Wide, hard floor-boards sustained a great

16

weight, even our roller-skating, which produced quite an alarming noise and was only permitted when my parents were out.

Four attic rooms lay tucked under the large sloping roof. They were the apple room, the Christmas store room, the bedding room and the smoke room.

Three of them would have made lovely bedrooms, but they became too hot in summer and too cold in winter. Looking down from the attic windows one saw the village from an unusual angle. One looked down upon the red tiled roofs of the cottages and their neat gardens of flower-beds and fruit trees. The dreaded farm dogs appeared small and insignificant, the ferocious gander was a small speck. Only the church spire stood as usual, dominating, grey and large, reaching out to the sky.

The apple room was the second largest of the four rooms. White muslin bags full of dried apple rings, prunes and hazelnuts hung from the ceiling. Apples and pears, carefully sorted into their varieties, lay, not touching each other, on the shelves. Little tags nailed onto the shelves told their names. Each fruit had been carefully picked in the autumn by my mother. Most of the apple trees in the garden were of a dwarf variety, but the pear trees were tall, old and dangerous to climb. This did not deter mother from climbing into them, completely fearless, and determined to get every pear, however impossible and dangerous it seemed to the onlooker. Precariously, she balanced on the brittle branches, not giving in until the last pear was safely and carefully put into her basket.

Twice a week in the winter months, Mother went up to the apple room and selected the ripe fruit and took away what was rotten or wormy. She had chosen her fruit trees so carefully that we had a variety of ripe fruit right up until the spring. The nicest were the "Christmas pear" and the "Napoleon's butter pear", so large and juicy that one was too much for one person, but too little for two. It was a ritual to eat them, either after lunch or in the evening in father's study just before bedtime, off fruit-plates handpainted with a golden rim. They were peeled with delicate fruit-knives with blue and white Meissen handles. They were delicious fruits and deserved precious things.

Next to the apple room was the small Christmas store room. Labelled boxes contained everything to do with Christmas: painted crib figures, candleholders and tree decorations. There was also a flat box full of long narrow silver strips, called "Lametta" which were hung from the Christmas tree branches like frozen rain.

The smell of honey wax candles and the faint fragrance of pine needles never left that room and was powerful enough to transmit a Christmas mood, even on a hot summer day. At the other end of the loft was the biggest room. In it stood enormous wooden boxes. One of them had father's name written all over it, and it was lined with pages and pages from exercise books in Greek, Latin and Hebrew. They seemed to me like drawings of crosses and dots and circles. This box had been father's book trunk and had followed him to every university he had been to. Now it contained heavy winter coats and furs, sprinkled with anti-moth crystals and camphor. Other boxes were filled with feather duvets this was of course during the summer only. In the winter they were almost empty except for the light summer eiderdowns. I did not like this room very much. The smell of mothballs was unpleasant and the contents of the boxes uninteresting, except for one bit of furniture. It was an invalid commode of mahogany whose lid bore a monogram. The fascinating thing about it was the huge chamber-pot inside, decorated with delicate bunches of roses and green garlands. Every time my brother and I went into this room we lifted up the lid and admired this beautifully painted but incredibly large vessel. Once I heard my brother, when he was closing the lid, murmur, "Quite impossible!" and he shook his head at the same time.

I was much more interested in the small room in the middle of the loft where most of the house's flue pipes met and went into one big chimney. Around it a small room had been built. This was the smoke room, into which led a tiny door made of gauze to keep out the flies. Here the smoked sausages were kept and the hams hung from large hooks. They were wrapped in muslin bags, yellowed from pepper and fat. It was the only room with a padlock; only mother had the key and it was mother only who decided which sausage to take down. I had never seen anybody else cut the ham except mother. I hardly ever missed this occasion and watched her, fascinated, as she took down the ham and put it onto the little table to take off the bag. Carefully she scraped off the powdered pepper with the big sharp knife and then cut into the pink ham bordered by strips of white fat. I liked it best when she started to cut a new ham. Once the bone appeared the ham became ugly, for she skilfully cut around the bone, so that eventually a nasty stump, like an amputated limb, stuck out, and this repulsed me. Each time mother sprinkled the newly-cut bit with fresh pepper before she put it back into the muslin bag. But before it went into the bag she looked smilingly at me, cut a very thin slice and handed it to me on the knife. This was the moment I had waited for. The ham was so tender and delicious, it melted in my mouth.

One big treasure stored in the loft was the toboggan. My grandmother had bought it in Lausanne for us. Its front was gracefully curved like the horns of a ram, its slats were thick and round. It was not a piece of factory work, as my grand mother pointed out to us, but a piece of craftsmanship. My brother was not very keen on tobogganing, but I was. From the first snowflake until the last bit of snow had melted the toboggan and I were inseparable friends.

There was also the old sledge, a Victorian bygone, like a wheelchair, only on rails and was painted in green and gold. It was pushed from the back. Once my brother and I took it out for an airing in the winter. I sat, wrapped in a blanket on the cast-iron seat and my brother pushed. It was hard work at first.The runners were rusty and left narrow brown marks in the snow, but after a while they glided easily over it and my brother began to try all sorts of tricks, like sharp turns, to upset me, but the sledge was well-balanced. We had great fun but it was spoiled by the village children, who almost killed themselves laughing and shouting rude remarks at the unusual sight. This stopped us from taking it out again, but we soon found many other purposes for it. We imagined it to be our tram, train, plane, even our pony cart.

One of the greatest secrets my brother and I ever shared was the "preaching". An old, disused lectern started it off. My brother began to preach in the loft. Later in his life he never had the slightest wish to become a parson, but at this stage in his young life it must have been there. One day he appeared in my father's long winter coat, a Bible pressed against his chest. Slowly he walked towards the lectern and began to preach. I was his sole congregation, sitting on a footstool below him with folded hands. Almost in the same voice as my father, he read a short text from the Bible and then began to tell stories, keeping up his parson's voice throughout his favourite stories, such as "Winnetou", "Quo Vadis", and, for my own special benefit (or the Sunday school children's benefit, as he announced), a fairy story. I was fascinated. A more ardent listener no parson could have wished for, but then, not all sermons were as interesting and captivating as my brother's stories. Alas, everything comes to an end. After a while his repertoire petered out and the stories repeated themselves a bit too often and I became bored. One day my footstool remained empty and there was no congregation. I think my brother must have been aware of his lack of inspiration because he made no attempt to claim me back. I often wonder for how long he went on preaching to himself in the attic.

As much as I loved the attic, I hated the cellar. There was no real cellar underneath the house, but a small dungeon-like vault with immensely thick walls. It had been built onto the house, halfway above ground. A pair of stone steps led from the kitchen into this dark, dank place. Two small windows with iron bars let in very little light. Along three of the cellar walls were shelves, on which were stored wine and bottles of fruit juice. I had a real horror of this place. Little did I know that later I should have to spend the greater part of three years in there.

* * *

My earliest childhood memory goes back to the age of two. I was

20

lying in a cradle: somebody I did not know bent over me and gave me a wooden spoon. I started to play with it and banged it rather too hard on the edge of the cradle (it must have been a fairly rotten spoon), and it broke in half. Silver stars and a large orange moon with a grinning face looked down on me. My mother explained to me years later when I mentioned these memories to her that an amateur dramatic group of our village performed the play by the well-known German author Matthias Claudius, *The Moon has Risen* – for which I was borrowed. Of the play I remember an enormously tall man with a top-hat trying to take me out of the cradle into his arms. Naturally, I was terrified and began to scream. The play had to stop and mother rushed from the audience onto the stage to pacify me, without any result. I refused to get back into the cradle and soon was fast asleep on her lap and the play had to go on without me. Father referred to my little episode as the *Intermezzo* and burst into laughter every time he was reminded of it. I was never borrowed for any acting again, but a certain dismay of men in top hats remained.

Gewi and Renate in The Rectory garden

21

The next thing I remember happened six months later. My brother had been very ill with a kidney complaint and needed my mother's sole attention. I was very much in the way with my liveliness, so it was decided that my father should take me to my maternal grandmother in Schleswig-Holstein, a long journey for a two and half year old who could not sit still for one minute.

The actual train journey I can't remember, but apparently, after a short period of looking out of the window I said in a loud and urgent voice that I had to spend a penny. Father was at an absolute loss. Never in his life had he been confronted with such a problem before, and despite all the advice mother had given him, she had forgotten to mention this vital detail. Luckily, a very nice woman in the compartment had watched this situation smilingly and offered to take me. I do remember sitting in a large waiting-room in Hamburg afterwards with a glass of milk in front of me and father urging me to drink it. I did not want to and no coaxing, pleading or bribing helped. I sat with my mouth tightly shut, refusing to take even a sip. Then my father had a brilliant idea. He remembered how much I loved clinking glasses, and so with every sip a beer glass and a milk glass met and the milk was drunk. It was a long process but it kept me occupied.

I can't remember anything of my stay with grandmother, except that I missed my mother dreadfully. It was obvious that I was homesick. Apparently I ate little and was, much against my nature, very quiet. At last mother came to fetch me (I think father dreaded another journey alone with me). I can remember the immense joy in my heart when I was told of her coming. When finally we fetched her from the station, I was wearing white knee socks, a thing for special occasions only, and I was skipping for joy beside grandmother. It had rained during the night, and this had left little puddles on the path, over which I jumped, not always missing them, and my white socks became splattered with mud. Grandmother's scolding could not stop me, nothing could stop me, for my mother was coming. And then I saw her coming towards us. I can remember so well the thought which came into my head — it hurts me to think of it now. I suddenly thought, why should I run towards her? She had sent me away and I did not like it. A few feet away my mother stood with her arms outstretched and I stood stock still, pretending not to know her.

With tears in her eyes mother cried: 'Don't you know your mummy any more?' "Oh, yes I do!" my heart cried out, but I shook my head and took grandmother's hand and didn't talk to mother at all, only looked at her.

That night mother and I slept together in the big double bed. When I woke next morning I saw her looking lovingly at me. I could not restrain myself any longer, but flung my arms around her neck and sobbed all the homesickness of the last few weeks out of me. I wouldn't let her out of my sight or let go of her hand for the rest of our stay.

CHAPTER 3

When my brother was well again, mother wanted to surprise my father for his birthday with a professional photograph of his children.

She took us to Hannover on a sultry August afternoon. Dark clouds hung from the sky and looked menacingly through the vast glass roof of the studio. Lightning illuminated the whole of it and frightened me. I buried my head in my mother's lap. Nothing could persuade me to pose for the picture. The photographer had to wait until the storm was over. My dress was of white organza with red embroidery, and I wore a little necklace of tiny moonstones. My brother wore a white sailor's suit. For the first time, mother had put a white ribbon into my unruly blonde curls. I did not like this at all and constantly tried to get it out. In the end mother lost her patience with me, especially as the photographer began to get impatient too as the thunderstorm went on and on, and she slapped my hand. This produced tears and an even longer wait. Finally the portrait was taken and all of us smiled happily, and the white bow in my hair stuck out like a starched white pigeon. I remember the photographer asking mother if she would allow him to take a few more photographs of me for advertisements, because I had "such lovely eyes." Mother was horrified and refused with great certainty.

One Winter morning – it must have been in 1933 – our house was suddenly full of people. It was at the time of the great unemployment. The church was trying to help. With a group of volunteers mother had sewn clothes until late into the nights, and now every room was stacked with coats and jackets and all sorts of other garments. Father had been to his former parish and collected food from the farmers. They had given so much that he had to hire a van to transport it back. He had also been given clothes, material and shoes from three drapers' shops in

Portrait of Gewi and Renate

our town. These were owned by Jews, called Simon, Maschekatz and Meinrath. Their generosity had been overwhelming, and there was no doubt that most of the gifts had come from these three.

More and more people crowded into the house, men and women with pale drawn faces, dressed inadequately for the winter cold. An unpleasant smell spread about the house. Unpleasant also was their behaviour; their manners were rough and they could become dangerous. They took the help offered as a matter of course. They became angry and rude if a garment given to them was not exactly the right fit or to their liking. My brother and I had been told not to leave our nursery on that day, but of course, I did and tried to ascend the crowded staircase with my favourite doll under my arm.

At that very moment the riot started. I saw fists lashing out everywhere; blood squirted from noses and mouths. The shouting drowned my frightened crying, especially when my doll was snatched from me. I most certainly would have come to harm, had not two strong arms lifted me up and carried me to safety. They were the arms of a policeman. Suddenly all was quiet: the police soon restored order and stayed in the house until the last person was fitted-out, which was late at night. My parents were both so tired that I never got told off for leaving my nursery. Losing my doll was enough punishment in itself.

When I was five years old I started to go to the Kindergarten. My brother had been going to school for quite a while now and the mornings had become lonely and boring for me. I must have had a few playmates, though I can only remember two. The funny thing about these two was that they were uncle and nephew. Their father and grandfather respectively, was a crude and enormously large person, who wore a shiny leather apron. I never saw him without it. He was a pub owner and a coal merchant at the same time, and lived not far from our house, His loud, unpleasant voice could be heard for miles, and every child in the village was afraid of him, as were his own five children and his wife. His youngest son, Ernstchen, the same age as myself, had been an after-thought, and Alex, a year younger, was the illegitimate son of his eldest daughter. These two were my friends. Ernstchen's mother had a small sweet shop, but although he tried to convince me that lollipops and gobstoppers were far cheaper in his mother's shop, the fear of meeting his father led me in my early childhood to the extravagance of spending more for my sweets at another shop.

Unfortunately, I sometimes had to take shoes to the old shoemaker who lived in the attic of Ernstchen's house. Steep, narrow wooden stairs led to his workshop. Ernstchen's father, hated a lot of people in the village, but mostly my father. Soon after our move to Lehrte, my father turned one of our barns into a church hall. Up until then Ernstchen's father had been allowed to store hay for his horses there and he also made use of the lovely fresh eggs our hens had been laying. All this came to a stop with the conversion of the barn and he resented it. He completely ignored my father but got his own back on me.

Every time I had to go to the shoemaker I tried to sneak into Ernstchen's house without being seen, but most times I was unlucky – his father was lying in wait for me. I even tried taking off my shoes and going up the stairs without making any noise at all, but every time he had seen me going up and waited for me to come down again. He stood at the bottom of the stairs, legs apart, his fleshy arms tattooed with snakes and naked girls. He grinned when he saw me hesitating to come down with my shoes in my hands.

Sneeringly he shouted, 'Are you afraid, you little holy one?'

Every time I thought my last moment had come, but he never touched me, and he moved just a little to let me pass. A shiver went through me when my arm came in contact with his dirty leather apron. Then he turned triumphantly round and shouted spitefully after me: *Pastoren Scheisser.* (Shit of a parson's daughter).

It was I myself who made this situation even worse. On a fine Autumn morning I was collecting acorns in the yard with Ernstchen and Alex. We were going to sell them to Frau Kruse for her pig. I liked Ernstchen very much but not so much Alex, and with this his uncle agreed heartily. As I was putting acorns into my basket next to Ernstchen, his little round face came close to mine, and I suddenly had the desire to kiss him, which I did. I don't know what came over me next, but I bit him also. He at once let out a piercing yell and ran home with his hand over his cheek.

It wasn't long before his father, with a still frightened Ernstchen beside him, rang the doorbell and triumphantly showed my parents the tooth marks of their vampire daughter. I can't remember if he demanded compensation, but I was sent to my room for the rest of the day and was given "prison food", as we called it – dry bread and a glass of milk.

Ernstchen did not come to play with me again for a long time, nor did his nephew. When he finally came back, he always kept a certain distance from me.

As I grew older, I grew less frightened of his father. I even dared to make some extra loud noises going up the stairs to provoke him. He gave up waiting for me at the bottom of the stairs, but never failed, when he saw me, to shout a rude remark after me.

I loved seeing the shoemaker and always spent a considerable time with him. He lived alone. Sometimes mother gave me some soup for him, which I carried in a little white milk-can. Every time he said politely, "Please thank Frau Pastor for me," and he emptied the contents into a very dirty saucepan which he put onto the small round cast-iron stove next to a pot of hot liquid glue, in which stuck a blackened wooden spoon. I loved the smell of this glue, and always asked if I might stir the delicious, yellowish, almost transparent mixture. He let me, but only a couple of stirs and then he said quite firmly, "That's enough". The mess in the little room was incredible. Shoes and boots of all sizes lay in a big heap beside his chair, but the funny thing was that one never had to wait for more than a couple of days for the repair of one's shoes. The repaired ones stood ready for collection on a small table, some highly polished, some as dirty as they had been on their arrival.

In spite of being a very busy man, he always seemed to have time for a chat and he knew exactly what I was waiting for. He

29

had a parrot which lived in a cage near the window above his worktop. One could ask anything under the sun, and the bird always knew the correct answer. Each time I thought of something really difficult which he could not possibly know, but the bird was a miracle: he knew the answer, and replied correctly in a very human, slightly hoarse voice.

By and by I noticed a certain resemblance between his voice and that of the shoemaker, who always sat with his back towards me when the bird answered. One day I told him of my suspicion but he laughed and, with some nails between his teeth, said in the parrot's voice, "No, no, it isn't true." I knew it was.

The highlight was his zither which lay on the bed next door. It was a beautiful zither of ebony with mother-of-pearl decorations. Every time I went into his bedroom to fetch it, gooseflesh came all over me, for on the chest of drawers, in a large dome-shaped jar filled with methylated spirit, coiled a dead adder. Without once taking my eyes off this extraordinary bedroom decoration, I fumbled for the instrument and went backwards out of the room, and shut the door very firmly behind me, then handed Herr Domeier the zither.

He stood up, wiped his dirty hands on the even dirtier apron, which still showed, here and there, the original green colour. He pushed aside the boots on the small table and very carefully put the instrument on it. He twiddled with the numerous pegs, and then plucked all the strings with his thumb to see if it was in tune. I could not judge if he played well or not; but for me it was heavenly music. I looked, fascinated, at his fingers with the long dirty fingernails as they pressed down on the strings for an extra loud and impressive vibrato.

Anyway, to the Kindergarten I had to go and I didn't like it one little bit. I loved Tante Lisbeth, the Kindergarten teacher, but I didn't like any of the other children. I can't remember why, I just did not like them and refused to join in any of their games or to sit down at the same table with them. For a while they let me be, thinking I would get used to them, but I didn't, and after a few weeks I became so impossible that I was allowed to stay at home again.

30

Once in a while I stayed a weekend with Tante Lisbeth, mostly when mother had one of her migraines. Tante Lisbeth lived at the other end of the town and our maid took me, pushing her bicycle, on which she had fastened my small suitcase. She held on to the bike with one hand and to me with the other. I carried a little basket into which I had packed my nightie and my toothbrush and my doll. Tante Lisbeth had so many things in her flat which delighted a child's heart, but the nicest thing was her voice, and she kindled in me the joy of singing and of listening to music. Her brother, who lived with her, was very amused by my singing. There were one or two letters I could not yet pronounce properly, like the "sch" which I pronounced as "s" only. He always asked me to sing: *Soene Luefte, soener sall, soener Fruehling ueberall.*

Not only could Tante Lisbeth sing well; she told stories most beautifully, and all three of us sat after supper in the cosy kitchen, I in my nightie on her lap, sucking my two middle fingers, until my eyelids dropped and Uncle Herrmann carried me to my bed, both of them tucking me in tenderly.

One night it was not quite so peaceful. I had a great dislike of onions and there were plenty in the fried potatoes for supper. Tante Lisbeth insisted that I should eat them, but suddenly I took my plate and emptied the contents onto the floor. This earned me a severe smack. On top of it, I was sent to bed early without a story. Above my head hung a luminous cross which looked menacing in the dark and frightened me. I had told Tante Lisbeth I did not like it, but she said it was there to comfort people. Every night I pulled the blankets over my eyes, so that I could not see it, but that night I kept on looking at it out of the corner of my eyes, and instead of feeling frightened, let alone comforted, I felt very, very miserable and homesick. I began to weep quietly. I was used to saying my prayers with my mother beside me, but this night two small hands folded by themselves and ardently I prayed: "Please, God, deliver me from these unjust people."

Next morning deliverance came. Everything had been forgotten and I was playing happily, when my brother suddenly

31

arrived to take me home. Tante Lisbeth was very surprised. I should have stayed for another few days as arranged, but my brother, Gewi, insisted. I packed my little basket, and hand in hand, Gewi taking his duty to look after me very seriously, we walked home. Everybody was surprised to see me, but all the same, mother, more or less recovered, took me into her arms and said how nice it was to have me back. It turned out that my brother had acted entirely on his own because, as he confessed, he had missed me.

* * *

When I was five years old I still sucked my fingers, which, as a result, had started to grow crooked. When I developed measles and the doctor came, mother asked him at the same time to look at my fingers. I have always had a most unnatural horror of doctors and illness. Once, when mother had helped a woman who fainted in the street, I asked her afterwards: "With which hand did you touch her?" and avoided that hand for a long time.

The doctor gave mother two small wooden splints for her to fasten on to my fingers with a bandage. Furiously I looked at the doctor, took the splints from the bedside table, jumped out of bed, and before anybody could stop me, threw them out of the open window. But it had done the trick. The horror of the splints was enough to make me stop sucking my fingers.

My terror of illness was so vivid and exaggerated, that the sight of a drop of blood would drive me into hysterics. One evening when I could not get to sleep I heard voices and footsteps going backwards and forwards across the hall. I got up quietly and opened the door and saw our maid coming out of my father's study carrying a basin of blood. I shot across the hall, shouting, "What has happened to my father?" When I burst into his room I saw him sitting in his armchair, with a woman whom I did not know holding under his arm a basin into which dripped blood. I was almost beside myself on seeing this. Mother, startled and horrified by my sudden appearance, tried to explain that this nice woman was only putting leeches on father's arm and that he was perfectly all right. In fact he smiled quite happily at me. But what did I understand about all that? I started to scream and actually went for the woman, who after a few quiet words from mother, packed her bags and hurriedly left the house. Only then did I start to calm down. I was pale, I trembled all over and my heart was beating wildly. Mother wrapped me in a blanket and carried me back to bed, gave me a sugar lump dipped in milk, and sat down beside me until I fell asleep. I don't know whether father had any more of such horrid treatments, but most certainly not in our house.

CHAPTER 4

My parents were a handsome couple. I was very proud of them. Both were tall and slim, with dark, almost black hair. Mother's was curly, but father's was straight, with a parting to one side and the other, fuller side resting in a slight swoop on his large forehead.

Not only was I proud of their handsome looks. I was proud for what they were, that they were our parents. In my childhood I took for granted everything they did, but when I grew older, perhaps from the age of ten, I began to realise how much of their lives they devoted to us children and to everybody who needed their help. I have seen them utterly exhausted in the evenings, especially during the war, not just with physical fatigue but mainly with worries, never about themselves, always about others. In spite of this, they never failed to show us and give us their love. They found time to go for walks with us, to play games with us and read to us.

The nicest thing was when mother, before our bedtime, sang with us from the big old song book, called *Kinderland,* which showed in colourful and descriptive pictures the content of nursery rhymes and folksongs. I can still see mother's fingers hovering, slightly shaking, over the keyboard of the harmonium when she tried to read the music and text at the same time. Gewi and I sat each side of her on the tall and slightly sloping oak bench, I resting my head on her shoulder. I loved singing the cheerful songs, but oh, when it came to the sad ones like *Haenschen klein* or *Morgenrot Leuchtest mir zum fruehen Tod,* or *Nun ade Du mein schoen Heimatland* – where the picture showed a young man leaving home to earn his living, waving a last farewell to his mother, who stood crying at the small wicket gate, drying her eyes with the corner of her apron – then I could not sing any more. Tears choked my throat and I moved even closer to mother. But even mother's clear voice (or was it perhaps the mournful sound of the harmonium?) seemed to fill me with utter sadness. I suffered badly from homesickness every time I went by myself on a holiday, and the older I got, the worse it became.

I adored mother; I thought everything about her was beautiful. Her oval face with the delicate complexion could go very brown in the summer. Her nose was thin and perhaps a little too long. Her lips were always a fraction parted by a front tooth which slightly overlapped the other. Her large blue eyes gave her face a sunny, kind expression; they were also sympathetic and laughing eyes. Very rarely did they appear otherwise, but when there was a very good reason they could suddenly look strict and penetrating. Then it was no good to tell a lie – when those eyes looked at you like that, you had to tell the truth. It did not happen often; we almost loved it. We actually sometimes asked mother to make her *Polizeiaugen*, (policeman's eyes) as we called them. But it wasn't the same when there was no reason for it. She over-exaggerated, and we all, including mother, burst out laughing.

Mother dressed well. She loved nice clothes though she was by no means extravagant. On the contrary, she was very thrifty. Father was utterly hopeless with money, so mother looked after the finances. We were not rich but comfortably off. Twice in their lifetime after each of the last two wars, my parents lost their savings through inflation. We did not often have luxuries, only on very special occasions. My parents had their annual three week holiday, which they spent mostly in Bavaria. Father's "luxuries" were books and concerts in Hanover, and mother's were the occasional new dresses, and plants for her garden. Mother worked hard. With the help of one maid and, once in a while with the help of a gardener, she looked after the house and large garden.

A lot of guests filled our house throughout the year; friends and relations and parishioners. Mother did all the cooking; she was an excellent cook. Flowers and pretty things made the house look cheerful and cosy. Parishioners sought not only father's advice but mother's as well. Her training as a nurse came in handy. I remember one girl coming to her in a very distressed state of mind. Mother found poison in the girl's handbag. She took her in and looked after her for several weeks. When the girl got better she went back to her own flat but committed suicide a few days afterwards. These things made mother very sad. She grew grey prematurely, and I often wondered if it was because of all the sadness she saw, especially during the war. Like father, she was loved and respected in the parish: people sought their comforting and help and they were always ready to give it.

Father called mother mostly by her Christian name, but in the diminutive *Paulinchen* as she was also called by our friends and relations. Gewi sometimes called her *Paulinchen* as well, but I liked to call her *Dotte* once in a while.

She once looked after a small boy suffering fromTB. He could not pronounce her surname, which was Gotthardt before she got married, so he called her *Dotte*. Mother had been very fond of the little boy, who died, and she still talked about him once in a while. Perhaps because of a little jealousy on my part, I sometimes called her *Dotte* and mother smiled every time I did so.

Physically I felt closer to mother than to my father. I loved it when she stroked my hair with my head in her lap or when she kissed my forehead or cheek, or when she hugged me and tucked me up in bed at night. That physical contact with mother made me secure and happy. When I was about 8 years old I wrote a poem about her which ended with;

Mein groesster Wunsch ist, denn ich bin klein,
ein Kangeruh Baby bei Mutti zu sein.
(My biggest wish, for I am tiny, is to be a Kangaroo baby with Mummy).

I adored my mother but I worshipped my father. To him I went when I was frightened, when I wanted advice, when I had done something wrong. I sat on his lap with my arm around his neck but I did not cuddle up to him. Father treated me from an early

Portrait of Renate's mother

age as a pal, a friend.

Many years later, on his death-bed, he stretched out his hand to me and said, "We have always been good comrades and understood each other. It has been one of my greatest joys."

Father was very sensitive. He knew when something bothered me. He would put his arm around my shoulders and ask, "What is it?"

I could tell him everything. He gave advice, comfort, faith to me, the child, with the same seriousness and conviction as he did to all his parishioners. Comforted, relieved and cheerful I left his study many a time, skipped across the hall and slid down the bannisters back to the nursery downstairs.

Besides being handsome, father was also very clever. A scholar of theology and philosophy, he was also a scholar of ancient languages. He spoke Greek, Latin and Hebrew fluently, and talked four European languages. His greatest hobbies were reading and music, his greatest gift his sermons, which were powerful, faith-giving and uncomplicated, so that young and old could benefit. Father's sermons were printed in numerous booklets all over Germany. He took the greatest trouble to prepare his sermons on Saturday nights until late into the morning. It was the only time when nobody was allowed to disturb him, not even mother. But on many a Sunday morning at 3 or 4 o'clock she would quietly open the study door and whisper, "It's time for you to go to bed."

From when I was about six years old, I used to accompany father on his way to Matins. To avoid the churchgoers we took a different route, and a slight detour took us along the little river, over the bridge, through an alleyway and across the patch of grass with the tall elms to the vestry door at the apse of the church. I walked beside or behind him, carefully carrying a mug, half filled with a raw egg beaten with milk, which father drank just before the sermon to lubricate his throat. We never talked on our way to church. I knew father was preoccupied with his sermon and I would not have wanted to disturb him. In the vestry, on cold winter days stood a small electric bar heater over which we warmed our hands. A churchwarden usually waited

Portrait of Renate's father

for him and, after discussing one or two things went back into the church. The organ quietly played an introduction and muffled coughs and clearings of throats came from the waiting congregation.

Father put on his black gown, gathered from the yoke in many folds. When I was still too small to reach up to him, I climbed onto a chair to tie the white starched bands around the collar, carefully tucking in the ends. Whenever I was not there to do this, father forgot about the ends and they remained sticking out from under the collar. Having done this, father wanted to be alone. We shook hands solemnly and I went home.

My brother had his Sunday duty as well. His job was to light the candles and to put out the collection plates. He then took up his post in the porch and, of his own accord and, if I remember correctly, against father's will, counted the arriving congregation, nodding a good morning to those he knew, continuing with his counting which he recorded in his private notebook. He always had (and still has) a passion for records.

After church I once again went to the vestry, and untied father's bands and put them carefully into the big, fat Bible which lay on the table. This time we walked hand in hand the usual way home, father raising his hat non stop because everybody knew him. Sometimes he stopped and talked to somebody. When it took too long I grew impatient and tugged at his sleeve. We continued our walk in cheerful chatter. Sometimes we hummed one of father's university songs which he had taught me, sometimes we played a game when father put his large soft hand over my eyes, leading me along, going this way and that way, sometimes turning around in a full circle, and I had to guess where I was. Yes, father and I were great friends.

Father had a lot of female admirers. In no way did he try to charm them – he had a natural charm which women found irresistible. He enjoyed female company, especially intellectual female company, but he always preferred mother's though she was not an intellectual. Her common sense, sound opinions and fairness father valued more than anybody else's.

41

Ever since his student days father wore a small moustache until one day in Hannover, at the beginning of the war, a man mistook him for Adolf Hitler, who indeed had the same moustache, haircut and even the same mackintosh, a light brown one with a wide belt. Father was wearing one on that day. He was taller than Hitler, but the man undoubtedly thought it was his idol. He jumped off his bike, saluted him with an out-stretched, rigid arm and shouted: "Heil, my Führer!" He was most disappointed when father put on an expression of loathing and then looked into a shop window to discover that his reflection looked indeed a little like Hitler's. Without losing a moment he went to the nearest barber shop, had his moustache removed and his lock of hair over the forehead cut very short. He then bought himself a black mackintosh with a thin belt and burnt the other on his return.

* * *

I very often heard mother complain about our maids; how troublesome they were and how she wished she could do without them. I could not see anything wrong with them at all. I liked them, but looking back I can understand that often they must have been more trouble than help.

Apart from our first three maids, mother took in young girls who came from Homes for unmarried mothers; some had been in prisons, some in mental homes.

One time this proved to be almost fatal. This particular maid was called Marie. I liked her because she was always smiling. As I was only five years old at the time, I could not distinguish between a cheerful smile and an insane grin. I thought it funny when one day, during a Bible reading her face became very red and she could not control her giggle, which started me off, of course, and we were both sent out by my father. She went on giggling in the kitchen, until I got fed up and went into the garden. Gewi knew that she was slightly "round the bend". Mother had a soft spot for all unwanted girls, but this one proved to be a bit too much.

42

Once my parents went away for the weekend and left us in Marie's care. Mother had given Marie some money to buy cream cakes for our Sunday tea. On Sunday afternoon Marie put a large bowl of whipped cream on the tea table and nothing else. We had been looking forward to our cream cakes and did not know what to do with this large heap of whipped cream. We piled it onto slices of bread, but the three of us made only a small impression on the mountain in front of us. As it was summertime and we had no fridge, the cream would have gone off by the evening. Suddenly I had an idea. I fetched as many of my village pals as I could find; it was a great treat for them to have whipped cream and in no time all the cream was demolished on slices of brown bread with sugar.

But it was in the evening that Marie frightened us. I must have been asleep for a while when I suddenly felt something touching my throat, and when the pressure became greater I opened my eyes and looked into Marie's grinning red face, which came very close to mine, and her hands tightened around my neck. Gewi slept next to my room, and he must have heard some noise because he appeared just at that moment. He threw himself upon Marie, small as he was, being only ten years old, and Marie rushed out of the room and left us, totally shaken, sitting on the bed.

Then Gewi had the bright idea that we should leave the house as quickly as possible and quietly we crept out of the garden door and knocked on Oma Thiele's, our neighbour's, window. We spent the night on her sofa.

My parents were horrified when they heard of the danger we had been in, especially when they saw the marks on my neck. Marie went back to a mental home and it was the last time mother took in mentally unstable girls.

But of course there were others: Helene, for instance, who came from a prison and swore that she would never steal again. Father called her "Die fromme Helene" (the pious Helene) after a story by the writer and caricaturist Wilhelm Busch, whose work he liked very much. Indeed, Helene sat during our Bible reading at lunchtime with a very pious expression on her face.

She loved reading aloud from the Bible. Once a day, a leaf from a religious calendar was torn off and a short text from the Bible was read out by each of us in turn. Once, when my parents weren't present, Gewi insisted that Helene should read from Genesis, chapter 10. Helene was thrilled and with no idea what lay ahead of her, started to read, only to give up after the second verse; but Gewi was adamant that all 32 verses had to be read. Her enthusiasm for reading the Bible was very much less after this.

One day a friend of mother's, who was staying for a few days, missed a considerable amount of money from her handbag, which had been in her bedroom. It turned out that Helene had once again succumbed to her old habit, and confessed that she had taken quite a few other things as well, which we had not even missed up till then. That was the end of Helene's stay.

The other memorable maid was Hilda, from Cologne. She came to us with a large tummy, three months before she had her baby, which she had adopted, much against mother's advice. Hilda and I got on very well until one day, after she had had her baby, I told her that she had lost a great deal of her beauty. It was a cruel thing to say and quite untrue; it was something I had picked up from my friends who said that mothers lose their beauty when they have had babies, and I, six or seven years old, believed it. After that announcement our good relationship was spoilt. Hilda did not stay long with us. She was vain and man-mad. One night mother saw a man climb into Hilda's bedroom window, and that was that.

Our first two maids were super. Emma had come with my parents from their previous parish and she stayed for four years until she got married. When she left I cried my eyes out. On the day when Emma left and Else started, I sat outside, underneath the kitchen window, and sobbed for Emma. Else noticed me and came out and sat beside me. She put a small package into my lap. "It's for you," she said. I unwrapped it with tears still dropping onto the paper. A rat made of dough, with two currants as eyes, real whiskers and a tail appeared. "You can eat it," she said, but I shook my head and said that I would rather not. I

44

rats but I did not like to tell her that. She came from Hamelin. Else and I became good friends and she stayed with us for six years. She got married to the local carpenter and called one of her two daughters Renate, after me.

Every summer, Dina came and helped in the garden. Dina had a room in an outhouse belonging to a farmer. Once when I was "exploring" the village with some friends, we came upon a very narrow path between two barns. It was almost too narrow to squeeze through even for us children, and it was dank and dark and unpleasant. A window with iron bars in front of it caught my eye. "Dina lives in there," I was told. I looked through the bars. Dina was not there. The room looked more like a cell with its bare white-washed walls, a neatly-made bed with a crucifix above it, a chest of drawers, a small table and a chair, all the furniture Dina possessed. Dina was a very ugly person with a heart of gold. Her greasy grey hair hung in strands over her face. Her nose was large and crooked; she squinted and the only tooth she had left was one enormous front one which stuck out onto her lower lip. She was tall, even with a hunched back. She must have been about 55 years old. She wore long skirts with an equally long apron on top, and man's boots with thick socks. She was deaf and partly dumb, for there was something wrong with her throat. From the bottom of her neck to the top of her chin hung loose flesh, like a turkey's neck, and when the sun shone sideways on to it, all that flesh became transparent. Poor Dina could only make some peculiar gutteral noises and nobody could understand them, but she managed to make herself understood by sign language. Dina worked hard in the garden and was utterly reliable. She was an ardent Catholic, and when she had tea with us she crossed herself before she slurped from her tea mug and dipped the bread into it. She was feared by some village children and made fun of by others. Gewi and I did neither; we were very fond of her. When she first smiled at us we thought she was crying but it was just the way the muscles of her face worked.

One day Dina stayed on after work to look after my brother and me whilst my parents had gone out for the evening.

45

It was a warm summer's evening and just beginning to get dark, but it was still too warm to go to sleep, so Gewi and I were reading. We suddenly heard somebody singing and we tiptoed out of our bedrooms towards the sound. The door to the drawing-room was wide open. To our amazement, we saw Dina sitting on the low window-ledge, her head leaning against the wall. She looked dreamily out of the open window at the full harvest moon, singing in a low, soft voice, a song about Mary and Jesus. Dina, who could not talk and made the grunting sounds of an animal, was singing! We could not believe our ears; not only was her voice beautiful but it was clear as well, and we could understand every word she sang. I wanted to go to her, but Gewi took my arm and shook his head. She could not hear us, of course, but we withdrew a little so that she could not see us either, and we stood devoutly listening to her singing. Then we went back to bed leaving a lonely, dreaming Dina gazing at the moon and the stars.

* * *

Twice a month mother went to Hannover to shop. When we needed new clothes, or perhaps as a treat, we went with her on the 13.29 train from Platform 5. Taking us firmly by the hand, she confidently crossed the Ernst-August Platz and the even busier Georgstrasse where trams and cars in an almost continuous stream missed each other by a hair's breadth. On a peninsula, jutting out into the traffic, stood Hannover's most-frequented *Konditorei* (café) called *Kroepke*, or as father called it: *Der Ziegenstall* (Goat-stable) Heavily made-up ladies sat at small tables near the windows. *Kroepke* was a dome-shaped building, entirely made of glass, so everybody knew what went on outside and inside. Here sat ladies dressed in furs and large hats drinking mocha and eating lashings of cream cakes, smoking cigarettes from long holders and gossiping. I never had the chance to go inside. It was destroyed in the first air-raid on Hannover.

Mother always shopped in the same shops. *Karstadt und*

Saeltzer for our clothes, *Werner und Werner* for father's shirts; *von der Linde* for linen and material; the *Reformhaus* for any special food; and, last of all, the *Markthalle,* an enormous building with a glass roof where every kind of food was sold: citrus fruit, precariously stacked in pyramids, vegetables scrubbed and artistically arranged, a hundred kinds of various breads and cakes, fish and meat. Going past the meat stall, I turned my head aside. Rows of deer, hare and wild boar stared with glassy, sad eyes at the passers-by. Every year in the Autumn wagon loads of hare and deer were driven through the village after a day's shooting, a most depressing sight.

Mother steered towards the stand which said *Arberg's Delicatessen.* Sausages of I don't know how many varieties hung above the counter. Mother bought *Fleischsalad* (meat salad) and thin smoked *Frankfurters,* my favourites. We could smell the fish stand from a long way away. A fishmonger with a cart and dapple-grey horse came twice a week to our house to deliver fresh fish. But the fish stand here offered more: Lobster and crabs, crayfish, smoked eels, smoked salmon, buckling, rollmops and *Kieler Sprotten* (smoked spratts), shrimps and prawns, wafer-thin slices of smoked haddock twisted into a long curl, and rows and rows of salads in milky glass dishes. Mother bought shrimps for our supper, a small shiny black smoked eel for father and *Kieler sprotten* which lay tiny and tightly packed, golden and smoked, in a wooden box which had in black lettering *Kieler Sprotten* written all over it.

Our next stop was the *Sprengel* sweet shop. *Sprengel* was the best chocolate in the whole of Germany, and it was made here in Hannover. Mother bought a small bag of liqueur beans, and for Gewi and me chocolate drops covered in hundreds and thousands.

We would put our noses against the glass partition of the counter and inhaled the aroma of the extremely good and bitter chocolate. We were given one drop each by the shop assistant, a good habit all German shopkeepers have. A sweet here, a slice of cheese or sausage there, even a tiny curled-up shrimp, children were always given something. Mother put a bag with the chocolate drops into her bag; "For later," she said. Our treat before we caught the train home was tea in the *Kakao Stube*, a smart and well-known *Conditorei* in Hannover, of Art Nouveau style, crammed full of little round tables and customers, in a hazy atmosphere with a small orchestra playing sentimental music.

Gewi and I always chose the same – hot chocolate, the café's speciality, with mountains of whipped cream on top and a slice of cake made of layers of meringue, sponge cake, whipped cream and ice cream, topped with thin curly bits of chocolate. We ate every scrap of it and made it last as long as possible. We ate the cream on top of the hot drink with a spoon with a little of the liquid. In the end we stirred it into the cocoa and drank it the proper way, not leaving a drop in the cup.

Portrait of Renate, Gewi and their mother

On the way home in the train mother opened the bag with the chocolate drops and in spite of our large tea we ate them as well.

If mother had bought a dress or other garment for herself she presented herself in it to father after supper. Father approved every time. He stood up from his chair behind the desk, put his arm around mother's shoulders and said lovingly: "My beautiful little Paulinchen".

Gewi and I looked at each other, giggling. We were very happy, lucky children.

CHAPTER 5

Two lovely old farms touched our grounds on both sides, but the many trees in the garden hid their buildings. Each boundary fence had a little gate which let us communicate with each other in an intimate and friendly way without having to use the formal front door entrances from the road.

On the right lived "Oma" (granny) Thiele with her husband in a couple of rooms of the large farmhouse. Her son and family occupied the rest. Oma Thiele's drawing-room window was low to the ground. We hardly ever bothered about the formal entrance but climbed through the window; the first time I stood in front of her window she lifted me over the low sill. She immediately went to the cupboard in the corner and took out a smoked sausage and cut off a thin slice for me. This sealed our friendship right away. Oma Thiele's sausage tasted far better than ours, I thought. Many times when I was playing in the garden, I stopped suddenly to knock at her window and ask for a slice of sausage. Sometimes, when I had been knocking too often, she gave me an extra thin slice, but she never refused it, not even in the war.

In the winter months she spent most of her time at her spinning wheel. I used to watch her through the window. Of course she had seen me, but pretended not to, and when I finally knocked, she always appeared to be completely taken by surprise, which made me laugh. When she was spinning, she took off her right shoe, and her small foot in the thick black stocking pushed the treadle up and down in an even rhythm. She sat slightly bent over the wheel, and wore golden half-rimmed spectacles. On her lap lay a lump of uncombed and unwashed fleece from which she plucked a thin thread to feed into the little aperture and an even thinner thread wound itself onto the spool. When two spools were full she stuck them into two long needles of an upright stand and plied them together into hanks. These hung from her mahogany secretaire, waiting to be washed, before they were made into thick winter socks for her husband and herself.

The nicest thing about Oma Thiele was her chestnut brown hair. Not a strand of grey in it, always shiny, and there was lots of it. She wore it in a tight plait coiled on top of her head, and two combs kept any stray bits of her hair in a tight grip around her temples.

A large seashell lay on the chest of drawers, white from the outside, a delicate pink leading into its mysterious inside. I was compelled to lift it to my ear every time I saw it because Oma Thiele said that one could hear the roar of the sea. Indeed I heard it, first faintly, then more and more until I thought the waves would take me with them out to sea and I quickly, but very carefully, put it back onto the chest.

Her room always appeared to be sunny and warm. A stove of green tiles reached as far as the ceiling. Its lower half had two iron doors with brass knobs for coal and wood and ashes. The top part had three different compartments, each with a decorative double door of cast iron. In the lowest and hottest stood a kettle with ever-simmering water. The second was for baking potatoes or apples and the third, which was only just warm, had an oval-shaped shiny black warming stone which periodically went on to Opa Thiele's lap to warm his hands in the winter.

Oma Thiele's kitchen was tiny, and there was no running water, but two enamel buckets stood full of spring water on a low bench, with a large ladle hanging from one of them. All her cooking was done on a *Grude*. This was an old-fashioned, but most efficient cooker used in almost all the farmhouses. It was about six feet tall, with an oven for baking and roasting and another compartment on top for keeping food warm. A tank on the side with a tap gave constant hot water. A tray on rails full of hot ashes was pulled out twice a day, and very carefully the ashes were pushed to the sides with a shovel on a long handle, until the red ash appeared and a new lot of small anthracite was put on top. Once again it was embedded with the ashes previously pushed aside. This kept it going for about ten hours and gave enough heat to cook on. It required careful handling, otherwise the fine ash would cover everything with dust. I liked to watch Oma Thiele replenishing her *Grude* with new coke. In the winter, when for a few moments the glowing ash lay exposed, I warmed my hands over it. To my great joy my grandmother presented mother with her *Grude* when she moved house. Mother was very opposed to this old object, but my arguments that it was ideal for warming hands on, and even more Oma Thiele's advice, made her change her mind, and it was installed. For the first week Oma Thiele came twice a day to show mother how to "feed" it, and soon mother got used to it and never regretted having it. Especially during the war it proved to be most economical, and it always kept the kitchen warm because it never went out.

Whenever we had turnips, bread soup or one of mother's peculiar North German dishes, I went to eat with the Thieles. As soon as my face appeared at the window at lunch time Oma Thiele knew why I had come and she got a plate and spoon for me. I sat down at the table on which stood a large white terrine. They always had soup and it was always bouillon. Little stars and letters of the alphabet were the only visible contents, but it was delicious. Opa Thiele had a long white beard. He sat on the black oilcloth-covered sofa, a napkin tucked into his collar, and he slurped his soup very noisily, leaving stars and letters hanging from his beard. He had had a stroke and could not help it because he could only put his spoon sideways into his mouth. On that side the spoon had worn away and one could always tell which was his spoon.

On a warm day his wife would lead him to the stone seat in front of the house where he sat hour after hour, his hands folded over his walking-stick which he had dug into the earth in front of him, his chin and beard resting on his hands, his eyes fixed on the approach of every passer-by, following them until they were out of sight. Sometimes Gewi and I sat with him, but we hardly ever talked. He didn't talk much to his wife either. He was what one could call a laconic person.

One summer day I saw Oma Thiele working in her vegetable garden, in her large old-fashioned sunbonnet. I liked giving her little surprise presents when she was out and which she would find on her return, such as a drawing I had done or a bunch of flowers. This time it was a snail made out of plasticine which I put on her table. I suddenly saw a long plait of chestnut brown hair hanging from her secretaire where in the winter hung her spun wool. I had never seen anything like that before and didn't know what to make of it. Quickly I fetched my brother and quite out of breath pointed to the plait.

'Well,' he said, 'That is Oma Thiele's artificial hair,' and softly he stroked the shiny plait. I myself could not touch it. I had thought her beautiful hair so much part of herself, and when I saw her wearing it the next time, I could not keep my eyes off it and was puzzled how she managed to glue it on to her head every day, but I never asked her about it.

The neighbour on the other side was also a farmer, called Busch. Frau Busch was almost completely deaf. On my arrival I always managed to startle her. It didn't matter how loudly I knocked at the door or banged it shut. I remember her standing at an old-fashioned stone sink tackling a mountain of plates and saucepans, the sweat dripping off her forehead into the washing-up water. In the summer, swarms of flies settled everywhere in the kitchen; the sticky flypapers hanging from the ceiling were full of them. Frau Busch seemed quite an old woman but I never saw anybody helping her, except in the war when she had a Polish girl. Years of hard work and sorrow had aged her prematurely.

The Busch's had three children. One daughter was married a long way away, and two sons were helping on the farm. Heinrich, the younger one, was weak in the head since he had meningitis at the age of sixteen. He seemed quiet and harmless, which indeed he was, except when it "took him" which happened about twice a year. Then he got into such a state that he smashed everything in sight and went for people, except for my mother who was fetched every time he had one of his attacks.

I remember once he had climbed to the top of the house and sat astride on the ridge, dismantling tiles and throwing them down. We tried not to let mother go, but she was fearless. She had a ladder fetched and climbed to the top of it and talked to Heinrich. We could not understand what she said, but after a while the distraught young man came down and let himself be led into the house by mother.

Every time he ended up in the lunatic asylum for treatment. When he was released, after about four weeks, he returned home pale and very quiet, avoiding any human contact, hiding in the barn. For quite a while he never walked, but always ran like a hunted animal. I could hear him talking to the calves in the barn in a gentle voice, and he looked after them beautifully. After a while he became more himself and started to communicate with his family again. Heinrich and I were very good friends.

Two large cherry trees stood in their garden, and when it was time for them to be picked, Heinrich fetched me. He climbed into the tree and threw down into my apron underneath, the most delicious ripe black cherries. Once he took a couple of cherries, whose stem was still joined together and put them behind my ears. They dangled and bounced like two heavy rubies when I moved my head. He was also most anxious that I should spit out all the cherry stones, but sometimes I had so many cherries in my mouth at once that I did swallow some. I did not tell him.

Heinrich's hobby was reading; he was always carrying a book in his pocket. He told me many a story. Some I understood, some I did not. I can't remember seeing very much of Heinrich in the winter, but in the summer we used to sit on a bench in front of a well from which they drew their drinking water. It was covered with a wooden lid with a hole in the centre, large enough to let a bucket through. The bucket was fastened onto a long rusted chain, coiled umpteen times around a beam with a handle which, when turned anti-clockwise, let down the bucket under the clanking of the chain until it hit the water with a dull thud. It was not quite so easy to get it up again, and when I sometimes turned the handle, Heinrich put his hand over mine to help me wind it. The chain would creak and wind itself slowly back onto the beam until the bucket appeared, full of cool, crystal-clear water. Several times I asked Heinrich to lift me up and let me look at into the well, for I was eager but afraid at the same time to see the mysterious inside of it, but Heinrich always refused. It even made him angry. His brother once took off the lid and lifted me up, because I was not quite tall enough to look over its rim. He held me tightly when I leaned over to look into it. At first I could not see anything at all of the water, only stones, slightly green, with bits of ferns and grass coming out of their cracks. When my eyes got used to the darkness of the well, I spotted the water far, far below. I became frightened and closed my arms tightly around Heinrich's brother's neck and asked urgently to be put down. But sometimes, when nobody was looking, I took a little stone and dropped it through the opening, quickly put my ear against the well and waited for the splash. It was hardly audible, because the stone was only small and it sounded far away and hollow. Whenever I read Grimm's fairy story of *The Princess and the Frog* it was this well that I imagined.

CHAPTER 6

The day came when I had to go to school. I was six and a half years old. My brother had just finished his four years at the *Volkschule* which every German child had to fulfil before changing to another school. He now started at the Gymnasium for Boys in Lehrte where Latin was the main subject. French and English were also taught as foreign lauguages. Pupils of this school wore a cap indicating which class they were in. It started with a dark blue one for the first form, the *sexta* which my brother was now proudly wearing. The eighth and last form was called *prima* and once the *Abitur* was successfully passed, University followed. I looked with the greatest respect upon anybody wearing a school cap. It was the only sign that showed the difference between schools.

My first school year was spent in the old church opposite our house. Ever since the new church had been built, in 1860, the old one had been halved and one part was used for school beginners who lived in the village. These first year pupils were known as the "A.B.C. Archers", of which I now became one.

I was fitted out with a brand new leather satchel which was worn like a rucksack on the back. All it contained on the first day was a small blackboard, a wooden box for the thin stick of chalk and an oval case for a small damp sponge. It was a very special case of thin wood, heavily lacquered with black paint. The lid showed a landscape with a windmill, a couple holding hands and a lamb grazing beside them. It was given to mother on her first school day, then to my brother and now I became the proud owner of this little box. (I still have it, standing on my desk; I keep elastic bands in it).

It was the custom that on the first school day mothers took their offspring to school. About fifteen little children walked demurely alongside their mothers, holding on to their hands, in their Sunday best, with new satchels on their backs. Some of the children were so small and the satchel so large that the sight from behind was a comic one. We all waited in front of the solid oak door of the church which was still closed. The sight was not a happy one; it looked more like a funeral than a happy occasion. Mothers were constantly wiping their eyes and making remarks like: "This is my last one", or "This is my first one". I couldn't make head or tail of it. I was as happy as a lark, and so was mother beside me.

I was dressed in my favourite dirndl and wore white knee socks. For the first time I wore my hair in plaits. I held my head very upright lest they might come undone. I kept on glancing at mother, in case she might be overcome with tears like the rest of them, but was reassured by her happy smile.

There was one thing I was not happy about, though. Every child held a large object under its arm, called a *Zuckertuete:* it was a cone of cardboard filled to the brim with sweets. It was the custom that on this "sad" and important first school day every child should be comforted with one of these – except, of course, me. "Dreadful things," mother had said, when I mentioned *Zuckertuete* a few days before. "Quite unnecessary." I had been looking forward to one of them and had spent some time looking into shop windows where these sugary comforters were displayed in gold and silver paper, like enormous ice-cream cones, topped with a white rufflet and silk ribbon of a garish colour. Some even had an inscription written on them such as, "For our little darling". It was one of this kind I had in mind and I was most disappointed when I did not get one at all. At the same time, I think I must have been the happiest child on this first school day.

A partition divided our small cosy classroom from the rest of the church, of which we had a horror as we were told that it was full of skeletons and other frightful things. A peep inside through the windows was impossible because they were too high off the ground and the door to it was always locked. Our teacher told us, on the first day, that whoever did not behave would be locked in there – and I was very nearly the first one to

58

experience this.

We were taught on the first school day how to write the small "i" and our homework was to write ten rows of these on our blackboards. Full of enthusiasm, I threw myself into the task after lunch. Crooked and drunken-looking i's appeared, laboriously written, with penetrating squeaks from pressing the chalk too hard. After the third row I had had enough. The sun was shining and beckoning and I wanted to play on the swing. My blackboard was shoved back into the satchel with the idea of finishing off in the evening. But I forgot all about it until bedtime when sleepily I took out the blackboard and saw, to my surprise, ten neat rows of i's. My brother had written them. Should I wipe them out and write my own? I decided against it. Next day when the homework was inspected, the teacher looked at me sternly: "Who has written this?" he asked. "My brother," I answered in a small voice. And it was then that he told me if it ever happened again I would be locked into the next room. I made sure I never gave cause for this threat again.

My special friend of the first school year was Ilse Rust. We looked very much alike. Both of us were skinny with lots of curls, only Ilse's eyes were blue and mine brown. "You even laugh in the same annoying way," our teacher used to say, as we were always giggling.

One thing Ilse took very seriously was her family name – Rust. There were numerous "Rusts" in the village, all well-to-do-farmers. Every one had an additional name like: Great-Rust, Dr Rust, Zacharia Rust. Ilse's father worked for the railway, and they lived in a small house near a large meadow, so Ilse invented her own double-barrelled name and even insisted at school on being known as "Meadow-Rust".

Beside Ilse's house stood one of the largest old farmhouses, surrounded by lime trees. The childless widow Klunder lived there with her old maid Else. She was so rich, Ilse told me, that she went shopping in Hannover by taxi, which was after all, 28 kilometres away. Ilse also confided in me that one day she would inherit Frau Klunder's fortune, because she was so fond of Ilse. She had given her permission to go into her large garden any time she felt like it and eat the strawberries and greengages – so Ilse said.

One afternoon we did just that, and as we were sitting in the tall grass stuffing ourselves with the delicious fruit, and I was once again being told by Ilse of the great wealth awaiting her one day, a threatening shadow fell upon us, and behind us loomed Frau Klunder dressed in the deepest black, all six feet of her.

She grabbed us by our shoulders and pulled us up in front of her. "You wicked little thieves," she shouted, and pushed us away disgustedly. Completely surprised, I looked at her and then for Ilse, who was nowhere to be seen.

I was very much ashamed and stammered, "I thought it was allowed to come here".

"Why should it be allowed?' she thundered. "Ilse is a very wicked girl and now she is leading you astray too."

I wasn't quite sure any more if Ilse was going to inherit her fortune after all. I was terribly afraid that Frau Klunder would go straight to my parents, but this did not happen until a little later when, once again, she caught us at our misdoings.

* * *

The winter was the time to empty slurry pits on all the farms. Every day horses pulled long containers plastered with muck, along the village street. Through the opening at the top overflowed the smelly dark juice which trickled onto the snowy white road leaving a nasty brown track behind.

Now Ilse had the bright idea of opening the tap at the end of the barrel, which lets out the slurry. She thought it would be such a laugh if the farmer arrived at his field and found the slurry had all gone. She dared me to do it – and I did. Little did I know with what tremendous force the liquid came out. I was at once covered from head to foot and stood dripping in the road, surrounded by an evil-smelling lake of slurry. To my horror I saw Frau Klunder witnessing it all. Now she was steering in the direction of my parents' house. I followed her shivering with cold and trepidation. Ilse was again nowhere to be seen.

Needless to say, my parents were horrified when they heard what I had been up to, and when the proof of it stood small and very unwholesome in front of them, I was severely scolded and punished.

I am sure Frau Klunder meant well in telling my parents that Ilse was not the right sort of girl for me to associate with, but they did not stop me from playing with Ilse or the rest of the village children. My parents pointed out to me what was good and what was bad. Young though I was, they told me that they had faith in me and were sure that I would not do the many wicked things in which the village children indulged. As a matter of fact, it was the village children themselves who would not let me take part in their naughtiness. When they decided to go and steal peas or carrots from the fields surrounding the village I was not actually allowed to pick the fobidden fruit, but was posted as sentry to give a whistle when somebody was approaching. Or should they all decide to pile into the little outhouse – the loo – I was pushed aside and told to wait outside. When I asked what they were doing in there they would not tell me.

Group of village children, including Renate
(with her hands folded in front of apron)

61

It may have been because they lived in awe of my father. In 1934 the position of a parson was still revered. Although religion as a whole did not mean much to these youngsters – their parents were certainly not of the church-going type – at the same time they were brought up to show respect to the clergy, which was also combined with a certain amount of fear. Nobody could have been kinder to children than my father, but as soon as they saw him they scattered. So I gained a certain protection from them. They put up with my going about with them but I never became a "sworn-in" member of their gang.

The people I was afraid of, and almost started to hate at an early age, were the farmers' widows, dressed in black, opulent and corpulent, trotting to church every Sunday, and then gossiping maliciously about their neighbours for the rest of the week. They appeared to me like gangsters in black uniforms who spent their time behind lace curtains spying, especially on me. Frau Klunder was their ring-leader!

* * *

My school pals came from the poorest families. Many lived in houses, long condemned, belonging to farmers. Their mothers came from Poland or Silesia after the first World War to work on German farms. They were known as the "Beet-Girls", as they were cheap labour to help with the sugar-beet harvest. Most of them married farm workers and settled down. Their German was poor, their husbands, mostly, were communists. I remember the men, and their children copying them, greeting each other with tight fists, shouting: *Heil Moskau*.

The wives had a raw deal. They were bound to the farmers in return for living rent free in their miserable houses, and each had to look after a large plot of sugar-beet land. The work started in Spring with singling out the small plants, keeping them free of weeds during the summer,and in the Autumn pulling the beet out, cutting off the leaves and throwing them into the carts beside them. From the age of six the children had to help, and the younger ones stood shivering in their inadequate clothing beside their mothers. The Winter started early, the ground became hard with frost, and often the beets were pulled out in snow and ice. No wonder the classroom in the winter was filled with constant coughing from the children's infected chests.

Their fathers led a lazy life. Often laid-off by the farmers for their slack attitude towards work, they lay on their sofas in the kitchen, foul tempered, yawning and belching. Just as their children were afraid of my father, I was afraid of theirs. They looked at me mistrustfully, but at the same time I liked going to their houses: their wives could not have been kinder. In spite of being poor, they ate well. All their money was spent on food and nobody in the family was undernourished except the mothers, who always looked ill and thin.

Every morning I went to fetch Helga to walk to school together. She had a twin brother, Willi, and her mother was a particularly kind and hard working person. Every time I was given a lovely warm crisp roll with lots of butter and jam. (At home we only had rolls on Sundays). The husband looked at me begrudgingly, but the mother urged me to have another roll. I never saw any plates on the table. All slices of bread and rolls were prepared by the mother on the not too clean surface of the kitchen table and delivered into the ever outstretched hands of the children and husband. The main meal was cooked in one large stewpot on the stove. At mealtime the pot was put in the centre of the table, tin spoons put beside it and everyone leant over and started to slurp the stew into their mouths as fast as they could. I avoided going at mealtimes, for I could not have got myself to join them.

Apart from the awful smell which dwelled in these kitchens, they were very cosy in the winter. It was always warm on dark winter mornings. The smell of the paraffin lamp on the table mingled with the boiling cabbage and fat meat, already prepared for lunch and the lamp's dim light hid the grime on the walls. The small windows were never opened in the winter and thick condensation formed behind the dirty lace curtains and trickled down the inside of the panes. A white enamel bowl with greyish water, a few small soap bubbles and some hairs floating on top, was the evidence of the family's morning wash. This same bowl was used afterwards for washing-up, washing the clothes and for making cakes. The mugs were of enamel too, with chipped black patches showing through.

Once or twice I had a glimpse of their bedroom. The whole family slept in the same room. It smelled very damp, with peeling wallpaper, straw mattresses and dirty red and white checked bed linen. There was a large chamber pot under the bed. Their pride and joy was the parlour, mostly facing north and therefore sunless. A sofa, a few rickety chairs, a table with a black oilcloth upon which stood a cheap crystal bowl, a sideboard with Woolworth china, and vases with garish coloured paper flowers. On the window-sill stood well-looked-after geraniums and a myrtle tree, and always a jam jar of cut flowers, filled with daffodils or asters according to the season, deprived of their stems with only the heads sticking out like drowning children.

There was never enough money for clothing or fuel. Nobody helped them except the church. Later in 1936, when Hitler had come to power, they were offered work, new houses and a better life. They took it and all the other advantages that came with it. Suddenly they turned from being communists to socialists and large and small fists unclenched into a thunderous "Heil Hitler".

* * *

These were my friends until I was ten years old. I took them into our house but they didn't feel at home, in spite of my parents' kindness. They talked in whispers and unlike their usual behaviour, were quiet and bashful. Once they entered the garden they became their natural selves again. We climbed trees, set the swing into such violent motion that the frame began to rock and we ate all the plentiful fruit, forbidden or not. We were told to eat only the apples and pears and plums which were lying under the trees, but we had a cunning way of throwing ourselves against the tree trunk or branches so that the fruit fell off and showered the ground underneath. Sometimes we teased

Heinrich from next door, who was watching us silently from behind the fence.

When we became too loud and boisterous we were told to go to the meadow at the end of the garden, where there were tall trees and a hazelnut grove. Two large mounds, where once weeds and rubbish had been dumped, but were now overgrown with grass, were excellent for our little handcarts to roll off or for us to race down with scooters and bicycles. These were things my friends did not possess and were a very good reason for my popularity.

On a hot summer's day, father sat in his arbour after lunch, reading. This was a small lawn surrounded by tall yew trees with an opening cut into it which looked very appropriately like a church door. He sat in a large cane armchair, surrounded by books, smoking a cigar.

Mother also had her private little corner in the garden; a sunny retreat surrounded by mock orange and lilac. It was quite large and every year on mother's birthday, the 21st July, when the weather was good, we had tea there with guests arriving all through the afternoon. It was nicest there in the summer evenings, when my parents sat with friends in the secluded arbour drinking. I could hear the clinking of their glasses, their laughter, and the faint, drowsy twitter of birds when I was lying in bed. Through the open window drifted the scent of the orange blossom.

Sometimes I heard the clanking of the chain when Heinrich or his brother drew a bucket of cool water up from the well. I used to get up and stand at the window, looking down into the garden. I could not see anybody, for the trees and bushes surrounding the arbour were too high. The garden looked so forlorn, the only traces of the day's activity were the watering-can left on the path and the hosepipe with its tap still slightly dripping, coiled like a sleeping snake on the lawn. The sky was still pink from the setting sun. In the distance, behind the garden gate over the little river, rose a thin blanket of mist.

Sometimes I did not go back to bed but dared to creep up to the arbour in my nightie and tell the grownups that I could not go to sleep. Mother lifted me onto her lap, wrapped her shawl around my knees and I cuddled against her warm shoulder. I hardly ever remember being carried back to bed, but I do remember the feeling of complete happiness the heavy scent of blossoms and the drowsiness which slowly came upon me, making the voices and laughter of the people around me go further and further away.

I had my own little summerhouse of wood, painted green with white windows. It even had white lace curtains and a white picket fence gate. In front of it stood a large magnolia tree whose stem had split in half, but each half was a thick trunk, large enough to climb onto. My brother was the owner of the one on the right and I of the one on the left.

The summerhouse was furnished with a small wooden nursery table, four matching chairs and a bench, all painted green. Every year in the Spring, when my maternal grandmother stayed with us for four weeks, she gave them a fresh coat of paint. A miniature stove of cast-iron, about a foot square, was my pride and joy. It had belonged to my grandmother in her childhood, and it had a real brass rail in front which from time to time I polished. But the great thing was that you could really cook on it. A methylated burner heated up the small enamel saucepans. Raw fruit was boiled to a pulp and sweetened with plenty of sugar and presented to our guests, who mostly consisted of our long-suffering maid and mother, who sat on the uncomfortable small seats, praising our cooking.

My brother and I had our own little garden where we could plant and sow whatever we fancied. My brother's was always the same; every Spring he planted his wallflowers and forget-me-nots and sowed radishes and parlsey. It was well looked after and always weed free.

Mine was different every year. Once I transformed it into a rockery and wished for a gnome. Mother was horrified, but I pleaded with her to let me have one, and next time she went to Hannover she brought one back for me. It was only a small one, but I was terribly happy. It had the usual red nose and a hood and wrinkled trousers. I had to promise mother that he would not stand in a prominent position, so he found his home behind a rock. I planted flowers around him and held conversations with him. He became a very good friend. I even gave him a Christmas present, a little frog of stone which from then on sat at his feet.

Beside my small garden was the swing, which was also used by mother and our maid for beating the carpets on once a week. A large sandpit, surrounded by a wooden seat, a see-saw and, my favourite, a merry-go-round, made out of a huge waggon wheel which squeaked incessantly, kept us happy for hours. The garden was a paradise for me and my friends. Careless hours we spent in play, not always peacefully but always happily.

The nicest part of the garden for me was the meadow in summer, when the long grass swayed in the breeze together with daisies and wild cowbells, buttercups and dandelions. The grasshoppers chirped all day long until late into the night. I was always longing to walk through the long grass, touching the stalks and petals and finally lying down in it, completely hidden, smelling the aroma of the various herbs and looking up into the blue sky.

Alas, it was forbidden, as the grass was cut once a year by a man from the village as hay for his goats. After it was cut it became coarse and uninteresting, and it was no fun lying on the shorn meadow. After a couple of weeks it was green again and flowers and grasshoppers returned. When the man came to cut the grass, he brought along his son, who was a little older than I was. I did not like him at all. He always stuffed his pockets with our plums and pears and he was very rude. Once he took a cotton sanitary towel from the washing line and held it, like a dead fish, in his fingers waving it in front of me.

'Do you know what this is?' he asked.

'Of course I do,' I said, 'that is a flannel.'

'That's just what it isn't!' he shouted.

'It is . . . ' but before he could explain it to me, his father had grabbed him by the collar and told him to get away, and boxed him behind the ear.

* * *

My brother Gewi, perhaps because he was four years older than I, very seldom played with us. He was by nature much quieter than I was; he was a dreamer. He sat for hours reading books. His favourite occupation was going to the end of the garden to the wrought-iron gate from where he gazed towards the horizon. There he stood every evening, with his hands in his pockets, looking at the sky and the clouds and drawing his own conclusion about the weather for the next day. He was mostly right. When we were expecting guests, I was the one who fetched them from the station, whilst he sat, next to Opa Thiele on his stone bench, waiting for us to come down the road. As soon as he had spotted us, he got up and went indoors. He was very shy and hated any sort of demonstration, and never showed his feelings openly.

He was very sensitive. Once he knocked over a little boy when riding his bicycle. The boy unfortunately was laid-up with a damaged knee for a couple of weeks, but there was not a day on which Gewi did not go to inquire about him, and he used all his saved-up pocket money to buy him presents.

Sometimes he had funny ideas. On one very hot day in the middle of summer, he noticed a pair of ear mufflers lying in the corner of a shop window, obviously overlooked and forgotten after the clean out of the winter displays. They were of black buckskin on the outside and of red velvet on the inside. He had just enough money to buy them. He then walked about on a hot day proudly wearing this contraption on his head. He was about eight years old then.

I was apt to tease him when he did these peculiar things. This made him angry and he would pull my pigtails, until I apologised.

One Sunday morning we were alone in the house as everybody had gone to church, I had unfortunately been teasing him again, and he put a toy clockwork bird onto my head. It got entangled with the masses of curls. Eventually it stopped

68

turning. Its pointed beak, however, went on pecking into my scalp and I shrieked with pain. My brother put his hand over the bird to stop it and so we sat, with the bird in my hair and Gewi beside me with his hand on my head, until my parents came back from church. Mother had to cut a great chunk out of my hair to free the bird.

* * *

One day in the autumn of 1934, father was raging through the house. The black, white and red old German flag had to go; instead every household was compelled to display the red and white Nazi flag.

'This Hitlerflag and a rectory don't go together,' father shouted. 'I won't have this rag hanging from our house.'

Mother tried to pacify him. 'We will buy a very ordinary small one,' she said. And a very ordinary, small one was bought, and when this miserable rag hung for the first time from the centre window of the house, the string with which the long handle was fastened to the window-ledge became loose and the flag slipped to halfmast. 'Leave it like that,' father said. 'That's just right.'

On the eve of this particular autumn day I saw a torchlight procession for the first time. An endless column marched through the street, men in brown shirts and black breeches, displaying on their sleeve the Nazi emblem, in long shiny, highly-polished black boots which kept in step with the song they sang: *S.A. marschiert, Die Fahne Hoch*. Their left arms swung backwards and forwards like stiff pendulums and in their right hand they carried a torch. I ran out of the house into the street and was fascinated by this sight. Never before had I seen anything like it. The light of the torches illuminated the faces of the men, who looked sternly ahead and sang. This was almost as nice as the Easter bonfires, I thought, and I couldn't understand why my parents had not told me about this wonderful procession. Suddenly my brother appeared beside me. He grabbed me by the arm and pulled me away.

'Come home,' he said, and when I tried to resist, he whispered into my ear: 'These are the Nazis and we are not joining them.'

'Why not?' I wanted to know, 'and who are the Nazis anyway?'

By and by the circumstances were explained to me, that a man whose name was Adolf Hitler was ruling Germany and that the Nazis were his followers, but that a lot of people were not, and we were amongst them. I really didn't understand very much of it, but I soon learned that I was never to tell anybody what was discussed in our house.

CHAPTER 7

One morning everybody in the street stood and gazed up into the sky. The "Graf Zeppelin" was supposed to fly over the town and they were waiting. I too stood and looked eagerly upwards, putting my head so far back that I nearly fell over.

It was a breezy Autumn day; large white clouds hung like puffy featherbeds from the sky. We expected the airship to make a tremendous noise and were taken by surprise when suddenly a large oblong object emerged silently out of a cloud and floated like a shiny silvery fish. We saw the undercarriage clearly and some said they saw the people inside. It was a breathtaking moment, gone in almost a flash before the tail end disappeared into another white cloud. It was the first and last time we saw the airship. A few weeks later it went up in flames.

After a happy first school year we were moved up to the big school, an ugly building opposite the new church. We had been guarded by our teacher like a shepherd guards his small flock of first-year lambs. Suddenly we were released into a large field with four hundred sheep. We felt forlorn and orphaned, but not for long, because our new teacher was equally nice, a small man with a round red face, smelling very strongly of drink.

To my joy I discovered some of my older playmates in the new classroom, though I could not make out why they should be in the same form as I, when they were two and three years older. It was explained that they were hopelessly stupid and would soon have to attend a different school, which our teacher referred to rather ironically as "the Academy of the Elite" (a school for educationally subnormal children). I had always looked upon them with such respect, but now they presented quite a different picture as they sat sheepishly and uncomfortably at their desks, which they had long ago outgrown.

There was "Lanky Emil" whose arms and legs were far too

71

long for his age and could not be accommodated by the infant desk any more, so he sat sideways. Next to him sat two sisters, called by the surname of Grosskopf (Big Head); both of them were the despair of the teacher. "Such big heads and nothing in them," he used to shout. There was only one year between their ages, but they were as different as day and night – one enormous, the other tiny, both completely gormless. They reminded me of two monkeys, one an Orang Utan, the other a Marmoset.

Very quickly I made new friends. There was Annemarie, who was frightened of almost everything. There was Anneliese, whose father was a teacher at the same school. She had long blonde pigtails and deep blue eyes which filled with tears at the slightest upset. And there was Gabi, dark-eyed and dark-haired. I liked her best but, unfortunately, I could never become her best friend because Anneliese had got there before me.

Going to tea with the Boedeckers (Gabi's family) for the first time was a great treat for me. They lived in a large, beautiful old farmhouse. A huge glass double door divided the entrance hall from the inner hall. When I rang the door bell two older girls, one blonde, the other dark, opened the door. Gabi had told me proudly of her two sisters – how very clever they were and that they went to a school in Hannover every day. I soon envied her for having two such nice sisters. They obviously adored their much younger sister and showed great kindness towards her new schoolmate. From the first moment I felt happy and very much at home at the Boedeckers.

In the same house there also lived their spinster aunt whom everybody just called *Tanta*.

Tanta looked after the cattle and, when Gabi showed me around the farm and we came to the cowstall, I asked Tanta if I might scrape the "Pennies" from the cows' rumps. These were small round bits of dried dung and Heinrich had taught me how to remove them, so that the cows were made more comfortable. Laughingly she handed me the scraper and they all stood around me watching, bemused at their small guest enthusiastically cleaning the cows.

Gabi dragged me away to see the horses just being fed by her father. Out of a large oval-shaped shallow basket he poured the chopped oat-straw into the manger, and the horses, hungry after their day's work, put their heads into the cribs, shaking their manes with pleasure and pulling at their chains to get their heads closer to the food. All we could hear was a rhythmic munching and the clinking of their chains.

It was a warm, sunny Spring evening when Gabi showed me her own small garden for the first time. It was full of pansies and wallflowers, and the butterflies moved gently on the dark red and brown blossoms as we sat on her rickety self-made garden bench, a small plank of wood balanced on some bricks.

Gabi was a serious girl, Anneliese was sentimental, Annemarie timid and I was always cheerful. We made a good quartet for many years.

For three years we stayed together in this school, adoring our teacher except on the days when he smelled even stronger of drink and his red face took on a purple colour. We soon learned when he was not in the mood for any sort of a joke and that we had better sit quietly and do our work, so Ilse and I refrained from giggling. The slightest noise upset him and whoever was responsible had to suffer. Of course we were punished when we deserved it, and quite a few times I had the cane, which fell upon my outstretched hand with a whistling blow. With my head bent so as not to show my tears I went back to my seat and immediately put my hand on the cool metal lid of the built-in inkpot. I never showed my hand to my parents, for fear of being punished once more, but our maid was most sympathetic, and my punishments earned me pieces of chocolate and biscuits.

One day Herr S. said, "Who would like to learn to play the mouth-organ?" About six small hands shot up – mine was amongst them. On the next day we carried a Honer mouth-organ of one octave in our satchels, copied notes of music from the blackboard with special attention to the in and out blowing. It was not difficult and soon six little Larry Adlers were happily blowing away.

At the same time my grandmother gave me a violin. Because

I was still rather small it was a half-size one and music lessons were arranged for me with Fräulein Pook. My first lesson disappointed me for I had thought I should be able to play a tune the same day. That did not happen until weeks later, and when finally I was able to play a fairly recognizable one, nobody wanted to listen.

Fräulein Pook had a great rival, who was naturally her enemy, in the town. It was Herr Posen, who also gave violin lessons. He was a very handsome young man, very popular with the ladies, so quite a few mothers preferred to send their children to him. Fräulein Pook referred to him as a five-o'clock tea fiddler, and father dismissed him with one word: shocking.

It took me half an hour to walk to Fräulein Pook's house at the other end of the town. Proudly I carried my violin case for the first time, together with my music satchel, into which I had put the Mozart Sonatas which father played from time to time. I had never met Fräulein Pook before and when Emma, her maid, opened the door to let me in, I thought she was my new music teacher. I was horrified to see that she looked almost like a man, with a very visible moustache and long hairs on her chin, but when she told me in a deep stammering voice that Fraulein Pook was in the music-room, I was most relieved.

But not for long, because Fräulein Pook also looked like a man, except that she did not have any excess hairs on her face. Her hair was certainly cut like a man's, her voice was as deep as Emma's and she was smoking a large cigar. Her fingertips were brown from nicotine, and her breath smelled of tobacco. I had to sit close to her on the sofa. She drew an apple on a piece of paper, halved it, quartered it, divided it into eight then sixteen pieces and in this way explained the timing to me.

She took my violin out of its case, held it in front of her and sighing deeply, said, "Ach, Gott," and told me the names of the strings, what a fret-board was and introduced me to the frog on the bow. I was allowed to hold the violin under my chin, together with the blue velvet chin cushion and she led my bow by pushing my elbow across the "E" string. A most excruciating noise was the result and a cloud of dust from my bow, which I had rubbed

74

with resin for half an hour before I set out. Her four canaries started to object and had to be covered-up. I could never understand why she had to have canaries in her music-room anyway, as they spent most of their lives being covered-up with a blanket. Even if one played well, they objected and made more noise than violin and piano together.

It took a long time before I enjoyed playing the violin and I wanted to give it up lots of times at the beginning. My mother practised patiently with me, until I started to practise on my own regularly every day and began to enjoy it. When I finally played my first small pieces by the great masters, modified for beginners into the first position, I grandly wrote to my grandmother, "I am now playing Mozart, Beethoven and Bach."

The highlight of the school year was the day's outing. I remember one to the Harzmountains, which stands out as a specially happy one, because both my parents came. It did not often happen that both of them were free at the same time. Apart from visits to my grandparents in Hannover, I can only remember one holiday in Berlin with both parents.

A group of 25 children, most of them accompanied by their mothers, stood excitedly on the platform on a July morning. Each carried a small rucksack and was fitted out with tough walking shoes which by the end of the day caused everyone painful blisters. The weather was promising and the sun was still low and rosy as the train sped along, past woods and meadows where cows were lying on the dewy glistening grass, chewing the cud.

Shrieks of joy and amazement broke out at the first sight of the mountains. Our own countryside was as flat as a pancake for miles and miles. Not the smallest hill broke the monotony of it, though there were woods. I kept on glancing with pride at my parents who looked so different today. Father appeared years younger in his travelling suit of salt and pepper tweed with matching cap, such a nice change from his usual dark suits and hat. And mother, who mostly wore smart dresses, was today dressed in a dirndl. All this made me very happy.

When, after two hours, the train finally stopped at our

destination, Bad Harzburg, a small town surrounded by wooded mountains with patches of green fields here and there, our excitement had reached its peak. A four-hour walk to Goslar lay ahead of us. Our teacher went on in front, swinging his walking-stick as he strode along. Taking out the mouth-organ from his jacket pocket, he began to play the *Happy Wanderer*. Everybody followed, singing and trusting his sense of direction. We looked like the children following the Pied Piper of Hamelin. We started along the small but fast-running river called the Ocker, but soon our steep narrow path led us far above it and we looked down onto the white foaming water as it rushed over the rocks into the valley.

Parents shouted to their children to be careful, hanging on to them for most of the walk. Thank goodness I was not one of them. Ilse and I were in our element, darting from one rock to the other, always discovering new things, running back from time to time to our parents to make sure that they also were enjoying themselves.

Our own enjoyment was rather dampened when we saw "Lanky Emil", his face deathly white and his eyes half closed, walking slowly beside mother who had put a helping arm around his waist. He had already been sick on the train. He suffered from migraines. It had been suggested on arrival that he should stay with his mother at the station and catch up with us by train when he felt better. This was very much opposed by his mother, a robust person, who said quite firmly that she had saved up and paid for this trip and was jolly well going to enjoy it. And this she did, leaving her son completely in mother's care.

After a two-hour walk we stopped to rest and to have our lunch in a *Biergarten*. Poor Emil flopped onto the grass; there he lay outstretched, not able to live or die. A small group of grown-ups and children stood around him looking sympathetically at this heap of misery. Mother knelt beside him, wiping his forehead with her handkerchief soaked with Eau de Cologne, whilst the rest of us sat under cheerful sun umbrellas eating our sandwiches and drinking lemonade through straws.

The day became hotter and hotter, our walking after lunch

slower and slower. The singing had stopped altogether and Herr S. had put his mouth-organ back into his pocket. His face had become redder after lunch and was beginning to take on the alarming purple colour, but he stayed in a good mood. Father caught up with me, took my hand and told me to walk slowly for a while beside him. He brushed the curls from my damp forehead and demonstrated how to breathe in deeply the delicious mountain air and the sweet scent of pine trees. It was good for the lungs. I did not stay beside him for long, as I was still charged with plenty of energy. Herr S. shook his head when Ilse and I overtook him and said to father, "These two are doing the whole walk twice over."

We arrived at the old Imperial town, Goslar, in the afternoon and were dragged to see the castle, in which we took not the slightest interest. We were beginning to get very tired. We got our second wind on the way home in the train when we talked incessantly of our adventures. Even Emil had sufficiently recovered to join in, though his memory of it all must have been rather hazy and unpleasant. By and by we became quieter and one by one dropped off to sleep.

When we arrived at our station our eyes were small and blinking. In a daze we got out of the train and walked stiffly down the platform, because of blisters and aching leg muscles, a different little group from the boisterous one in the morning – quiet and tired but carrying in our young hearts a memory of a very happy day which stayed with us for a long time.

CHAPTER 8

In the Winter of 1938 for the first time I heard an all-male choir perform in the church. The choir members, all dressed in black, looked like cut-outs silhouetted against the lit-up altar as they grouped themselves in front of it. The rest of the church was dark. They wore a peculiar get-up: wide-sleeved blouses held in by leather belts over loosely-fitted trousers, which were tucked into high black boots. Their hair, beards and moustaches were equally black. They were Cossacks. Never before had I heard such wonderful voices. Their deep richness not only filled the church but penetrated into one's inner self and it sent shivers down my spine.

After the concert they were invited to supper at the Rectory. Silently they followed mother and me through the dark evening, dressed in long black coats and fur hats. During the meal they became more talkative and their dark eyes began to sparkle. The choirmaster stood up, raised his wineglass towards my parents and with a deep bow expressed his gratitude for their hospitality. Their faces became relaxed and cheerful and the hall filled with the vibration of their laughter, which was as deep and rich as their voices. Their German was not very good but good enough to tell us stories about their homesteads in Southern Russia, about their families and ponies. One of them performed a dance in a peculiar squatting position; with his arms stretched out in front of him he danced to the rhythmic clappings of his comrades. When they said goodbye they kissed the sleeves of our coats. Some of them had tears in their eyes.

* * *

I can't remember ever being bored. Admittedly I had my brother and friends to play with, but if they weren't around I was quite happy on my own. In the winter I played with my dolls; this was before I was able to read. Once I could read, at the age of seven I think, my dolls became very neglected. I adored reading. My grandmother had given us lots of books which once belonged to her children. Fortunately, my brother loved reading too, and we both sat for hours completely engrossed in our books. The only maddening thing sometimes was that Gewi insisted on reading aloud: when this happened I put my fingers in my ears and tried not to listen.

The lovely old books we read, could not be found anymore. Most of the children's books in the shops at that time were Nazi-orientated. My first spelling book at school started with: "Heil Hitler, Toni, how is your cat?" I need not mention my father's remark on this. It became a standing joke that every time he asked me what I had learned at school that day, he said: 'Oh I know, Heil Hitler, Toni!'

"Christening" was one of our favourite games. It started with the actual birth when I had to recline on the sofa with a blanket over me and Gewi was the doctor delivering the child.

When I was twelve years old mother enlightened me about the facts of life. Until then I drew my own conclusions, altered at times by horrendous information from various pals. I am sure my brother, being that much older than I, must have known more about it, but he certainly did not let on.

Until I was about eight years old I believed in the stork bringing the babies. There was a stork's nest on our neighbour's chimney, and every May Mr and Mrs Stork returned to the same nest. Sometimes they raised a family, sometimes they didn't, but the storks standing in their nest on one leg became a familiar sight. It was supposed to be good luck to see a stork in flight and it was then that one had to express a wish like: *Stork, Stork Guter, bring mir einen Bruder,* or *Stork, Stork bester, bring mir eine Schwester.* [Bring me either a brother or a sister]. I was longing for mother to have another baby, and I shouted and pleaded my utmost whenever I saw a stork in flight. Once, when mother and I went for a walk and came upon a lonely gypsy caravan beside the road, we heard a baby crying from within. I was quite sure its mother had abandoned it and begged mother to go and fetch it so that we could take it home, but mother assured me that its own mother would come back soon.

Gabi's father had told her that the foals lie under the cobbles in the stable and that the horse paws them from underneath the stones. Once we saw a horse doing just that. Gabi and I sat quietly with pounding hearts on the feed bin, watching it. The noise of the horse's hoof was alarming and sparks started to appear. 'It's coming soon now,' whispered Gabi, but the horse gave up and continued feeding out of the crib. I asked mother where babies came from and was told that each mother, before the baby was born, carried it under her heart.

Once, when coming home from school, my friends and I passed a cottage from which suddenly came a most dreadful yell. 'It's Frau Albin having her baby,' one of my friends said knowingly. Now I knew two things; that I had to put the doll next to my heart and let out a fearful scream when Gewi pulled it away from under the blanket. The christening followed in a grand style, and Gewi was once more in his element acting as a parson.

* * *

There was always something to look forward to throughout the year; festivities like Christmas, Easter, Whitsun and birthdays. Christmas was the nicest. It started with the beginning of Advent when a large wreath of fir branches was hung from four wide red silk ribbons suspended from the ceiling in the hall. Four fat red candles were stuck onto it. A smaller replica appeared on the dining-room table. For each of the four Advent Sundays a candle was lit at tea and supper time. Two Christmas calendars, one for my brother, one for me, hung against the nursery window. The scene they showed was mostly a little town with snowy roofs, where each window had a number corresponding with the date up to the 23rd December. Finally, on the 24th the double stable door was opened and the Nativity appeared.

81

Each Advent Sunday night we were allowed to put our slippers onto the window-ledge for *"weihnachtsmann"*(Father Christmas) to fill during the night. Even when we did not believe in Father Christmas any more we kept up this practice until the war put an end to the supply of presents. I tried to keep awake to see Father Christmas come, but fell asleep every time and dreamed instead of the slipper overflowing with delicious things. Sometimes I got up during the night, felt for the slipper on the window-ledge, pulled out a chocolate Father Christmas and indulged in a midnight feast. Of course I was disappointed in the morning when I saw a dismantled Father Christmas and crumpled-up silver paper beside the almost empty slipper.

The 6th December was a dreaded day for me. It was St Nicolaus Day, and St Nicolaus appeared in person. He came towards the evening, dressed in a red coat trimmed with white fur, a long white beard and a red hood. He carried a sack on his back and in his hand a switch of birch twigs; this of course was only for the naughty children. I always had a bad conscience and hid behind the sofa as soon as I heard his voice. He always found me and dragged me out from behind it, told me not to be frightened but to be more obedient and more diligent at school. It was marvellous how exactly he knew about all our shortcomings, especially about father who sat in the armchair, very much amused by it all, smoking a cigar and putting a couple of them into the large coat pocket of Father Christmas. Gewi and I had to say a poem which went like this:

Lieber Guter Weihnachtsmann
Sieh mich nicht so boese an
Stecke deine Rute ein
Ich will auch immer recht artig sein

(Dear Father Christmas, please be kind to me, put away your stick and I promise to be good from now on.)

After that he began to unpack his sack. Everybody got a present and it was always just what we wanted. How did he know? When we had thanked him and promised to be good children he went, but not before giving father a friendly tap on his shoulders with the birch twigs and telling him to go to bed earlier. (Father did most of his writing at night and never went to bed before 2 or 3 o'clock.)

Later, of course, we knew that Father Christmas came from a large department store called Karstadt, in Hannover, and that mother had hired him, telling him exactly what to say and what to bring. When the war started he stopped coming. He most likely had to enlist and ended up somewhere in Norway or Russia.

Early in December mother started baking ginger biscuits and a special kind of dark treacle biscuit with lots of spice in it. Gewi and I helped her, cutting stars and half-moons out of the dough and decorating them with a hazelnut or almond. Just before Christmas the kitchen looked like a factory producing endless Christmas *Stollen* (fruit loaf), all of which found their way into the homes of the needy. Our own biscuits were stored in large tins and every day at tea time a plate of them appeared on the table.

Mother was in charge of the Nativity Play performed by the Sunday School children. Each year the play varied. My fervent wish was to be Mary, but it never happened. 'Your hair is too curly and fair,' mother said, and that was that. I hated my hair. So many of my friends had long dark hair, just right for Mary. I always played an angel, and Gewi was always a shepherd. He did not mind; he didn't like acting anyway and always had to be coaxed into it. Once he got the giggles. I don't know what started him off; it was so unlike him because he was always so serious. I was very easily infected by giggles and although Gewi controlled himself quickly, I could not, and was sent out by mother in the middle of the play. Of course this ruined my chances completely of ever being Mary.

My brother was very good with his fret-saw. I was hopeless with the needle. I tried to crochet but it was not much better either, and the saucepan-holders which were meant to be square turned out to be a peculiar conical shape. But mother made use of every little present we ever gave her. My favourite presents to give

83

were boxes of matchwood which I painted; fortunately they were very fragile and broke easily, so it didn't matter that I produced them year after year. I was very bad at keeping my presents a secret. Once I told father what his present was. As soon as I left his study I sat down and cried, full of regret at having told him. Father heard me crying, came out and said that he had already forgotten what it was. I believed him and was happy again.

A great treat before Christmas was the children's opera to which my grandmother invited us every year. It took place in the Opera House in Hannover. "Haensel and Gretl" was my favourite opera and "Frau Holle" came next. The Opera House was very beautiful: its chandeliers sparkled and the red plush seats in our box with its gold brocade felt soft and grand. I wore my best dress for these occasions, and grandmother lent me her delicate pair of binoculars made of mother-of-pearl.

After the opera we always had a quick walk around the Christmas Fair before we caught the train back. There were huge Christmas trees with white electric candles, brightly lit stands covered by canvas roofs on which the snow lay heavily and sparkled in the light, glittering jewellery, chocolate hearts hanging from silk ribbons, every kind of toy, and the lingering smell of roasted chestnuts and fried sausages served on a paper plate with a crispy roll and lashings of mustard. Father Christmas in his full regalia cracked jokes or kissed a frightened child. Above all stood the impressive Marktkirche, known for its green copper spire which was now floodlit. Its deep melodious bell behind the golden clock rang out every quarter of an hour.

A few days before Christmas a large Christmas tree was brought up the stairs into the drawing-room and from then on the door of that room was locked. Only mother was allowed in there. Happy were the days when I still believed that mother was working behind the door with Father Christmas or, as mother said, with the Christ Child Himself. She had a marvellous way of making me believe in things. I sat in front of the door with my ear against it, listening to the mysterious noises going on inside. Sometimes mother would ring a tiny silver bell which made me believe that the Christ Child had just flown in through the window. When I requested, in a timid voice, for Him to talk to me, mother answered in a thin sweet voice which for years I did not recognise as hers. Once she left a very delicate golden hair on the threshold which for a long time I treasured as that of the Christ Child.

My behaviour most certainly improved before each Christmas. The atmosphere in the house was so exciting and beautiful and I lived in awe of what went on behind the closed drawing-room doors.

The morning of the 24th was wonderful to wake up to — it was the most special day of the year. Gewi and I wrapped up the presents we had made. Mother was busy in the kitchen preparing the goose with apple and raisin stuffing for the following day, and the finely-shredded red cabbage to go with it was put onto the stove: the longer it simmered the better it was.

Tonight's meal was as usual, carp — "Carp Bleu" as it was called — with creamy horse-radish sauce and parsley potatoes. Our maid was scrubbing the tiles in the hall shouting angrily at us as we dashed backwards and forwards, hopping over the wet floor and her bucket, to get more wrapping paper from the chest in the hall. Father was typing in the study, preparing the many sermons he had to deliver during the next three days.

The day improved as it went on. At about three o'clock the work was done and a hush settled over the house. Two more hours to wait before Mass started. These quiet hours in the afternoon on the 24th were always very special to me. There was nothing much to do except wait, but it was just this that I liked, and Gewi felt the same. We were both completely different in temperament, but for certain things we had the same feeling. Confidently we sat in our nursery, our noses pressed against the double window. Looking out into the wintry garden, we watched the birds snatching the last bits of crumb or nut from the bird-table before retiring for the night. The clear sky got redder with the setting sun, until a pale first star appeared. Suddenly the sun set and the pinkness of the sky changed to a cold pale blue which very quickly became dark. The curtains were drawn and the tea brought in; all four candles on the advent wreath were lit, one had nearly burnt itself out but the fourth still had a long way to go.

I shall never forget the afternoon of one Christmas Eve. What was so special about it was that I had mother all to myself. My brother had gone out with my father and our maid was in bed with a cold. Mother was upset because she had broken a small bulb for the campfire of my brother's toy fortress which he was to get that evening. Apparently this bulb was very important. I knew the shop where I could get it, but as I was only five years old and the shop was a long way away, mother was very reluctant to let me go. I assured her I would be alright.

With the small bulb inside my mitten, I set off. There was hardly anybody about. Everyone, it seemed, had done their shopping and were now busy putting the finishing touches to the preparations indoors. The shop windows were lit up, but the shops themselves were almost empty. A dummy figure of Father Christmas appeared in almost every shop window; his head was continuously nodding and his eyes rolled from left to right, his grin from one ear to the other. They were not very becoming images, in fact they were rather frightening. I got the bulb from the electrical shop. Here and there I could see through the windows a lit-up Christmas tree. The light of the street lamps threw long shadows onto the pavement and the thin snowflakes danced and glistened in their light.

When I turned into our drive I saw mother's face looking out of the window from father's study and before I had reached the front door she had opened it and took me into her arms. She had obviously been very worried about me. I think this was perhaps the first time I realised how much mother cared for me, and it made me so happy that I shall never forget that moment. Mother took me to father's study where she had prepared tea just for herself and me, and my happiness was complete. I sat on her lap and she stroked my curls, and softly hummed a Christmas carol.

Christmas Vespers was at 5 o'clock and we all went to church, which was packed every year, mainly with children. It was said that mothers sent their offspring to Vespers because it gave them a chance to do the last preparations in peace at home. The only time mother sat in the "rector's pew" was at Christmas. It was right next to the altar. She hated to sit "in front" and usually had her seat next to the entrance. Tonight she sat here for our benefit so that we could get a full view of the two tall Christmas trees at either side of the altar. On their wide dark green branches stood white wax candles, all alight; they lasted exactly the length of the service. I found it difficult to listen to what father was saying. Thank God that for once he kept his address short. The last carol was sung with great fervour by old and young. Excitement and anticipation of the things to come that night were reaching their climax. But it was a long time yet before we had our presents and supper. Mother had prepared several small Christmas trees, beautifully decorated with candles and small silver balls, as well as presents of food and warm clothes for the sick and suffering in our neighbourhood.

One of these families was Mr and Mrs Rettich. I shall never forget the first time we took them a Christmas tree. They lived in one of the oldest houses in the village, shared with many others. Their two rooms, a kitchen and a bedroom were at the top of the house. A large wooden double door, through which a horse and waggon could easily fit (that was exactly what the door was for originally), had a smaller door on one side through which we went into a dark interior which had an uneven earth floor. A smell of goats and pigs, which were kept in little compartments on either side of the hall, filled the airless place. We climbed the rickety stairs and mother knocked at the door. A thin-faced old man opened the door, holding a small oil lamp in his trembling hand. His wife lay on a shabby sofa in the kitchen. The stove gave out ample heat; through the cracks in its surface, flames threw a red glow. Our shadows danced and quivered on the ceiling. The smell in the kitchen was unbearable. Frau Rettich had been paralysed for years and never left the sofa. The smell was of dirty clothes and urine, although the kitchen itself was very clean. I wanted to leave the room for I was beginning to feel sick, but Gewi caught me by my wrist and held it tightly until we

87

left. He was so much wiser and nicer for his few more years than I was. When the candles on the tree were lit and their light fell onto our faces, I saw tears rolling down the old couple's cheeks. They had never expected the Christmas tree, let alone presents, and would have spent this evening as all other evenings, alone and cheerless in their minute kitchen by the dim light of their oil lamp.

The sick woman held mother's hands and squeezed them and muttered something incomprehensible, for her speech had gone long ago. A lump came into my throat and, glancing at Gewi, I saw that he too had tears in his eyes. And now mother said, 'Let's sing "Silent Night"'. How could she expect us to sing and especially this, the most moving carol, but we did, and the old man joined in with his thin, quavering voice.

It was after having been to see people like this old couple that we had our own Christmas. By now we could hardly wait.

At last the little silver bell from within the drawing-room told us to come in. The room looked the same every year, and each year we greeted the tree and the crib with the same joy. The scent of the tree and the sweet smell of the honey candles filled the room. The tree reached the ceiling, under its lower branches was the crib, a thatched open stable about four feet long with Mary and Joseph kneeling in front of the manger, in which lay the Christ Child with His halo. Donkeys and cows crowded around, all the figures being made of plaster and beautifully painted. Fresh green clumps of moss and rocks, which I recognized as being from the garden, made up the fields around, on which sheep and lambs were grazing. Shepherds stood in awe looking up at the delicate wax angels which were suspended from the lower branches. The largest, the angel Gabriel, hung very low. They were all of different sizes and the one furthest away was the smallest, a tiny delicate angel not more than an inch in size. Every year a new piece was added to the crib. This year we spotted a well in the middle of the field; it had a small silver bucket on a lever which let the bucket disappear into the well. Behind the crib stood a cross of pale pink roses made of tissue paper. An electric bulb from behind illuminated it.

Mother started to play "Silent Night" on the harmonium and father accompanied her on his violin. He could play and sing at the same time, something which I found very difficult when I joined them with my violin. I could not possibly sing as well.

All the time we were singing, we could not help glancing towards the row of tables which were arranged on one side of the room. They were covered with long white starched table-cloths on which lay our presents. Finally, after what had seemed like ages, mother led everybody to their own table. A large plate of sweets, marzipan and chocolates stood in the middle of it and round it lay the presents, so many of them, that we did not know which one to open first. We shrieked with joy, on receiving the gift we had wished for, ran to our parents, embraced them wildly, and rushed back to open the next present.

Our maid was pleased with her table. In her clean white apron, she stood in front of it with a wide grin on her face as she opened her presents. Mother never failed to make us feel that our home-made gifts were, once again, just what she needed and wanted.

The meal followed, taken in the Christmas room. All the time the candles burnt on the tree. We watched as they burnt out, one by one, and when the last one flickered feebly in its holder, it was time for us to go to bed.

Getting up the next morning was easy. Still in our nighties we crept into the drawing-room, where a fire was already lit. The smell of the burnt-out candles from the night before still lingered about the room. We reassured ourselves that our beautiful presents had not been just a dream. When we were old enough – from the age of six, I think – we went to church with mother, but before that we stayed at home in the charge of our maid who was also in charge of roasting the goose.

Once, when I was still very young, I stood in front of the crib and looked at the Christ Child. For some reason it was made of marzipan. I had a passion for marzipan and I remember taking it out of the manger and nibbling a little at its feet and then its legs. It looked ugly without them, so I ate a little more and finally I ate it all. I did not tell anybody but felt terribly guilty.

When at tea-time the candles on the tree were lit, I went to the crib (no-one had noticed the empty manger) and I thought that Mary looked very sad as she gazed at the place where once her child had been. I burst into tears and confessed to mother what I had done. She did not scold me, but very quietly said: 'How sad'. For that evening the manger remained empty and my brother looked at me most reproachfully. The next day a little wax angel replaced the Christ Child, and Mary's face, I thought, looked a little happier.

* * *

A week later it was New Year's Eve, which I never liked. Going to church at 5 o'clock reminded me of Christmas Eve the week before. Now it was all over, this was an anti-climax. Instead of the cheerful Christmas Carols, mournful hymns were sung. Father's voice thundered from the pulpit: 'We do not know what sorrow is waiting for us in the coming year, therefore . . .' It all struck me as being very sad, and when I was small I put my head into mother's lap and went to sleep. I remember the smell of her leather glove as she put her hand on my head.

New Year's Eve is the time for fireworks, hot punches and doughnuts. Until I was ten years old I was not allowed to stay up, but I did not mind, and even when I was old enough I never really enjoyed it.

* * *

There was no particular time to take down the Christmas tree or decorations. We kept the tree and crib until the needles started to drop. When that time came, everything was taken off carefully, wrapped in tissue paper and put back into the labelled boxes which were taken to the room in the attic.

The tree was thrown out of the window. Without a sound it landed on the snow below and was put in front of the woodshed to be chopped up in due course for firewood. For a short time a patch of pine needles showed where it had landed but it was soon covered with fresh snow. The once-beautiful Christmas tree sometimes stood for weeks leaning against the shed, and bereft of its needles it awaited the end. The only sign of its former glory was a thin strand of silver paper which fluttered in the cold wind on one of the bare branches.

* * *

Birthdays were almost as exciting as Christmas. I always thought that father's birthday was even nicer than my own.

Every year he was serenaded by a group of young girls and women between the ages of eighteen and thirty, a Bible Group he had founded when coming to Lehrte, who met once a week. As soon as we heard the shuffling of shoes and whispering and stifled giggles, my brother and I rushed to the stairs. From the top step, dressed in our pyjamas, we watched as the early congratulants grouped themselves at the bottom of the stairs. Suddenly the whispering stopped, one or two cleared their throats. Then silence followed until one of them raised her hand. Immediately lovely voices in soprano and alto sang father's two favourite hymns. One was "Praise the Lord, the Almighty", and the other was about being carried on the wings of an eagle to heavenly heights. They were the same hymns every year. Father stood behind us in his dressing-gown. His birthday was the only time I ever saw him in his dressing-gown, except occasionally just after the war when he was very ill. When they finished singing he went down and shook hands with them and they presented him with a bunch of flowers and a book.

None of them could stay as they all had to dash off to their jobs but the next time the "group" met, they were given cakes and coffee. On fine summer evenings they persuaded father to have their meetings outside on the lawn and these evenings ended up with country dancing. I watched from my bedroom window. They saw me and waved their hands and called me to come down. In my bare feet and my nightie, I danced with them under the weeping willow to the sound of the accordion. Father and mother joined in too, but not my brother — he stood with his hands in his pockets all by himself. A row of village children sat on the stone wall under the oak, watching us.

Parishioners came throughout the day to congratulate him. In the evening he sank into his chair, saying, 'What a tiring day a birthday is,' something I could not understand.

One of father's birthdays turned out to be a sad one. My grandfather, who was in his 80th year, often came to preach to give father a day off. He had come to this birthday celebration to do just that. Matins was from 10 to 11.30 and Sunday School started at 11.45. I had arrived early and was surprised when suddenly the big double doors opened and the congregation appeared, sad-faced, some crying. A kind woman took me aside and whispered that grandfather had fainted in the pulpit. I rushed into the church and saw him lying in front of the altar on the deep red carpet, his head resting on the cushion which was used by brides to kneel on. He looked very pale and had his eyes closed. An ambulance took him to our house. Grandfather was a healthy man and after two hours he recovered. Grandmother stayed beside him all day as he lay on the sofa, and held his hand. He was told by the doctor not to preach any more but he continued to do so until he was 86.

He was of great help to father at the beginning of the war. We sat with trembling hearts lest he should faint again, but he never did. It was a touching sight when father and son, one tall and dark-haired, the other bent from age, his hair snowy-white, stood side by side at the altar giving communion. Father held the chalice with the wine, grandfather gave the bread.

Whose ever birthday it was, a garland of flowers surrounded the birthday King's or Queen's place at table. The presents were laid out on a small side table. In the middle stood a candle-holder indicating the age. It delicately refrained from revealing the age after eighteen.

CHAPTER 9

I didn't like the Summers nearly as much as the Winters, though I can only remember summer days as being hot and sunny. I always longed for the winter, the snow and all the joys it brought with it.

When the first snowflakes came floating down from the dark bluish-grey sky, I sat with my nose pressed against the window-pane watching them as they came faster and faster and bigger and bigger, settling on the frosty earth and covering the frozen puddles. Everyone was prepared for the snow and knew that it would not melt but would remain with us for the next four months. My sledge was waiting next to the front door, oiled and polished with a new rope to pull it. For the next few months we would be inseparable friends.

After the first heavy snowfall everything seemed trans-formed. The light in the house grew a shade brighter even when the sun was not shining. Outside, everything was quiet. Now the snow muffled the sound of the noisy cart-wheels, the large uneven cobblestones lay deep under a white blanket and the clatter of horses' hooves was silenced. Instead there was a jingle of harness, and the snorting of the horses produced a small white translucent cloud in the clear frosty air.

People dressed in fur boots and fur hats shuffled carefully along the footpaths. Soon the activity of shovelling pathways from front doors to the road set in. I, too, got hold of my small shovel from the sandpit and joined in. Our path to the road was a long one and several others had to be made to the woodshed, wash-kitchen and chicken-house. Hands began to get cold but by beating them across the shoulders they soon warmed up again. A large snowplough had pushed the snow to each side of the road, leaving high banks near the pavements. It was up to the pedestrians to make a break-through here and there.

Soon the beauty of the first snow was spoiled when ashes and sand were scattered and the snow became slushy and brown. Disappointed by the sight of it, I opened the door to the garden. Here the untouched snow lay feet deep in front of me. Its surface sparkled in the sun like a veil of diamonds. Trees and shrubs, shortened by several feet, emerged out of the white mass, their branches bent under the weight of the snow. Over everything spread a great stillness. Sometimes a very small branch succumbed to its sudden weight, broke with a brief sharp crack and fell silently with its burden on the ground, leaving a slight mark on the white surface, which, apart from a few traces of delicate feathery hopping marks of a bird, was still untouched.

Behind the garden lay my Winter paradise, a disused claypit-cum-rubbish dump with 50 to 100 metre-long slopes falling steeply to the lake below which lay dark, deep and menacing. It was an ugly place in the Summer but now it looked different in its coat of glittering white. These slopes were our only chance of tobogganing; mother very reluctantly let me use them and I had to promise only to stick to the smaller slopes, which I am afraid I did not. There was one slope of 100 metres, called the "death-track" leading straight onto the lake. The sledge zoomed across the ice until it was stopped by the slopes on the other side. Some daredevils had erected a narrow passage of drums at the bottom of the slope through which the sledge was steered at a tremendous speed. Of course these drums were empty, but inaccurate steering resulted in the most awful crashes with nose-bleeds and bruises.

It took a good twenty minutes to re-climb the steep slope, which had become icy from our constant use. Often, nearly at the top, one of us slipped, let go of the rope and the sledge shot down into the pit. We had to try again. Our coats and gloves were covered in snow and, as soon as the sun started to set, the snow froze, they became stiff and our faces went blue with cold. It was time to go home.

By the time I reached our front door, my hands were hardly able to clean the snow off boots and coat. The gloves became completely useless, small icicles hung from them, and my numbed fingers fumbled to unbutton my coat. My "snow suit" must have been dripping wet every time, but the next morning I found it hanging dry and warm on the hook in the hall and the woollen gloves were once more soft and comforting.

Mother was waiting with the tea in the drawing-room. Every time she said on my return, 'I am glad you are back safe and sound,' and she rubbed my cold red hands until they were warm again. After I had drunk the hot cocoa my cheeks began to glow with the warmth of the room and the contentment inside me.

A sizzling noise from the stove promised baked apples filled with raisins and topped with sugar. Through the outer double window, which was covered with "ice flowers", came the last rosy glimmer of the setting sun. Mother got up and drew the curtains and pulled the lamp low over the table. In a very definite voice she announced: 'Time for homework'. The cuckoo clock ticked noisily as we sat at the table, my brother and I bent over our books, mother over her mending and our maid shelling dried beanpods or helping with the mending. These were the winter days and evenings I loved and longed for.

Neither my brother's nor my bedroom had a stove and they were icy-cold. It was so cold in winter that the walls glistened with thousands of tiny particles of ice, which I could scrape off the walls with my finger-nails. The bathroom was equally cold except on two days a week when we had baths. The water cylinder was a two-foot wide copper container about five foot high, a small cast-iron stove underneath heated the water to such an extent that the cylinder started to bulge dangerously. When the hot water was drawn it spurted out of the tap in alarming gurgling spasms so that the bathroom filled with dense steam and the electric ceiling light appeared like a full moon on a misty night. It was highly dangerous: what's more, the electric light switch was in the bathroom itself. It was a handsome little switch of brass, which gave us all shocks, more than once, but we survived.

On non-bath nights we had a good wash in my parents' bedroom where an old-fashioned tiled stove gave out ample heat. In front of the fire stood a large, low, rubber tub into which a large basin with warm water was put. We stood in the rubber tub to wash ourselves and could splash as much as we liked. Our nighties were put on top of the stove and were lovely and warm to slip into. I remember one evening when my parents were out, and my maternal grand-mother, who was staying, supervised our washing. She had, like my mother, some peculiar ideas about health. One of them was to plunge one's feet into icy cold water after one had just washed them in warm water. I refused to do this and she gave me a smack on my bottom, whereupon I called her the dreaded word "*Arschloch*" [which meant "arsehole"]. That was too much for my grandmother. She took out the hot water bottle which warmed my bed and I spent a freezing night without it.

The winter mornings were cruel. No stove was yet lit and the mornings were dark. School started at 8 o'clock. My dressing was done up to a certain stage under the eiderdown, a dash into the bathroom to clean teeth and have a quick wash. We ate in the warm kitchen. Hot cups of rye coffee, with bread and butter and honey revived us before we set off for school in a temperature not more than 15 degrees below freezing, with the pale stars still twinkling in the morning sky.

One day, in January 1938, I came home from school feeling very ill with a sore throat and aching limbs. Mother's remedy for colds was a drastic one, but mostly very effective. After a hot bath I was wrapped into an ice-cold wet sheet with only my arms sticking out; warm blankets were put on top with a hot water bottle. A glass of piping hot elderflower syrup ensured that I was bathed in sweat, and according to a famous doctor called Kneip, this was the best cure for colds.

But it did not work this time. My temperature rose and I felt more and more ill. The next day red blotches appeared all over my body. The doctor diagnosed scarlet fever. There were two dreaded children's diseases; one was diptheria, the other scarlet fever. In both cases the death rate in those days was high. Both were strictly hospital cases as they were very contagious, but mother pleaded with the doctor to let me stay at home. Knowing her ability as a nurse he allowed it.

96

Four weeks of complete isolation followed. I remember little of the first two weeks, except that when I woke up one day after a deep sleep, I found myself in my parents' bedroom. Father had been banned and was in the spare bedroom, and mother, in a white overall, was sitting beside me holding my hand. She had tears in her eyes. Apparently they were tears of joy as I had just overcome the crisis and was on the mend.

It took a long time before I was allowed out of bed. My brother and father appeared at the bedroom door waving to me from a distance. Outside the bedroom hung two white overalls, one for the doctor, one for mother; also a basin of water stood on a stool with some disinfectant, the smell of which lingered over the whole house. Mother had taken the utmost care that nobody else caught my illness. I lapped up all mothers' lavish attention. She carried me to the open window so that I could breathe the fresh March air. Sadly I looked at the vanishing snow, through which already peeped crocuses and pearl hyacinths. I had missed out on a lot of tobogganing. I felt weak and very tired. I had caught glandular fever as well, had become very thin and the mere thought of food nauseated me. Cod liver oil and malt was forced down me, which made it worse.

The Summer came and I was still poorly. Mother decided that sulphur baths would do me good, so off we went – mother, Gewi and I – in the summer holidays to stay with my grandmother in Bad Segeberg (Schleswig Holstein).

Every morning mother took me to the pump rooms where I was immersed in a horrid-smelling bath. For the first week I felt like dying. It was a long walk to the pump rooms from grandmother's house. I felt so weak after the baths that mother almost had to carry me back. Indeed, one day I fainted. Mother gave up taking me and from that day I felt better and became stronger.

One of the nicest things was the scent of the lime avenue in which my grandmother lived. Every morning, Dollie, her maid, swept the pavement in front of the house which was covered with white lime blossoms; the scent drifted through the open windows and the house was filled with it. At night the street lamp in front of the house threw mysterious shadows onto our bedroom ceiling, and my brother and I watched from the window when the man came to light the gas lamp.

Through my illness I had missed a lot of school and I had to catch up on a great deal. My Godmother in Westphalia, who had spent some time teaching in England – she was an Oxford graduate – invited me to spend a few months with her. I adored Aunt Emmie and her adopted daughter, Hanna, who was much older than I, and I was most enthusiastic. They lived in a pretty little house in Buer, where my parents lived before we moved to Lehrte. I had been there several times before and I knew it well.

I was meant to go to the local school for two months and Aunt Emmie was to give me lessons in the afternoons as well. The schoolmaster was a fanatical Nazi who proudly wore the Party emblem on his lapel. He was very friendly when Aunt Emmie introduced me to him on the first morning. The trouble started after she left. He made me stand in front of the class with my right arm outstretched in the Hitler salute.

Three times he made me say, 'Heil Hitler', and when my voice wasn't loud enough, I had to shout it another three times. It had not been made compulsory at that time to use the Hitler Gruss, and it was the first time that I had been obliged to use it. When I finally got it to his liking and wanted to take my seat next to a girl I knew, he shouted that I could not sit there, and pointed to a desk at the far end of the room at which I had to sit by myself. For the rest of the morning he completely ignored me. I did not mention this to my aunt, but when the next day he pulled my pigtails in a very painful way, I burst into tears. My only comfort was that now I had a deskmate, a curly-headed gipsy boy, who had been treated in exactly the same way by the young Nazi when he appeared that morning. Finally I began to understand why we were given this unjust treatment. Again he came and pulled my pigtail so hard that my face hit the desk and he shouted: 'We will teach you a lesson or two. Gipsies, Jews and parsons are all alike, they are the vermin of Germany.'

Ignanz, the handsome gypsy boy, shrugged his shoulders; he could not care less. Had he not shared in my misery at school, I should have complained to my aunt about the teacher. Ignanz and I became good friends; he was my first love and what could have been more romantic? Alas, it did not last long.

Every day after school I went with my new friend to his gypsy waggon which stood at the edge of the village near the stream. His mother was not a bit surprised when she saw me and she showed me his tiny baby sister who lay on bulging pillows asleep in a cupboard – which served as a bed. I kept very quiet about my friend to Aunt Emmie. I knew she would not approve. For nearly a week after school I went back to his home with him. Once I saw his sister being breast-fed; she had enormous black eyes and her hair was as curly as her brother's. On her tiny wrist she wore a silver bracelet. Ignanz had a habit of scratching his hair. I soon did the same and when Aunt Emmie noticed it and looked into my hair, to her horror she discovered lice. She was almost beside herself when I told her about my daily visits to the waggon and she forbade any further visits.

I did not tell her that I was sitting next to Ignanz at school. I wanted to pay one more visit to the gipsies to say goodbye. In my ignorance I told his mother that I had caught lice off them and that my aunt had forbidden me to come any more. Somehow the kind gipsy woman took umbrage at this and she took the frying-pan with potatoes from the stove and threw them at me. This was the sad ending of my first romance. Two days afterwards, Ignanz did not come to school for the gipsy waggon had moved on.

School without Ignanz was unbearable and then I told my aunt about the treatment I was receiving. The very same day she took me away from school, but here she met with opposition from the teacher who was not prepared to let his little victim go as easily as that. Aunt Emmie produced a doctor's certificate that I was still not well enough to attend school, and he had to let me go.

* * *

In the Autumn of the same year I noticed that my parents often looked worried and sad and talked in whispers to their friends.

I overheard words like "Jews" and "Concentration Camp" mentioned. I did not ponder on it; the last word was completely new to me and I did not know its meaning. But I knew of the Jews who played quite an important part in our small town – did not four of the largest shops belong to them? Most of the population bought their shoes in Herr Simon's shop, including us, and dresses and materials were found in Herr Maschekatze's at a very favourable price.

Herr Maschekatz was a particularly generous and friendly man; he never failed to escort mother out of the shop, bowing deeply and opening the door for her. He did not overlook me either, called me, "my Little One" and gave me remnants of material to make into dolls' dresses. His son Daniel went to school with my brother and his younger son, Herschel, an enormously fat boy, was in my form. He was always being teased, not because he was a Jew, but for his size and clumsiness. We did not know any difference between the Jews and ourselves; the only difference was that, like the Catholics, they went to their own church. Quite a few Jewish families had left the town since 1935; gone to America, it was said.

Father was often seen in long conversations with the male Jews; they looked a bit alike in their sombre suits and black hats. Oma Thiele, our neighbour, sold most of her vegetables to them, and in summer, her fresh strawberries.

On the evening of 9th November 1938, the telephone rang whilst we were having supper. Father answered it. When he came back, his face was sad and he looked pale. In a quiet voice he said, 'They are burning the synagogues in Hannover.' Whenever he used the word "they" it meant the Nazis. We went outside and looked to the west towards Hannover, where the sky was blood red from the fires.

Father said: 'There will be revenge'. I took his hand, which I did whenever I was frightened and he was near. His hand was so big and comforting.

'Why do they burn them, father?'

Before he could answer my questions, a group of S.A. men in uniform marched past us shouting in unison: 'Exterminate the

Jews, get rid of the vermin'. I had heard that before and gripped father's hand tighter.

They were marching in the direction of the town and going to do just that. All night they beat up the Jews, plundered their shops and houses, made bonfires of their books and enriched themselves with their valuables. Sleep did not come quickly to me that night; had not the teacher mentioned gipsies and parsons as well as the Jews? Was it to be us next?

* * *

The town looked a sad sight the next morning with broken glass everywhere and the smell of the dying bonfires. The broken shop windows were crudely repaired with planks of wood on which was written: "Who buys from Jews is a traitor". Daniel and Herschel never came to school again. I only saw them once again when they walked with their eyes downcast beside their mother, completely ignoring me. All visits to theatres, cinemas or any other public performance were forbidden to the Jews. They found themselves not only unwanted but homeless, jobless, penniless, and compelled to wear a large yellow star on their clothes, so that everybody recognised them, despised them and even spat at them.

When I met Herr Maschekatz some time later, I hardly recognised him, for the handsome middle-aged man had turned into an old man, walking bent with a stick. As always, I curtsied to him and bade him good day. He stopped, looked around him and, as nobody was to be seen, put his hand on my head and said: '"Little one", it is better you ignore me from now on.'

When I told my father he looked at me sadly and said: 'He is right, you had better not greet him any more, but you can pray for him.' This I did, and for Daniel and Herschel too. At that time I thought of so many people I had to pray for, it became something like a compulsion. Eventually my list got so long that I often fell asleep before I could mention them all.

101

* * *

The only holiday we ever had with our parents, except the North Sea holiday when we were very small, was when we celebrated the golden wedding of my grandparents in Berlin in the summer of 1939.

The golden wedding took place at the summer residence of my uncle in Berlin-Sacrow, a district for the rich with beautiful houses and large gardens running down to the river Havel.

Uncle Claus was the eldest of my grandparents' eight children (six of them were still alive). Like his brothers, he was tall and handsome. I liked him very much indeed, but unfortunately I only saw him twice. He was married to Aunt Clarutschka, who had a German mother and a Russian father. She was very fond of children and young people. They never had any children of their own, so Aunt Clarutschka invited children of her numerous friends to come and stay with her. Gewi was a frequent guest and spent at least one holiday a year with her. He felt very much at home in these beautiful surroundings. I was quite unaccustomed to the wealth and luxury of my uncle's place. For the first half of the week my parents and I stayed at the large and comfortable flat in Berlin-Charlottenburg in the Nymphenburgerstrasse.

A butler looked after us, Annie, the cook, provided scrumptious meals and Louis, the chauffeur, drove us wherever we wanted to go in the open "Opel Admiral" . Father's brother and wife led a completely different life from that of a country parson. Uncle Claus had studied under Max Reinhardt to become an actor, but changed his mind and went into Science and Politics. He became Manager of the Chemical Industry in Germany. Uncle Claus was very different from his brothers and sisters; he hardly ever smiled and seemed to be miles and miles away with his thoughts. He loved sport, the only Ungewitter who ever did (apart from myself). Every day before breakfast he trained with a professional trainer in swimming and rowing.

102

On my first evening in Berlin I was taken by Louis to fetch my uncle from his office. I waited for him in a large hall with a fountain. I sank into one of the voluptuous, soft leather chairs and I was so tired by my journey and all the new impressions that I curled up and went to sleep. When I met him for the first time he asked me what my name was. I thought it was a silly question because surely he ought to have known what his niece was called. I told him my name was "Renate".

He said, 'Are you sure? How do you know that this is your name?'

I told him everybody called me so, and then added as an afterthought, 'And anyway, I also know myself.' He thought that was very funny and laughed. I think that was the only time I ever heard him laugh.

I fell head over heels in love with Uncle Claus. Unfortunately he was a very busy man and did not spend much time with us, but when he was present I watched his every movement. I thought him most terribly handsome.

On the morning of the golden wedding, the family foregathered in the conservatory for a short service taken by my father. I even watched Uncle Claus through my folded hands during prayers. He did not believe, like us, and whilst everybody else had their heads bent in prayer, he looked out of the window and seemed far away with his thoughts.

I was overjoyed when, on my last evening with them, he told me to sit on his knee. He asked me how old I was and if I had learned to speak English yet. I told him that I was changing school that Autumn and would then begin to learn other languages. He told me to make a special effort with the English language, and once I could speak it well, he would buy me a beautiful new dress. These were almost the last words he spoke to me and it was the last time I saw him.

The golden wedding was on a lovely summer's day but the clouds of war hung low. The grown-ups sat in the garden until late in the evening. From their anxious faces we could see that all was not well. Uncle Claus had more inside information than any of his family and his absent gaze and his seriousness, I am sure now, were there for a good reason.

Uncle Claus

Aunt Clarutschka was the complete opposite. She was small, vivacious and always laughing and she talked with a foreign accent.

One afternoon I went with my parents to Dahlem to visit the wife of Pastor Martin Niemoeller, the former submarine Commandant, who since 1931 had been the leader of the "Bekennende Kirche" opposing Hitler. In 1937 he was "put away" by the Nazis. After his imprisonment I included him in my nightly prayers, and countless Germans prayed for him throughout the war, until his release in 1945.

After the first week my parents went to Bavaria, and Gewi and I stayed with Aunt Clarutschka in Sacrow. With us stayed another boy, the same age as Gewi. His name was Heinz Goering, a nephew of Herrmann Goering. Heinz was full of fun. One morning he came to breakfast in an embroidered Russian dress which he had found in a cupboard, and nobody recognized him until he started talking.

Under Louis's guidance we rowed across the River Havel to Posdam to the impressive Schloss which belonged to Frederic the Great, called Sanssouci. Terrace upon terrace, each with its orangery, stretched up to the castle, a beautiful building in baroque style. Louis took me to see the *Bradenburger Tor, Unter den Linden,* the *Zeushaus* and the Zoo, and we watched the changing of the *Wache* (Guard) in front of the *Neue Kanzlei* on a Sunday morning.

The highlight of the whole holiday for me was when he took me to see Leni Riefenstahl's film of the Olympic Games of 1936 in Berlin. Gewi and Heinz had been taken by my aunt when the Games actually took place. I had, up until now, only seen pictures of it in magazines. I had a very good reason for going. Besides Jessie Owens I looked for another person, called Trudi Meier who had won a gold medal in gymnastics and who came from Hannover. Not only did she live there, but I had become one of her pupils. After the Games she started to give gymnastic lessons in Hannover as well as in our small town. Every Thursday afternoon thirty girls stood in pale blue tunics in a straight line in front of her. The age group was from six to sixteen. Trudi Meier, in a white track suit which bore the emblem of the Olympic Games of five coloured rings, greeted us with "Heil Hitler" and taught us to use the parallel bars and the horse, to climb the rope and to do movement to music. Trudi Meier had dark bobbed hair; the older girls copied her hairstyle in admiration, and once again I cursed my own curly blond hair.

When she appeared in the film, standing on the rostrum receiving the gold medal and shaking Hitler's hand, I felt proud to be one of her pupils.

In the evenings Aunt Clarutschka told us stories of her childhood. We sat at her feet on the terrace and listened to her adventures of when she toured Russia with her father, who had been a well-known architect, and had designed the main railway station in Moscow. The river was below us. Once in a while a pleasure steamer with rows of windows lit up, Chinese lanterns swinging in the breeze to the music, glided past. Then the only noise was the lapping of small waves from the swell of the passing steamer against the rowing-boat anchored at the bottom of the garden.

There were always guests at her house, mainly actors and politicians. Uncle Claus was not a Nazi. His high position in Berlin compelled him to get on well with many fanatics of the Party but he did not care to entertain them. His sad face and silent behaviour revealed to those who knew him well the conflict he was in.

Although my father and my grandfather implored him for information he shook his head and would not talk about it. He had probably been sworn to secrecy and knew what was at stake if any information should pass his lips. Families had started to disappear and innocent children were drawn into the punishment of their parents who had disobeyed the orders of the "Führer".

Uncle Claus was determined not to bring any unnecessary suffering upon his family and remained silent like so many others.

I remember meeting Robert Ley and Herr von Ribbentrop at

my uncle's house. Herr von Ribbentrop suddenly pulled a bright red yo-yo out of his pocket and began to play with it, and then gave it to me.

This was our last holiday in Berlin. A month later, on the 1st September 1939, the second World War started.

CHAPTER 10

The 1st of September 1939 was a beautiful sunny day with a definite tinge of autumn in the air. During breakfast we heard a voice from the road shouting through a loudspeaker: *'Achtung! Achtung!'* We rushed outside; a van covered with the Nazi flag was parked just in front of our entrance gates. Again the voice shouted: *'Achtung! Achtung! In the early hours of this morning the Führer's troops have invaded Poland. Germany is at war!'*

The national anthem and the Horst Wessel song followed, blaring out of the loudspeaker at full volume. The van moved on, leaving groups of people behind standing dazed and silent in front of their houses. The silence was very noticeable after the din of the songs and the impact of the grave announcement. Shocked, everybody stood for a while and then went on with what they had been doing. Just when we were about to do the same, our neighbour's nephew who came every summer from the Ruhrland, came running up to us, dressed in the Hitler Youth uniform. His arm shot up in the Hitler salute, his heels clicked and he shouted at the top of his voice: 'Great Germany has declared war. Long live the Führer!'

Father's face suddenly became very red. He took one step towards the boy and said in a very angry voice: 'Shut up, you stupid boy, you don't know what you are talking about!' Father was so angry that I feared he would hit him. This would have been a grave offence because anybody in the Führer's uniform was not allowed to be punished. Instead, father turned round in disgust and walked into the house.

Mother followed father into his study. My brother Gewi stood as usual with his hands in his pockets, thinking. I was thinking too. School had not yet started. What was going to happen now? I was nearly eleven years old and I had no idea what was going on between the countries; of course I had read of wars but it had

109

never occurred to me that war could happen now, right now. What was it all about?

I knew about the Jews and I felt sorry for them; I knew of Pastor Niemoeller and I prayed for him; I also knew that the Nazis were dangerous and that father said Hitler would destroy Germany one day. Was this going to happen now? I was very muddled. I suddenly remembered that I was invited to a birthday party that afternoon, but now there was a war on, was I still able to go? Would it be wrong to go to parties in critical times like this? It worried me and I decided to ask father's advice.

Father smiled, put his hand on my head and said, 'I am sorry for all you young people. Of course you must go to the party.' Then he drew me towards him and said, 'Promise me, never to lose your cheerful smile, whatever happens.'

I went to my friend Irmela's party that afternoon. To start with we sat and talked in whispers about the war. We decided how we would help; we could knit socks and mittens for the soldiers and perhaps we could even help to nurse them.

'That will not be necessary at all,' said one girl, whose father was a Nazi. 'The war will be over long before we are old enough to nurse the soldiers.' Little did I know that six years later I would actually be helping to nurse not just German, but French, Italian, Serbian, Polish and Russian wounded. During the course of the afternoon we completely forgot about the war, and were happy and carefree.

But when I walked home by myself, I found as I always did, that the red evening sky, as beautiful as it was, tightened my heart just that little bit. That evening it reminded me of blood and I remembered father telling us a short time before, that when he was staying in the Harz mountains with mother, they had seen some red clouds in the sky in the shape of a large sword. I suddenly felt very frightened and started to run towards home. Once inside I forgot again all my worries of the war.

During the course of the first week ration cards were dished out: blue ones for meat, red for groceries, pink for bread and flour, and yellow for butter and fats. Children under sixteen years received double butter ration.

The ration cards were delivered to the house by people (they all wore a Nazi button on their jackets) who, at the same time, took down detailed particulars of every member of the household.

On 3rd September, England and France declared war on Germany. Soon after that, a man came and taught us about air raid precautions. He told us where to put buckets of water and sacks of sand, and he also inspected our cellar and shook his head and told us it was not good enough. We were told to use our neighbour's cellar, which came up to standard. Mother pointed out the thickness of the walls and ceiling, but he did not agree with the cellar windows being above ground. In the end he compromised, and a five-foot wall was built in front of each window, leaving enough space for us to squeeze through if necessary.

Nothing else happened that was different from any other Autumn except that young men were called-up. Ernst, Heinrich's brother from next door, came one day in uniform to say goodbye, and many others came to do the same. Father's new colleague, who had been sharing the parish for the last year, was one of the first to be called-up. He was the father of six children.

The blackout needed quite a bit of organising with so many windows in our house. We started off with blinds made from blackout paper. On the first evening of a mock air-raid an outraged warden rushed into the house. 'For God's sake, turn the bloody lights off, your house is a direct target and a danger to everybody else!'

In some ways, mother wasn't very practical, and father had no idea whatsoever about practicalities. Apparently gaps either side of the blind let the light through, so now we used endless drawing-pins, until the sides became so perforated that the paper tore. From then on thick blankets were used; they hung from hooks at the top of the window and were held in place on the window-ledge by heavy books. Although no more light escaped, they weren't altogether satisfactory as they were cumbersome and an eyesore during the day. In the first few months we sometimes forgot all about the blackout, and would go into a room and switch on the light. Immediately angry voices shouted from the road and we felt like traitors. Luckily it was not until March 1942 that serious air-raids started. Then we all became so frightened that naturally everybody was extremely careful and not the slightest glimmer of light escaped anywhere.

The issue and trying-on of gasmasks was a frightening thing in the first couple of years. More frightening still, was the actual sound of the sirens. Hand-sirens were distributed to various parts of the town and village. They were funny-looking things on tripods. The village one was handed out to my friend Ernstchen's father. Although the sound was alarming, the sight of the massive Herr Kruse winding the handle of the siren in front of his house with his grumpy expression, was an amusing one. He never took very long over it. In fact, people complained that they had not even heard the sound, when he took the machine which was still humming, the last notes becoming lower and lower, under his arm, and put it back into the corner of the bar and continued drinking his pint of beer. One day Ernstchen pinched the siren and gave us a demonstration. Unfortunately, the sound was louder than he expected. Herr Kruse came and gave his son a good hiding in front of all of us, and then disappeared into the house, with a howling sound from Ernstchen and the fading humming of the siren trailing behind him.

Changing to a new school was, for the time being, much more important to me than the preparation for war. When the holidays came to an end in the middle of September, Anneliese, Gabi and I said goodbye in floods of tears to our teacher for the last three years, and prepared to go to the local boys' school. Originally we were supposed to go to Hannover, to a girls' school, but our parents thought it safer, now there was a war on, not to travel daily to a large city. The boys' school had recently changed its name, under Hitler's orders, from "Realgymnasium" to "Oberschule". Many things had changed by Hitler's orders. No more morning prayers were said; instead the national anthem was sung and some lines from "Mein Kampf" or some "impressive lines" by the Führer were recited. Scripture lessons were made voluntary, and to make it difficult to attend them, they were tagged on the time-table after 1 o'clock, when it was time to go home.

The Oberschule was a good half-hour walk from our house. It was a large, ugly building dating from 1820, but at the same time it was impressive with a large well-equipped gymnasium built onto it in recent years. A large courtyard with old elm trees surrounded it.

The headmaster was just about to retire when the war started, and like so many others, he stayed on. His name was Dr Pol. He was well over six feet tall with long white hair, and he walked like a stork – very deliberately picking up his legs higher than necessary and holding back his shoulders, he walked slowly and upright. He was very keen on posture and stopped students who slouched and made them do exercises. Immediately anybody saw him they straightened up and walked stiffly and unnaturally past him. He and his wife, who was also a teacher (she taught me English for six years), rode on their ancient bicycles to school every morning. They rode with their backs completely straight, looking intently ahead of them, ignoring all the "Heil Hitlers" that students on their way to school shouted at them. They were both anti-Nazi and Dr Pol confessed to father one day that the reason for cycling to school was because it saved them from acknowledging the Hitler salute as they needed both hands on the handle-bars.

Our Biology teacher was an old man who was also due to retire at the beginning of the war, but stayed on. He was like a Teddy Bear to look at, round and small with fuzzy grey hair and he "grunted" a lot. He was known as Opa H. He never let on that he was anti-Nazi, but his ironic grin during the hoisting of the flag in the courtyard each morning, and the slack Hitler Gruss he gave, barely lifting his right hand, suggested what he thought of it all.

It was clear to us that Opa H. was fed up with teaching, and he let us do what we liked, provided we were quiet. Whilst he read, or more exactly murmured, from the Biology textbook about the

113

theory of heredity by Mendel or about the functioning of the kidneys in the human body, we did our homework. Sometimes a skeleton was brought in to show anybody coming into the classroom that some serious research was going on, but it stood grinning and completely ignored in front of the desk for the whole of the lesson.

Our history and German teacher was the exact opposite – vivacious and strict. She was also an anti-Nazi but very diplomatic in her attitude. When she entered the classroom we stood up. Briefly raising the right arm and saying, 'Heil Hitler,' in a soft voice as she had taught us to, we took our seats again. Her name was Dr Schaumann or "Uschi" as we called her.

Physics and Chemistry were taught by Studienrat R. whose nickname was "Paule". He was a very nervous man and flew into a rage at the slightest provocation, so we were more than careful not to provoke him. He had been known to take a chair and throw it amongst the pupils. His wife was known in town as "Rosa Luxemburg". He did not share her communist beliefs but he was not a Nazi either. On entering the classroom he took on a clownlike posture; his arm was gradually lifted in the salute and without saying a word he glared at us, sometimes coming very close to our faces. If anybody started to giggle he received an *"Erdnuss"* which was performed with the knuckle of the right index finger at the back of the head, a painful experience. We learned to outstare him; this performance lasted for about three minutes, after which he suddenly dropped his arm, and everybody, without having uttered a single word, took their seats.

Apparently he boasted after the war that the "Heil Hitler" had never passed his lips, and he got away with it.

The only two Nazi teachers we had at the beginning of the war were our Art teacher, Herr L., who was small and spiteful and who was known as "Giftzwerg" (poisonous dwarf), and Herr Offenhausen, known as "Offi" who taught Literature, Music and Mathematics. Offi was the biggest Nazi in town and did more harm to my father throughout the war than anybody else.

114

Yet I only remember him as a warmhearted, kind man with a great sense of beauty and humour. In fact, he was my favourite teacher, whereas Giftzwerg was the most loathsome man I could think of. I must confess I did not have much talent for drawing but he never even tried to teach me, and looked at my attempts with the utmost contempt, teasing me mercilessly about being a parson's daughter. I ended up by doing the shopping for him. One day he made me go for miles to get some asparagus.

The sandy soil in our area was ideal for growing asparagus and farmers had large plantations outside the town. The asparagus was delicious, long white tender stalks, every bit of it melted in one's mouth.

During the war, farmers were committed to surrender most of their crop to the nearby canning factory, so unless one had a "tame" farmer or "connections", it was impossible to get any. A kind farmer supplied us during the season with two to three pounds for our Sunday lunch. Mother used to peel the stalks very thinly; a soup was made with the peel and the stalks were strictly rationed out, so that everybody got a fair share.

It was almost impossible to get any asparagus in towns. Giftzwerg, who lived in Hannover, was on to a good thing when he sent me to get some. The plantations were a good two miles from the town and each had its own small hut where the asparagus was sorted before it was taken to the factory. I knew where the farmer who supplied us with the vegetable had his hut, and as I didn't dare return to school without it, I asked him for our own weekly supply. There was no asparagus for our Sunday lunch that week. I confessed at home what had happened, but it was really up to myself to stand up to the teacher and tell him that I would not get any a second time.

Luckily, the season was a short one. He tried it again, but unsuccessfully, though I had to suffer for it in other ways. He made me clean the basins in the art room into which everybody tipped their unused paint and cleaned their brushes. I had to sharpen his pencils and empty wastepaper baskets – anything but do drawing or other exciting things which everybody else was doing and which I should have liked to have done, too. One day he did not come back to school. His house in Hannover had received a direct hit from a bomb and he and his family were killed.

As the school was not geared for girls we received the minimum amount of teaching in Needlework and Sport. The young sports teacher had been called-up like all the other young teachers. Instead Frau S. taught us, but after the age of fourteen there was no more sport. The only games we played were rounders and football. Frau S. was a very tough person of about 55, with grey hair in a bun and the beginnings of a very definite white moustache. With the football under her arm, a whistle in her mouth and dressed in a tracksuit, she led boys and girls onto the football pitch. On rainy days she gave us demonstrations of how to climb the rope or pole. She looked so comic that we nearly killed ourselves with laughter. It was very unkind as it was a brave undertaking at her age and she was obviously untrained for the job.

She was not very good at teaching needlework and I learned next to nothing. We had made a pact between us few girls that one of us would forget her needlework in turns, and as she was a person who could not bear to see anybody sitting idly by, she allowed that person to read aloud to us. We made sure that all our favourite books were read, and after the first ten minutes, our knitting or crochet work came to rest in our laps and even Frau S. got absorbed in the stories. Our most favourite one was *The Wonderful Adventures of Nils Holgerson with the Wild Geese*.

In every classroom hung a large picture of the Führer. In fact it had become compulsory for every household to have at least one picture of him. Father had been very clever. He had chosen a "diluted version" as he called it, of the Führer. It was a photograph in which he and the former Chancellor, Hindenburg, were shaking hands and it hung in the darkest corner of the hall.

116

* * *

That Autumn I saw a dead person for the first time. Opa Thiele, next door, had died. When Oma Thiele asked me if I would like to see him laid out, and say a final farewell to him, I did not have the heart to say no. Secretly I was afraid to see a dead person and, with a heart full of fear, I followed her up the stairs into the bedroom where he was lying.

I am glad that my first contact with a dead person was Opa Thiele. It took from me a great part of the fear I had of the dead. We entered a room in which the curtains were drawn, but a gap in them let in a shaft of the afternoon sun which ended in a pool of light on the wide brown floorboards. Opa Thiele lay on a massive oak bed with an expression on his face I had not seen on him before. He looked so much younger, so peaceful and so clean. His white hair and long beard were beautifully combed, and his hands were folded across his chest. He wore a long white starched nightgown, and on his feet thick black stockings which stuck out from underneath his gown like two pointed rocks.

'His feet were so cold,' said his wife, with tears in her eyes, 'I put some socks on them.' And she lovingly rubbed the stiff, cold feet of the old man. Two candles burned at either side of the bed and below his hands lay a bunch of dahlias. It was very quiet except for the buzzing of a fly which settled on Opa Thiele's face. Carefully I wiped it away. I said my farewell, and when we went out of the room we shut the door quietly behind us, so as not to disturb the peace we had left behind.

117

CHAPTER 11

I was only ten years old when I had to join the Hitler-youth. Of course my parents were against it, but there was nothing they could do. It was not compulsory for grown-ups to join the Party, though most of them did. Sometimes their profession forced them to, but it was compulsory for every German youth between the ages of 10 and 18 to join this youth organisation.

When it started on a voluntary basis in 1936 it had 100,000 members. During the war it rose to 8 million.

For quite some while I had secretly looked forward to joining. The uniform, the marching and the singing appealed to me. I went to the first meeting turned out to Hitler's liking, in a uniform consisting of a short blue skirt, white short-sleeved blouse with a black triangular neck-scarf which was held in place by a brown leather knot, white knee-socks and a light brown suede jacket, like a windcheater. My pigtails were neatly plaited and I brimmed over with enthusiasm.

Every Wednesday and Saturday at 3 p.m., the Hitler youth met on the tarmac square in the town park, girls on the right, boys on the left. The boys' uniform looked very severe with black windcheaters. In the summer they wore brown shirts, thin leather straps over their shoulders. A wide black leather belt kept up their short trousers. A boat-shaped black hat was pushed under the shoulder-strap. Round the neck, they wore the same black tie as the girls with the leather knot.

Twice a week throughout the year we gathered grouping around the flagpole, raised our right arms and sang the national anthem and the Horst Wessel song, a lengthy ordeal. Fortunate were the ones in the second and third row, for they could rest their arms on the shoulders of the ones in front. Quotations from "Mein Kampf" were read to us as the flag, a small black triangular rag with the white Hitler youth emblem

119

imprinted, was raised to the top of the pole, where it remained until 5 p.m. when the same procedure happened again.

It very soon became rather boring for me and a few others. There was a small group, but only a small group, who thought it all a great hoot. We were the ones brought up by anti-Nazi parents, and were fortunate enough to learn from a young age that, behind the façade of this organisation with all the various opportunities it offered, stood Hitler's technique of indoctrinating Germany's rising generation, at its most vulnerable age, with his ideals and philosophy.

The Hitler youth was indeed able to give us the things that appealed to us, which our school, with its ancient teachers and lack of materials, could not offer us any more. Here the young were led by the young. Sport, travel, crafts, music – a chance to do it all.

It was easy to get sucked into it all without noticing. Hitler had the gift of cunningly starting a campaign just at the right moment. He took the unemployed off the streets at the right time. The youths adored him and flocked to him because he provided them with things which would otherwise have been denied them.

Once a year, just before the summer holidays, a two-day sports event took place in the vast new stadium in the town. Dressed in the shortest of black shorts and white vests, boys and girls competed in a miniature Olympic Game. The winning of 100 points justified a *Siegernadel,* a small silver pin, which the winner received on the evening of the second day, when he went onto the stage where the top nobs sat, and shook hands with the "Gauleiter" (political Head of the province), who pinned the award onto the vest. I think sport was the only thing I was good at. I received a pin every year, long-jump being my triumph – even my father did not mind my wearing it.

I made a new friend when I changed schools. Inge's father had been sent to Polen to reorganise the postal system in Posen. Inge played the piano very well, and we both qualified for the Hitler Youth Orchestra. It had its pros and cons. Pros because we were let off other things like marching exercises, cons because we had to perform at lots of functions; some were on Sunday mornings at the same time as church. Father forbade me to go. To start with, it didn't seem to matter, but as the war went on and the hatred towards the church became greater, I was commanded to appear. When I didn't one Sunday, a group playing drums and fanfares marched to the front door of the church during a service. Their blare drowned father's voice and he was forced to dis-continue the service until they moved on. It was repeated several times until I reappeared on Sunday mornings whenever the orchestra was playing.

I wished I had never joined it. I felt so sorry for father and, worst of all, I felt I was betraying him. Father never said one accusing word to me. He knew that whatever they were trying to teach us – to which we had to listen – would not enter into my heart. Inge and I were often reprimanded, when we did not take things seriously. Inge had a great sense of humour and was very good at mimicking others, especially those in uniform.

In 1941, Lehrte received its first *Ritterkreuztraeger* (a new war medal meaning: Bearer of the Knight's Cross). Hitler-youth and S.A. men formed a lane from the station to the house of this young hero. Every household hung out the flag, and a lifesize portrait of the Führer was hoisted onto the platform next to where the orchestra was sitting. When we took our seats, I unfortunately tripped over one of the ropes which secured the picture. It started to sway precariously and, for a moment, it looked as if it was crashing down on top of us just when the train was pulling into the station. Fortunately it was saved, but almost everybody thought I had done this on purpose.

I can still see the horrified face of the young *Ritterkreuztraeger* when he stepped out of the train. Instead of being greeted, as I am sure he expected, by his parents and fiancée, he stepped straight into the hands of the "Gauleiter" and his fellow leaders.

By the time he had listened to speeches, the orchestra playing and the ever-repeated national anthem and Horst Wessel song, he looked tired and cheesed-off. All the way home he had to acknowledge the "Heils" and "Sieg Heils" shouted at him. Oh yes, Hitler knew what would please heroes, but it did not go down

121

well with all of them.

* * *

Because I had changed school and made a lot of new friends, playing with the village children had become less frequent. Sadly it was they who withdrew, calling me posh and stuck-up, but I did not feel like that at all, but homework, music lessons and Hitler Youth took up a lot of time.

My tobogganing with them came also to a sudden and sad end. It was towards the end of February, when the temperature had suddenly risen for a few successive days, that I was trudging through the deep snow across the field to the tip. I suddenly saw a group of men coming towards me, rather slowly, carrying something between them, which at that distance I could not make out. They were followed by children pulling their sledges behind them. When they came nearer, I saw that they carried a stretcher covered by a blanket with two shapes visible underneath. Puzzled, I looked at my friends. One of them said: 'The Neumann brothers have been drowned'.

The ice had broken when their sledge hit the ice on the lake. One brother, aged nine, fell in. The other, one year older, tried to rescue him, but drowned as well. No grown-up was present. The other children, frightened and helpless, did not know what to do. By the time they had fetched help, both boys were dead. This had happened three hours before and all the time the other children stood and watched the men as they tried to get hold of the bodies from under the ice. Silently we followed the men on the way to the village to the home of the boy's parents.

I had never heard anybody scream with such pain as the mother did when she opened the door and saw the stretcher. Then she looked under the blanket and saw both her boys, her only children, dead. She threw herself upon them and remained motionless. Stunned from witnessing such grief, and the fact that we would never see our cheerful playmates again, we turned away and went home.

I could not eat my supper that night. I went to bed and cried in the dark bedroom. It was not for the boys I was crying; I believed that they were angels now, but it was for the mother and father. The pain-stricken cry, and the sight of the mother lying across her dead children did not leave me all night. When hours after I had gone to bed, my bedroom door opened and I heard mother and father come in, I pretended to be asleep. They stood for a long time silently at my bed. I had a feeling that they were praying.When father put his soft warm hand on my forehead, I felt comforted, but still very sad.

A couple of days later a group of children watched two white coffins disappear into the winter's earth.

From then on the pit was out of bounds to all children, winter and summer.

CHAPTER 12

In every classroom hung a map of Europe and Asia and above it was a large portrait of the Führer in uniform. "Offi", who had become our form master, had risen to be the town's highest Nazi official. On most days he wore the brown party uniform and shiny high black boots. He had fought in the first World War and a row of medals adorned his brown shirt. Offi produced minute swastikas on pins and on every schoolday morning from the start of the war, we marched with our soldiers and triumphantly stuck pins onto the map. Within twenty days, flags advanced towards Warsaw, and on 27th September the Polish capital capitulated. The war with Poland had come to an end.

'Nothing to fear from Russia,' Offi shouted. 'They are our allies and supply us with grain, cotton, oil and platinum.'

And Great Germany, he boasted, gave arms and steel in exchange; there was absolutely nothing to fear.

In his smart, brand-new uniform the 55-year-old, yet already white-haired man, looked suddenly young, as with shining eyes, full of conviction and enthusiasm, he told us, again and again, how wonderful the Führer was, how trustworthy and great. He would soon give us more *Lebensraum* [living space], and a rosy future.

During the winter of 1939-1940, German and French soldiers stood motionless on either side of the Maginot Line. Norway received Sweden's oil, and Hitler's eye was fixed on Narvik. His next move was towards neutral Scandinavia. Britain had the same idea, but the Germans got there before them, in April 1940.

For the first time the German losses were heavy. We had lost six submarines and several other warships. Offi was not worried. 'For Führer and Vaterland,' he shouted, and stuck a swastika flag with a black pin head over Narvik and Oslo. His chest swelled with pride as, with his thumb tucked underneath the highly-polished brown leather belt, he marched up and down between our desks in his noisy leather boots.

The nickname for any high Nazi official was *Pfau* [Peacock]: quite appropriate; small brains behind brilliant plumage, all miniature Hitlers with big mouths. But Offi was different. He had a good brain. He could be cruel and hard when in uniform but kind and soft when in civilian clothes, as we were to find out later. Now he shouted, 'Let us sing the England Song,' and we stood up from our desks and sang, 'Let us drink the cool wine and fly towards England'. Offi stood in front of us singing the loudest in his good bass voice, with a tight fist and his right arm stretched out towards England. Our singing drifted through the open classroom windows into the first warm summer's breeze which gently lifted the last blossoms from the budding fruit and blew them over the garden fences onto the pavements.

Every Monday morning we carried bags of scrap iron, silver paper, rags, bones, waste paper and other materials to school. Carefully they were weighed and entered into a book. Points were given for each item and those who had most points got a cheer. It slowly petered out. After two years there was nothing more to bring. At the beginning of 1941 things became scarce. Clothes and shoes were obtainable on coupons only; coffee, tea and cocoa were things of the past, and of other foods there was just not enough.

Those who had soldiers as friends or relations in the occupied countries were lucky. Woollen garments were sent home from Norway; coffee, chocolate and tea from Holland and Belgium, silk stockings and leather goods from France. The black market had started. Anything was obtainable provided one had something to exchange.

It was in the summer of 1941 that I met one of the nicest and kindest persons I have ever known. Her name was "Tante Krueger".

On a sultry July morning father had sent me to fetch his diary which he had left in the vestry of the churchyard chapel. The new churchyard was a long way from the town, and even further from the village. I had been given a bicycle for my tenth birthday. I loved it, looked after it well, and later even took it into the air-raid shelter with me.

The churchyard was at least 6 kilometres from our house. It was like a huge garden with high, well-established hedges of yews and rhododendron bushes. In the spring, nightingales sweetened it with their songs. People came out in the early morning, and, sitting on the numerous benches, listened to the melodic chorus. It was not possible to see more than ten graves at a time because each row was surrounded by a tall hedge, and at each end of the row was a well which was continually fed with clear water from a fish's mouth, so the sound of water was always present.

At the end of a large well-kept lawn stood the ugly red-bricked octagonal modern chapel, into which I dreaded going, especially by myself. Long stained-glass windows made it dark inside. To my relief no coffin stood, as it usually did – minus the lid – in front of the altar. I found my father's diary on the table in the vestry and was relieved when I was out in the warm, welcoming fresh air again. When I pushed my bike towards the exit, I noticed a middle-aged woman sitting by herself on a bench, completely dressed in black, a sign of the deepest mourning. She wiped her face continuously with a handkerchief.

I stopped. Courtseying, I said, 'Good morning', and asked if she was all right.

'I am feeling a little giddy,' she said. 'Would you like to sit beside me for a while?'

I rested my bike against a tree and sat beside her.

'Aren't you Renate Ungewitter?' she asked.

'Yes, I am,' I said, 'and what is your name?'

She told me her name was Frau Krueger and that her husband had died suddenly from a heart attack a month ago.

'He came home from work, my Hein,' she told me. 'He was just going to ring the doorbell when he collapsed.' She found him when she opened the door.

'I come every day, morning and evening, to water his grave, but mainly to be near him. And today is my birthday,' she added quietly.

'Haven't you any children?' I asked her.

'I haven't anybody,' she said.

I sat with her for a little while, and when she was feeling better, I said goodbye and cycled home.

I told father about meeting Frau Krueger and that it was her birthday. Father, of course, knew about her and where she lived, and in the afternoon I cycled to her house which was quite a distance from ours. In the basket on the carrier lay a bunch of roses, freshly picked by mother, and a letter from father.

Frau Krueger lived on the fourth and highest floor of a large apartment house belonging to the railway. Her husband had been an engine driver. I thought her house most depressing as I climbed the eight flights of stairs. There were two flats on each floor, and on every other landing I passed two small brown doors opposite each other. These were the lavatories and some of them were rather smelly.

At last I reached the top flat. Here the ceiling sloped and a step-ladder stood under the trap-door to the loft. A shiny brass plate said H. KRUEGER. I rang the bell. The huge house was completely silent and I felt a little frightened when there was no reply. A small slate with a crayon on a string hung beside the door. Should I write Happy Birthday on it and put the flowers on her doormat? I rang the bell once more and a shadow appeared behind the frosty glass door. 'Happy Birthday,' I said when Frau Krueger opened it, and I gave her the flowers.

She was very pleased and surprised and asked me to come in. Her flat was tiny, cosy and very clean. The drawing-room had two small dormer windows, but the kitchen had a large window and was full of sunshine. We sat on the sofa, drinking delicious Ersatz cocoa [cocoa substitute] and ate home-made biscuits. Frau Krueger showed me photographs of her husband: in fact they were standing everywhere, on her side tables and chest of drawers, and some were hanging on the walls, in all sizes. A black velvet bow was tied to each one of them. She talked about him all the time. They had obviously been very happy together. She suddenly asked me if I liked picnics. Picnics were something we hardly ever had, but I did like them. So we arranged a picnic for the following week.

We walked towards the wood, carrying between us the picnic basket, onto which two small canvas stools were tied. I had not noticed how small and round she was; she wasn't much taller than I was at eleven. She wore thick spectacles and her face was chubby, and though she was not attractive she was very kind and nice. We found a shady place at the edge of the wood and, sitting on our small wobbly canvas stools, we had our picnic. She must have saved her rations for the entire week, as the most delicious things came out of the basket. She herself had the appetite of a sparrow. My healthy appetite pleased her and she urged me again and again to take one more sandwich or a piece of cake. She told me that once a week, when the weather was good, she and her husband had come to this place for a picnic and how much they had always enjoyed it. We arranged another picnic for the coming week, and we kept it up all through the summer. Our friendship was sealed over numerous cups of cocoa.

Sometimes I went with her to the churchyard. Behind a large black marble tombstone she kept her watering-can and a small hand rake. On the right side of the stone was written: "Heinz Krueger, born 12.2.1885, died 7.6.1941". On the left it said: "Luise Krueger, born 8.7.1889", and then a blank.

'That's where I am going to rest,' said Tante Krueger pointing to the left side and quietly added, 'I will join you soon, dear Hein.'

In fact she lived for another twenty years. I always felt very embarrassed when she held her little private conversations with her husband. I turned away and raked the path in front of the grave in a very special pattern to please her. I tried hard to cheer her up with nonsense stories or jokes or other silly things. At the start of our friendship she insisted on walking home with me.

Before we left her flat, I sometimes wrote something funny on the slate outside her flat door, which she was not to look at until she came back. I hoped it would make her laugh then, when she returned to her lonely, empty rooms.

Tante Krueger refused to come into our house: she said she was shy, so we said goodbye at the gates of the yard. My parents would have loved her to come in, but even when invited she would not come.

One day I told her that mother was in bed with flu. Our maid had flu at the same time and father was looking after us and doing the cooking. He had no idea how to cook and everything was terrible. Without hesitation she came into the house, saw how badly help was needed, tended to the patients, put on an apron and started to cook. From that day she became a friend of the entire family, and she was in fact our dearest friend.

It was lovely to see her change once again into a happy, cheerful person. One of her greatest assets was her sense of humour. Maybe it was because she had no children, but she was most certainly over-anxious. She often said that one of my dare-devil acts would give her a heart attack. When she came with me to the local swimming pool, she could not bear to see me jump from the 5-metre board and turned her head away, but I waited until she turned around again and then jumped. Mother said she spoiled me, but I liked it.

Sometimes, when I practised my violin, she would be in the same room attending to the mending basket. I really believed that she genuinely liked listening to my playing. She was very sentimental but not very musical. I stopped practising the things I ought to have done, and played things she liked, such as the *Largo* and *Ave Verum*. I played them badly; nobody else wanted to listen but Tante Krueger said, with tears in her eyes, so that she had to take off her specs and wipe her face with the sock she was darning, 'It's quite wonderful.' But I thought it was Tante Krueger who was quite wonderful!

CHAPTER 13

Offi's reassurance that we had nothing to fear from Russia did not come true. On June 22, 1941 (Hitler had typically chosen the same date on which Napoleon had marched his troops into Russia), German troops were given the command to attack the Soviet Union.

It looked, to start with, as if a second *Blitzkrieg* was to follow. Offi's little swastikas rapidly moved eastwards and by the Autumn stood threateningly in front of Moscow. We ran out of flags and quickly had to make more.

German troops appeared everywhere. Le Havre, Scapa Flow, Spitzbergen, Narvik, Tobruk, Crete and now Moscow. Offi was beside himself with pride, but father shook his head and said, 'It can't go on like this.'

A lot of people believed that victory would follow victory, that the war would not last long. Hitler shouted himself hoarse convincing them that it was true. Masses flocked to see him whenever he appeared in public. "Hypnotic" was the word I heard mentioned in connection with his speeches. We were compelled to listen to them. Police patrolled the streets to make sure everybody sat next to the radio when Hitler talked to his people. All lessons stopped. We sat in our uniforms on these great occasions, on the hard school benches and listened to the voice which was so persuasive. We listened to the applause, wave upon wave of it, and finally we got up after two hours, stiff and bored, and sang the National Anthem with many thousands of others who had come to see him in the Berlin Stadium, finishing with a triple *Sieg Heil*.

Polish prisoners of war had arrived in our town. They were ordered to work mainly on farms. In the evening a German guard with his rifle over one shoulder collected them and took them back to the camp, a large building not far from our house, its windows secured with barbed wire. It was a sight quite new to us when, on a dark evening, this group of about sixty prisoners in their long heavy coats, walked slowly and silently back to their camp, with the guard and his rifle behind them. All we could see was a long dark line and the glow of their cigarettes.

Farmers soon came to the conclusion that they were lazy and always hungry. After a few months Polish girls arrived and were billeted on farms. A year later a number of Polish infants were born. In many cases the farmer's wife took charge of the infant during the day, when its mother was busy, but in the evening the Polish mother took over, feeding the baby with all sorts of unsuitable food, convinced that the German Frau starved her child. Very often it was sick the next day. All this presented quite a few problems.

Not long after the Polish prisoners, French and Belgian P.O.W.s arrived. The Polish prisoners were now billetted with the farmers (and even more babies were born) and the newcomers were put into the large building with the barbed wire. They too were put to work on farms. Like the Poles they wore a khaki uniform and their language was the only difference. They were very cheerful and friendly but apart from their employers, we were forbidden to communicate with them. The farmers preferred them to the Poles, since they worked hard and did not have babies. They made fun of the guard when he came to collect them in the evening, but he took no offence; a packet of cigarettes from the prisoners soon put him in a good mood. Chatting and joking, in no special formation such as the Poles used to adopt, they walked to the camp. There was never an occasion when the guard had to use his rifle, and they were given enough food and treated well. I never saw anything to the contrary, but perhaps some were luckier than others with their employer.

I saw Herr Busch, our neighbour, packing a basket full of goodies and warm clothes and giving it to his French P.O.W. (the French were always shivering with cold), who embraced him and warmly shook his hand. After a while, they became

132

part of the farming community. We began to chat to them and nobody minded.

All through 1941 the black pins moved rapidly forward on all frontiers. *Sondermeldung* [special announcement] upon *Sondermeldung*, introduced by fanfares, came through the radio.

Since the Autumn we had made a new friend. Hauptmann Alex, in charge of the large ammunition factory outside the town, was our frequent guest. Up until then he had fought at the Eastern Front; his reports were gloomy and his forecast of the future not encouraging. Only when he was alone with my parents did he dare to air his views. All was not well within the German Army in Russia. Hitler had fallen out with some of his generals. Hauptmann Alex had inside information. A deep crisis had arisen in the East and some generals had "retired", (which meant they had been given the push). Towards the end of 1941, Hitler himself took charge of the army.

With the beginning of Winter the Hitler Youth got busy. Boys and girls, in pairs, wearing uniform, collected gloves, woolly hats, ear muffs, anything to keep our soldiers warm in the unusually cold winter of 1941/42 on the Eastern Front. We went from house to house after school until every household was exhausted of any surplus warm garment. Every pair of skis was confiscated, and we spent most of our spare time knitting. But not only the Hitler Youth knitted. Every household sat knitting, and small cartons were issued with *FELDPOST* [Field-post], written on them in large letters. They were filled with biscuits and something warm to wear, with a weight limit of 500 grammes. Hitler Youth collected the boxes several times a week, and took the heavy canvas bags to the collecting centre.

The *Winterhilfswerk* [Winter-help Organisation] came into action. Shivering in the bitter winter wind, we stood in the streets in our inadequately thin but smart uniforms. Wearing white kneesocks, our knees red and blue from the cold beneath the short skirts or trousers, and with cheerful faces as commanded (because Hitler's youth had to be tough), we sold beautifully made carved figures, small enough to hang from the button of a coat. We sold, always in pairs, blue candles in aid of the Russian offensive, and blue candles and colourful figures adorned every German Christmas tree that year. Only Christmas was not called Christmas any more but: "The night of the Sun Light", as the Führer had ordered.

In the New Year it looked as if once again Hitler's plan was going to work. A new offensive on the German side had started at the end of June. The aim was the oil sources on the lower Wolga river.

On the map in our classroom the pins crossed the Don into the Caucasus, and at the end of August a triumphant swastika was stuck on the highest peak, the Elborus.

CHAPTER 14

There was a small room in our house which was hardly ever used. Its only window faced east and looked into the farmyard belonging to Herr Busch. It was tucked away between father's study and mother's green room. Once there had been a door into it from father's room, but a few years before, a bookshelf had been built to take father's ever-increasing store of books and put where the door had been, so there was no trace of it left. Now the only entrance to it was from the green room.

One day, when I came back from school, I noticed that the tall mahogany bookshelf with the glass doors and criss-cross wooded slats had been moved in front of the door; nobody would have guessed that there was a door behind it. I thought mother must have been in one of her furniture-shifting moods and did not think any more about it. A few days later I heard a noise coming from the room, but mother said, 'It must be the mice again.'

On another occasion, I heard a muffled cough and knew that somebody *must* be in there. And then mother explained it all to me.

In 1941 there were still several thousand Jews in Berlin. Without the help of the Church they would not have been able to survive. With the ever-increasing air-raids on Berlin, more and more people became homeless. A lot of Jews, who up till then had kept themselves hidden in the houses of friends, became homeless and had nowhere to go.

Throughout Germany an underground organisation, run by the Church, helped them to find further shelter. Up until now I did not know that my parents belonged to this organisation, the members of which risked the death sentence, not only for themselves but their entire family, every time they opened their door to a refuge-seeking Jew. Many Jews were discovered – by the Gestapo – and together with those who had taken them in, were transported to concentration camps. But in spite of that, a great number of German people risked their lives and were willing to help.

Nobody knew about the hiding place in our house. Since the beginning of 1941 a household which had fewer than four children no longer qualified for a domestic help. It was fortunate that we were now without a maid. Tante Krueger was the only one who knew, besides my brother and me, and she would have given her life before she would tell anybody.

For eighteen months the little room hid these poor, unfortunate Jews. The longest each couple or single person stayed was a week; sometimes it was for one night only. The Gestapo were looking for them everywhere. Frightened of being caught, haunted by the knowledge of the danger they brought upon those who took them in, they moved on to the next place at the slightest sign of suspicion. Every time they moved on to the next hideout, a new address was given to them, never more than one address at a time. Continuously they were on the move. I know of one couple who in 18 months went to 66 different houses, but they survived, as did thousands of others. They had no ration cards and no coupons for clothes. Whoever took them in shared their own meagre rations with them and gave them warm clothes and most importantly, gave them sympathy and hope.

My parents were well aware of the danger they had taken on, not only for themselves but for us children as well. They also knew how much they depended on my brother and I never to murmur a word to anybody, not even to our dearest friends. Sometimes this was very difficult. The worst occasion was when we were told by our Hitler Youth leader to come to his office and were asked question upon question: How many rooms were in our house? How many people lived in it? (which they knew perfectly well). Who came to visit us? The same questions over and over again. We did not let on. They allowed us to go after two hours, only to repeat the same thing the next week.

After the first interrogation I cried all the way home. Gewi took my hand and talked to me reassuringly. He was now nearly 17 years old and would soon leave school. He told me that I must not show that I was frightened; they might think there was a reason for it. I must answer their questions as casually as possible without telling the truth about the room and its inhabitants. I had to promise him not to mention the interrogations to my parents as it would have added to their many worries.

The Nazis in our town were very suspicious of my parents, but so far had no evidence that they were helping Jews.

Offi, my teacher, and now the local *Gauleiter*, was most anxious to find something out. Nothing would have pleased him more than to take my father away from his parish, but Offi never tried to get any information out of me or my brother. Indeed, Offi and I felt a great mutual friendship towards each other. There was nobody who recited Moericke or Lenau, my favourite poets at that time, as beautifully as he did, and he liked my German essays. It was he who opened our eyes to the beauty of nature; when on a summer's day the temperature being too hot for indoor lessons, he took us into the fields and woods and we sat in the meadows singing old German folksongs. On those days he wore civilian clothes. Could this man, who was so sensitive and kind, really hate and be unjust? Or did he, like so many others in uniform, just do his duty ?

On one school morning he took the hand of my class-mate, Ernst-August, and gently led him to the door of our classroom.

'Go home, Ernst-August,' he said, 'your mother wants you.'

His father had fallen under a train that morning and had been killed. Ernst-August was an only child, and Offi knew that his presence would comfort his mother.

Ernst-August's grandparents, on his father's side, were half Jews, which made him a *Mischling* [Jewish-Aryan – second degree]. From this day on, Offi was especially kind and caring for the boy, even though he had Jewish blood in him.

We tried hard not to draw any attention to the only east-facing window on the first floor which meant that no electric light or even a candle could be used in it. Whenever the room was occupied, which happened once a month or so, the bookcase was eased away from the door just a little, so that the occupants could squeeze through and use the bathroom. It could only be done in the evening when visitors were not very likely. Either my brother or I kept watch from the windows facing the yard. Provided everything was all right, they sat with us for a while sharing our supper, after which mother packed a basket with provisions which they took with them back to the little room. Their faces looked thin and pale from worry and lack of fresh air. How did they get about from one place to the other unnoticed? They were given money and false identity cards, and they mingled with the crowds as naturally as their anxiety allowed them to. At that time there were a lot of homeless people in Germany, and it was not difficult to be disguised as one of them.

The first time the Gestapo arrived at our house they could not find anything. With a pounding heart I followed them from room to room. The relief when they left was more than I can describe. But they came again: this time it was not all right. However Herr Busch, our neighbour, had given us warning in good time. By chance, he had seen an S.A. man scrutinizing the east side of our house over the garden wall. He, of course, had no idea what was involved, but he knew it could mean no good, so his warning saved our lives. The Jews left the house immediately; people constantly came and left, so that was no problem.

By the time the Gestapo arrived all was clear. There had been just enough time to move the bookcase away from the door to its usual place. Though there was no trace left of the Jews, the Gestapo were sure we had been collaborating with the underground movement. They took father away with them to be interrogated in Bielefeld. It all happened so quickly that there had been no time to say goodbye to him.

We waited anxiously for his return. He was released after three days as they could not find enough evidence. When he came back he was unshaven and very tired.

After they had discovered the little room we could not shelter the Jews any more. For the rest of the war the Gestapo kept an eye on us. Though there were no more Jews in our house, they could

138

perhaps still find out that we had sheltered them. Every time they came we feared that they had found out.

CHAPTER 15

There was fighting everywhere now. Japanese planes had attacked American ships in Pearl Harbour in December of 1941. Japan and the United States were at war, and Hitler declared war on the United States a few days after the attack. Since the beginning of the war, families had received letters with the dreaded official Government stamp on the envelope. They read: "We are sorry to inform you that your husband (son) has been killed in action."

Black armbands on coat sleeves became a familiar sight, but the population of Lehrte also increased. The first people made homeless through bombing started to arrive in our town.

In the Spring of 1942, German towns like Luebeck, Cologne, Bremen, Wilhelmshaven and Hannover had their first major air-raids. A massive automatic siren, higher than the two chimneys, now stood on our house, it being the tallest in the village. When it gave the alarm the whole house shook, and, for a minute, every other noise was drowned.

After the first air-raid on Hannover the sky was as red as it had been when the synagogues were on fire six years earlier. I remembered how frightened I had been then, frightened about something I did not understand. I was frightened now. Had the revenge Father had forecast come so soon?

No bombs had as yet fallen on Lehrte, except for two which landed a few kilometres outside the town. Hordes of sightseers had walked or cycled out the next day to look at the craters in the middle of a cornfield, and did more damage to the crop than the two holes.

Air-raid alarms were a regular thing now. Almost every night the sirens howled. After those nights, school started two hours late, and three hours' teaching was the most we could expect now. There was no homework for us on Wednesdays and

Saturdays or on those days when the Hitler Youth needed us.

A homeless mother from Cologne moved into our house with her two children. With the first sounds of the sirens they rushed towards the cellar, where all three sat trembling and huddling together until the all-clear was given. We had got used to the humming and droning of the enemy aircraft overhead on their way to Berlin, releasing their deadly weapons upon the unfortunate larger cities.

We had got used to the deafening noise of the anti-aircraft guns which were stationed near the village. The fragments of their shells hit the roofs and I collected some of them the next morning to take to school. We sat in our warm kitchen during air-raid alarms, feeling reasonably safe, as we were sure that bombs would not be wasted on a small and unimportant town such as ours.

But we were wrong.

One sunny July day, shortly before lunchtime, we saw hundreds and hundreds of enemy aircraft flying overhead in perfect V-formations towards the east. Leaving white fluffy tails against the clear blue sky, they sparkled in the brilliant sunshine like silver birds on migration.

'Poor people in Berlin,' we said. This was going to be one of the first daylight air-raids. They flew so high, we could hardly hear them. The anti-aircraft guns were silent, being unable to reach them because of their height. But suddenly they started to fire. White puff-balls appeared in the sky and we noticed a much lower flying formation coming towards us from the east.

'Into the cellar at once!' Father shouted. We had just reached the cellar door when the air was filled with hissing and whistling sounds. The cellar lights went out and immediately after that the cellar began to sway. We fell onto the floor as a tremendous sound of rolling thunder came over us. The children screamed. Their mother was lying on top of them, like a hen protecting her chicks. I was clinging on to both my parents, too terrified to mutter a sound. Several more times the hissing, followed by the thunder, repeated itself and every time the cellar heaved and plaster fell off the ceiling. Then all became deathly quiet.

Anxiously we waited for five minutes, then father went up the steps leading into the kitchen. The door made a crunching noise when he opened it. There was glass everywhere. Half of our windows were broken, but apart from that the house was all right. The heavy front door was blown wide open. We heard people shouting and crying and the sound of fire-engines and ambulances.

What a sight greeted us outside! The peaceful little village was like a battlefield. A large crater blocked the entrance to our yard, clumps of earth covered the lawn and the wrought-iron gate was doubled up. Fortunately, not many houses were destroyed in our vicinity, but almost every house was damaged. Torn curtains fluttered from broken windows and a cloud of dust lay over everything; even the green lime trees looked grey. Most of the bombs had fallen into the many gardens and streets. Our own garden was untouched. One house was burning and people stood in a long line passing buckets of water. Over the town hung a large dark cloud of smoke. 'I wonder if my house has been hit,' said Tante Krueger quietly. 'We will go and see,' said father, but somebody took him by the arm and said, 'Please come and help us. A family is buried under the rubble and we think they are still alive.'

My parents immediately went to help. Tante Krueger and I went off by ourselves. Gewi had gone on his summer vacation the day before, and I wished now that I had gone with him. We took the handcart out of the shed and pulled it behind us, just in case Tante Krueger's house had been hit and we might be able to save something.

The town was in complete chaos. 'Thank God, the Church has not been hit,' said Tante Krueger as we passed it. It took a long time before we reached her house. Buildings were burning and collapsing. People pulled handcarts piled high with dusty belongings. We saw familiar faces; some had been lucky, some had lost everything. I wanted to go home when I saw a row of corpses, charred and unrecognisable, laid out on the pavement. I had never seen anything so awful. Tante Krueger said she

143

would go on by herself, but I could not let her do that.

We were stopped once; the road was sealed off because of an unexploded bomb. We sat on the kerb and waited for two hours. We asked passers-by whether No. 21 Wilhelmstrasse was still standing. Some said it wasn't, some said it was. Tante Krueger's face was very pale, and I could not stop trembling.

Tante Krueger's house was completely destroyed. Everyone who was in the house at the time had been killed. 'I am so very glad you were with us,' I said and hugged her. She just stood there. She did not even cry, but said over and over again the name of her dead husband.

Suddenly, I saw something yellow sticking out from under the broken bricks. I pulled it from the rubble. It was Tante Krueger's large brass soup ladle which always hung, highly-polished, above her kitchen stove. Except for a few dents it was undamaged. Carefully I laid it in the handcart, but it was the only thing we could save. I put my arm around Tante Krueger's shoulder and said, 'You must now live with us,' which she did for the next ten years. She moved into mother's green room, and our friendship became closer every day.

From now on, we, like the mother with her two children, rushed towards the cellar at the first sound of the alarm. From then on until the end of the war we hardly had a day or night without air-raid warnings. The first attack on Lehrte was the worst, but others followed, and we lived in constant fear when, day after day, night after night, thousands of planes passed overhead and any minute death could strike. It was this which stretched our nerves to the utmost.

I always spent my Autumn holidays with my Godmother, Aunt Emmi, in her small Westphalian village, but after the air-raid on Lehrte, my parents insisted that I spent the rest of the Summer holidays with her as well.

It was sheer bliss to sleep through the nights, for no bombs fell on this tiny village throughout the war.

Aunt Emmi wanted to speak English with me at mealtimes. I protested, 'I don't like the Tommies one little bit,' I said. 'All they do is drop bombs on us. I hate their beastly language.'

144

Aunt Emmi said that they were a very nice, kind race and that she had many friends in England who suffered from our bombs as much as we suffered from theirs, and that Scotland was one of the loveliest countries she knew.

To please Aunt Emmi we spoke English at meal times.

Two of my best friends, Elisabeth and her brother Friedrich, lived in the same village. Their father was the Rural Dean and they lived in the largest and most beautiful old rectory I have ever seen. Their large park-like garden and the hilly wooded surroundings were paradise to me, and the thought of spending the next two weeks without air-raid alarms, the Hitler Youth and *Ernte Einsatz* was wonderful.

Two things put a damper on this holiday. There was a mental asylum in the village, a yellow-painted building with a large garden around it. It was a familiar sight to us as it was almost next to the rectory. Every time we passed it we waved to the inmates, who sat on the garden benches or weeded the flower beds. We knew quite a few of them by name. They waved back to us with an exaggerated and childlike joyish response. This time, I noticed, the garden was almost empty of patients. 'Where are they?' I asked. Friedrich shrugged his shoulders, but Elisabeth whispered into my ear: 'The Nazis have taken them away to bigger hospitals; there are only a few left now.'

We all knew what that meant. Hitler had started to exterminate the Jews, and was now doing the same with the infirm and mentally unstable. Anybody who was a hindrance was quietly "put away".

On the third day of my holiday I suddenly had an awful pain on the right side of my tummy. The doctor diagnosed appendicitis and I was taken to the hospital in Osnabrueck. Aunt Emmi came with me in the ambulance but had to return with it, so I was left alone in the two-bed ward with the horrid blue ceiling light. I was scared of the operation which was to be the next morning. I was also frightened in case there was an air-raid, Osnabrueck being one of the west German cities which had them almost every night. I felt miserable and homesick.

Once in a while, a nurse looked in for a brief moment; they

145

were all so busy. 'Try and get some sleep,' she said, but I was lying awake, imagining all sorts of dreadful things. It was quite late when the door opened again and instead of the nurse, my mother walked into the room. Forgotten was the pain in my tummy. I jumped out of bed and hugged her. Mother had caught the next train to Osnabrueck after Aunt Emmi had telephoned her. All was now well. Mother was allowed to stay the night with me and she was beside my bed when I came round from the anaesthetic the next morning. There were tears when she left in the evening, but she said she would come back the next day. The air-raid warning came at midnight. I heard nurses giving orders in the corridor, trollies being rolled past my door, hurried footsteps and the shuffling of feet; everybody was going or being carried into the cellars. Soon they would come and get me. But nobody came. Soon there was no more noise in the corridors. A hush had descended on the hospital. I began to realise that they had forgotten me. I rang the bell, but no answer. I tried to get out of bed but my tummy was hurting and I still felt weak and dizzy from the operation.

'Please, God, let there be no bombs tonight,' I prayed. But God was busy; too many people asked for the same thing.

Bombs fell that night on Osnabrueck. Their hissing nearly paralysed me with fear. Their impact made doors and windows clatter. A dazzling light illuminated my room. I pulled the blanket over my head and tried God once again. I was quite sure I was going to die. Suddenly I thought of the many Jews in their hiding-places who could never go to a shelter for fear of being discovered. I tried to be brave like them. I can't remember how long the attack lasted, but it seemed an eternity before the all-clear was given and the corridors filled with voices again. Eventually my bell was heard. The nurse was horrified when she realised they had forgotten me, and was full of apologies.

Mother insisted the next day that she should stay with me for the next two nights, and then took me back to Aunt Emmi, where we stayed for one more week before returning to Lehrte.

CHAPTER 16

Whenever the alarm was given during school hours, I sneaked out of the school buildings and ran as fast as I could towards our house. It was a good ten-minute run. My parents forbade me to do this, but I took no notice, and they could not stop me. The thought that they could die in the cellar without me was too much to bear.

Some people thought it safer to take refuge in the ditches in the fields rather than to be buried alive under the rubble. Most of the Polish and French P.O.W.s thought the same, and as soon as the alarm was given a clatter of wooden clogs (that's what all prisoners wore on their feet) was heard, as they ran down the village street towards the fields. Heinrich too, took his bicycle and, ringing the bell continuously, cycled furiously to the small barn which stood in the field where in the Summer he milked his cows, and where he now sat all by himself until the all-clear was given.

Farms and ammunition factories were given the greatest support throughout the war. People used to say the farmers never had it so good.

There were ample P.O.W.s to help – Polish, Belgian, French and now Russians. And then there was also the Hitler Youth and the *Arbeitsdienst,* an organisation of young girls in blue linen dresses and silver brooches, living in camps and put to work on farms, or into households with more than four children. Twice a week we, the Hitler Youth, worked as *Ernteeinsatz* [labour-force]. Four times a week no homework was given to us. We now only had three lessons per day, sometimes less, it depended on the "Tommies".

A horse and cart, sometimes a tractor, driven by a P.O.W. took us, always in groups of twenty, to the fields. In the Spring we freed the young corn from hedge mustard, carefully walking

147

up and down the rows pulling out the yellow flower by its roots. When the potatoes flowered we looked for the dreaded potato beetle, carrying an empty matchbox to imprison the little pest. 'The Tommies are dropping them from the planes,' everybody said, but we never found a single one.

In the other fields around us, women in headscarves hoed sugar beet seedlings, Polish and German women side by side. We enjoyed the Summer and Autumn work the most. We picked tender young peas, pulled up kohlrabi, cut off their roots, put them twelve to a bundle, and threw them into the trailers which took them to the markets. When we returned home in the evenings at 6 o'clock, our tummies were full of peas, our pockets bulged with kohlrabi and our arms and legs were stiff and sunburnt.

In the Autumn we gathered potatoes. Kneeling on a sack, we crawled in front of the loosened earth and fumbled for the potatoes in the sticky, heavy soil, putting them into wire baskets which were emptied into sacks by the P.O.W.s. It was not pleasant when it rained.

We made bonfires with the tops of the potato plants and roasted potatoes in the ashes. On the days when the farmer or farmer's wife did not come out with us, there was nobody to supervise us except for the P.O.W.s. When that happened, instead of having one stop for a tea break, we had several, sharing our roasted potatoes with the P.O.W.s.

"Tres bien," the French said and smiled at us. *"Serr gutt,"* said the Poles and moved closer to their girl-friends. They were always kissing and cuddling. The Russians did not say anything; they sat apart and made their own fire and ate their potatoes in grim silence.

We became very friendly with the French. We could speak a little of their language and we tried to teach them German words like, *"Ich liebe dich"* and *"liebling"*.

Sometimes we heard the sirens from the town. As soon as the planes came near and the anti-aircraft guns came into action, we flung ourselves onto the grass or sat in the nearest ditch. *"Merde,"* said the French and looked scared like us. *"Nix gutt,"*

148

said the Poles. "*Scheisse,*" said we Germans, and the Russians huddled together and looked up at the sky with worried faces.

We did not get paid for our *Einsatz,* but we got double rations; my lump of butter was the biggest in the little dishes, but it was the first to disappear. I was always hungry.

On the days when grandfather came to help father preach, I fetched him from the station. He had a very loud voice and as soon as he had spotted me he shouted: 'There she is, there she is!' which made me very embarrassed. I never felt very much at ease with him, especially when he insisted on talking to me in Latin for the first ten minutes. Mostly he gave up with a deep sigh of disappointment in my abilities. Grandfather wore pin-striped trousers and waistcoats. A golden *pince-nez* dangled from the waistcoat pocket. In the summer he wore a black jacket, and in the winter a heavy black overcoat, always unbuttoned, with a velvet collar and a wide-rimmed grey hat. He walked very slowly, taking tiny steps and dragging his feet slightly, always using a stick which had a silver handle.

Most of the people of our town and village knew him and were very fond of him. Every time he was greeted with, "*Heil Hitler,*" he stood still, took off his hat, turned towards the passing person and said in his loud clear voice, '*Guten Tag*' [Good-day].

My grandparents lived in a residential part of Hannover called Kleefeld, where they had a ground-floor flat in a large 19th century house. Lovely old furniture and pictures filled their rooms. In the music room stood the concert grand and an upright piano, both Bechsteins, and a clavichord which grandmother had bought when she was 75. Grandmother played mostly when she was by herself. Once a week, on the days when grandfather visited us, Professor Werner, a well-known concert pianist then retired in Hannover, came and played duets with grandmother. And sometimes, as a special treat, she played to Gewi and me. Schumann's *Scenes of Childhood* were our favourite pieces. Gewi and I sat quietly on the small embroidered sofa and listened to the *Traumerei* played softly and dreamily, the *Steckenpferd* [Hobby Horse] followed, happy and lively, and then the sad one called *Sick Child.* Grandmother's favourite

149

composer was Bach, and every year until she left Hannover, she went to the Bach Festival in Leipzig.

Grandmother was a very loving and understanding person. She was very quiet and always looked a little sad, I thought. There was a special bond between my father and his mother. Grandmother once told me that one day, when he was about three years old, she had found him sitting on the stairs in a pool of sunlight, with such a blissful and happy expression on his face as she had never seen on a child before. His large brown eyes were staring into the light. When she lifted him gently into her arms, he whispered, 'Mother, I have just seen God.'

Once in a while grandmother would lock herself into her sewing room for a whole day. Everybody knew that she wanted to be by herself and no one disturbed her. Father told me that he had seen her one day, after the first World War had been over for two years, sitting bent over a parcel, in one hand a letter, in the other a man's jersey, and tears were streaming down her face. The letter bore the news that her son, who had gone to Buenos Aires the year before, had died of pneumonia. The letter was on top of the clothes which she had just received. The official letter informing her of the death of her son two months previously had got lost. Soon afterwards, a 20-year-old daughter died. Two other children had died in their infancy.

Grandmother was one of the many German mothers who were honoured by the Führer with the *Mutterverdienstkreuz*, a large iron cross awarded to mothers who had had more than four children. Grandmother had given birth to ten.

Two officials in uniform brought the cross to her house, together with a document signed by the Führer, in which he thanked the mothers for their valuable contribution to the Aryan race, and encouraged the younger ones to give him more blond, blue-eyed *Nachwuchs* [rising generations] for the *Lebensraum* [living space] which Germany was fighting for. It was not difficult to burn the document, but grandmother had to go for a little walk in the wood in order to drop the iron cross into the nearest pond.

Grandfather was not a bit musical. His hobby was reading,

and like father's study his also was full of books. He read, lying on the chaise longue, one hand holding the book, the other under his head. His desk, covered with letters and photographs in ornate silver frames, took up the whole of the large bay window overlooking the square.

Grandfather was writing the family history and so far had traced it back to the 14th century. He wrote with pen and ink in minute and illegible handwriting, and father dreaded the day when he would be asked to type it for him. The wall beside his chaise longue was covered with miniature family portraits. Grandfather was very proud of his ancestors and pointed out to us, not once but many times, that we were descended from one of the oldest nobilities of Hannovaria, the *von Hinuebers* and the *von Papes*. One of the von Papes, my grandfather's great-grandfather, had been a friend of Goethe and had often been a guest in Goethe's house in Weimar. Grandfather still had letters which Goethe had written to him. Grandfather's mother, Justine von Hinueber, married when she was eighteen, and lived with her five children on the east bank of the Elbe on a beautiful estate which became the Ungewitter family seat. She was known as the "black" grandmother because of her very dark eyes and hair. Everybody in the family talked of this Justine Ungewitter, my great grandmother, with the greatest love and admiration. I wish I had known her. She died at the age of ninety when I was three years old.

Grandfather returned to the estate where he had spent his childhood and youth, together with his brothers and sisters, at least once a year. It was now in the hands of his nephew, the third generation, and would be inherited by his son, Carl Ungewitter, who was fighting in Russia. Usually grandfather went on his own. The flat landscape near the river, with the sharp east wind, did not appeal to my grandmother.

CHAPTER 17

Stalingrad, the Elborus in the Caucasus Mountains, and El Alamein were the turning points for Germany in the Autumn of 1942.

For the first time the little swastikas on the map moved backwards. Allied troops had landed in Algiers and forced Rommel to retreat.

The Red Army broke through the frontier at Stalingrad and cut off German troops. The word Stalingrad was on everybody's lips. 300,000 German soldiers were cut off. At the end of January 1943, Offi pulled out the pin over Stalingrad and told us, 'Hitler wants to withdraw his troops to spare them the hardship of another Russian winter'. What he did not tell us was that only 30,000 men escaped; the rest were killed or taken prisoner. There had been more bitter fighting for Stalingrad than for any other city during the war, and more letters with the official government stamp were delivered that Christmas than Christmas cards.

Ernst, from next door, came home on sick leave in March. He was one of the 30,000 who had come out of Stalingrad. We hardly recognised him. He looked like an old man and did not want to talk, and for the first week he stayed in his bedroom. Gradually he became more himself again. Before he went back to the Eastern front he came to see us. 'How you have grown,' he said to me. Yes, I was nearly 14 years old. 'Will you write to me sometimes?' he asked. Of course I would. 'It's all blood and mud and it stinks,' he told us. 'I envy my brother Heinrich who can stay at home.'

But poor Heinrich was not at all well. He was still cycling to the barn every night in the deep snow and frost to hide during the air-raids. There he sat, shivering and frightened, until it was safe to return home. His nerves had definitely taken a turn for

153

the worse. Sometimes I helped him feed his calves. It was so cosy in the large barn with all the animals under one roof. At one end Marie, the Polish girl, and the French prisoner, milked the 20 cows by hand. It was so quiet in the barn that I could hear the steady stream of milk hitting the foam in the milking bucket. Sometimes Marie would hum a little tune when she sat on the one-legged milking stool with her head pressed into the groin of the animal. The cows chewed their sugar beet pulp contentedly and the cats sat miaowing next to the churns, waiting to have their saucers filled with milk. Over it all spread the smell of hay and the sweet-sour smell of beet silage, which clung to my clothes for quite a few hours afterwards.

Heinrich spent all his time with the young stock. I stroked the soft noses of the calves and let them suck my fingers. Heinrich, with an unshaven face and a nervous twitch, stood beside me and watched me. 'What do you think of it all?' he asked me.

'Of what, Heinrich?'

'Of the war.'

'Oh, I don't know; it does not look too good.'

'They will come and get us, we are losing. Will they come tonight?'

'Who?'

'The bombs.'

'Probably,' I said. 'They mostly do.'

'I am frightened,' he said, his hands trembling as he cut the string around the sheaf of straw. I tried to persuade Heinrich to come to our cellar instead of sitting in the barn by himself, but he would not hear of it.

My brother finished school at Easter. He was now 17 years old and decided to become a farmer. For the last two years he had spent his holidays on the estate near the Elbe and had become very interested in farming. My uncle had lost his only son at Stalingrad and he liked having Gewi around; they were very much alike in character, and Gewi started to work on my

154

uncle's farm in April. Forty Russians worked on the estate, and my uncle and brother were the only German males on this isolated farm.

As soon as he left home, his room was occupied by a homeless lady from Hannover and her 25-year-old daughter, who travelled to Hannover every night and came back in the morning. Every time Elsa Barufke went off in the evenings she looked smart and heavily made-up, but when she came back in the mornings she looked exhausted and not nearly so glamorous. We also noticed that she always returned with a full shopping bag. We felt sorry for her; the night shifts must be strenuous and taxing, with the air-raids and everything. We asked her mother what her job in Hannover was, but Frau Barufke said she wasn't allowed to tell. We assumed it was a secret government job. When Frau Barufke cooked, smells of roasted meat and other delicious things came from her kitchen. Where did she get it from, we asked ourselves. Months passed before we knew what was going on. Her daughter became ill and stayed at home. No more delicious smells came from their kitchen. Finally we were told – Elsa Barufke was a prostitute and had contracted V.D.

After Easter our school was turned into a military hospital. We moved in with one of the other schools in the town. School now worked in shifts. Twice a week lessons were in the morning, the other three days in the afternoons. Our classes became smaller and smaller. A large number of my classmates came from the surrounding villages, either by train or on their bikes. The air raids made it difficult for them to travel, so as they reached the age of 14 many of them stopped coming.

A lot of subjects were cut out. Geography was combined with History. History concentrated on the Nordic race. We knew nothing about other countries' history but we were well informed about Hitler: Born on 20th April, 1889 in Braunau am Inn. *Landsberg, Mein Kampf,* etc., etc.

Other subjects fell by the wayside. No more Sport, Music, Art. Scripture had been struck off the list at the beginning of the war. Five subjects remained: German, English, Latin, History and Maths.

In May, Tunis capitulated. The Desert Fox was beaten. The pins on the map took a big jump across to Italy, and shortly afterwards American and English troops landed in Sicily. Would Italy stay our ally, we asked Offi. 'Of course,' he said, but some of us began to wonder if he really believed it.

At this critical moment a great crisis had arisen on the Eastern front at Kursk. We had lost the bridgehead of the Kuban and the Donezbasin, and there was heavy fighting around Kiev.

Meanwhile in the West, German aircraft bombed English cities. A hideous competition had started between the Allies and Germany to kill innocent people, destroy beautiful things and to lower the morale of the home fronts. German fighter planes, our *Sondermeldungen*blared out, had again sunk thousands of *Bruttoregistertonnen* in the North Atlantic, but we knew this was an exaggeration as our planes did not have the capacity to carry large amounts of fuel, and their fighting area was very limited.

Unless we could prove that we spent our summer holidays on a farm, helping with the harvest, we were not allowed to leave the town. I spent my summer vacation of 1943 on my aunt's farm in Mecklenburg. I had never been there before. I had met Tante Pauline only once before, when I was five years old. She was a very tall, handsome woman at seventy; in her long black silk dress and pearls she had made a great impression on me. I asked her if she was a Duchess. This flattered her and she kept a soft spot for me.

A cousin of mine from Hamburg, who was the same age as I, spent the holiday with me. We met at the station in Lueneberg and travelled on to Parchim, a pretty small town in Mecklenburg. The countryside was very different from ours at Lehrte. The train took us through woods of Scots pine, interrupted by clear blue lakes surrounded by soft white sands.

The houses were as different as the landscape, single storied, whitewashed and thatched. We got out at a tiny station called Domsuehl. There was nobody about except the stationmaster, and an elderly man with a long white beard leaning against a landau, which was pulled by a lovely Trakehner horse. The man turned out to be my uncle Fritz, whom I had not met before. I immediately liked this man with the deepset blue eyes which had a friendly twinkle.

Here there were no cobbled streets or asphalt, only tracks in the soft white sand, small woods of pine and in between, golden cornfields as far as the eye could see.

'How lovely it is here!' I said.

'Not in the winter,' replied Uncle Fritz.

We stopped in front of a long white house with dormer windows and a thatched roof. A wide flight of steps led to the front door. Two low barns flanked the grassy farmyard in which geese were grazing, and again, tall Scots pines surrounded the whole complex like a moat.

Tante Pauline ruled the roost, still elegantly dressed and bejewelled, although nearly eighty years old. With them lived Annemarie, their daughter-in-law, and her six month old baby boy. Their only son, Annemarie's husband, was fighting in Russia. I noticed that Annemarie's eyes were often red and swollen.

My cousin, Ingrid, and I slept in a small room in the attic, the only spare room left in the large house. Two evacuated families from Wuppertal, two mothers and their six children, shared the rest of the house with my relations. At one end of the house were the servants' quarters which were occupied by the Polish maid, Marie, and six other Poles, and ten Russians who came daily from the village camp, but had their meals at the farm. My aunt and Annemarie did all the cooking. The meals were simple but nourishing and a great treat for my cousin and me. They cooked for thirty people every day without getting much help from the evacuated mothers. Everybody in the house looked healthy and well, fed on a diet of meat stew for lunch, fried

157

potatoes and scrambled eggs followed by *Gruetze* (a sort of fruit mousse) with creamy milk for supper.

Each day, Ingrid and I helped Marie with the washing-up, which always seemed endless, dug potatoes and scrubbed two buckets of them before 11 o'clock, and picked fruit for the *Gruetze*. In the afternoons we helped with the bringing in of the harvest.

For the first few days we were exhausted and we sank onto our beds, nursing our sunburnt arms, not only sore from the sun but from the prickly sheaves of corn we had to stook. We got used to it and really enjoyed our work. We made friends with the Poles and Russians, who were much friendlier than the Russian P.O.W.s I had come into contact with so far.

Marie was our best friend, but soon I fell in love with Dimitri, the youngest of the Russians, not more than 18 years old. Dimitri's black eyes shone like stars and kindled in me my first passion. When we stooked the corn we paired up, Dimitri and I, and every time we stacked the sheaves against each other, our eyes met and our hands touched. *"Nix gutt"*, said Marie and shook her finger at us. Ingrid thought it very bad that I fraternised with our enemy, but I could not look on the handsome Dimitri as my enemy. Dimitri could only speak a couple of German words and I knew not a single word of Russian.

We never got closer than touching hands, except for once when I took a carthorse out to graze in the evening. I sat astride on it and my short skirt left a lot of my thigh exposed. Dimitri had taken hold of the halter and walked beside me. He looked up at me with his large dark eyes and his enchanting smile, his brown hand caressed my bare leg and moved slowly up my thigh. It was the first time I had been touched like this and I liked it.

I was afraid somebody might see us. *'Dimitri, nix gut,'* I said and pushed his hand away gently. *'Serr gutt,'* he said and looked disappointed. Quickly I bent over and gave him a kiss on his cheek. Now he was all smiles again, but I shook my head every time he wanted to touch me in that way again.

I shall never forget those summer evenings in Domsuehl.

When the washing-up was done after supper, uncle and aunt sat on the terrace reading the paper, Annemarie nursed her baby, crying all by herself in the bedroom, and Ingrid and I joined the Poles and Russians who sat smoking and chatting on the grass, waiting for the guard to collect them. The trunks of the pines were still warm from the sun. The sun's last rays filtered through the tops of the trees and left a rosy shimmer on their scented barks. Stanislaus fetched his balalaika and began to play. The others got up and started to dance. It was an energetic dance, not unlike the one performed by the Cossacks in our house some years earlier. There was plenty of stamping of feet, and dancing in a squatting position with legs outstretched. Ingrid and I clapped to the rhythm. The dancing got wilder and wilder and suddenly it stopped and the dancers flopped onto the grass.

The balalaika started up again, this time a different tune, slow and melancholic, and one after the other they joined in, looking dreamily and sadly into the distance. How they could sing! We guessed it was a song about their homeland and sweethearts. It was so peaceful, it was hard to imagine that there was a war on, that soldiers were being killed and that in England and Germany, thousands of planes were getting ready for their nightly killing of innocent people. Why could it not be as peaceful as this all the time?

The sun disappeared in a large fiery ball behind the golden cornfields, the midges still played in the warm air and the pigeons cooed from the more distant trees. Suddenly Uncle Fritz gave a sharp whistle. He had seen the German guard approaching on his bicycle. Ingrid and I withdrew quickly into the house. Reluctantly the others got up and walked slowly and silently towards the guard.

One night, Ingrid and I were woken up by the distant noise of thunder. For two hours the thunder continued, never coming nearer, never going further away. We realised that it was not thunder but a major air attack on a northern German city. 'I do hope it isn't Hamburg,' said Ingrid, thinking of her parents and two sisters. We got up and looked out of the window. Towards the

159

north a wide area of the sky was blood red. 'It is Hamburg,' said my cousin quietly.

It was Hamburg, the biggest attack so far on a German city, on that night of 23rd to 24th July, 1943. Uncle Fritz had heard it on the radio that morning. Eighty enemy aircraft had been shot down over the city, so the attack must have been made by thousands. Ingrid cried all day. All telephone communications to Hamburg were cut off, and she could only hope and wait. We all felt sorry for her. When the P.O.W.s saw her sad and worried face, they shook their heads and said, *"Krieg nix gutt"*.

The next day Ingrid's parents with her two sisters arrived in Domsuehl. Two suitcases were all they had left, but the main thing was that they were alive. Ingrid and I moved out of our bedroom and slept on the floor of the landing to make room for her sisters and parents, who stayed in Domsuehl until January 1945, when they decided it was better to go back to Hamburg than to fall into the hands of the Red Army.

On the day when the largest wheatfield was to be cut, Uncle Fritz sent us to the village to fetch Julika, a local woman who was a dab hand with a gun. We guessed what lay ahead. The wild boar had done a lot of damage in the wheatfield and Uncle Fritz was getting his own back. They had started to cut the corn in the morning, and when the patch got smaller and smaller, everybody on the farm, except for Tante Pauline and Annemarie, surrounded the cornfield with large sticks in their hands and forced the poor animals back into the corn every time they tried to escape. Uncle Fritz and Julika stood with their guns cocked and fingers on the trigger, ready to shoot. Two wild boar and six hares were the booty of that afternoon. Uncle Fritz and Julika had long drinks from the Schnapps bottle.

The Russians rubbed their hands and were already looking forward to roast boar the following Sunday. Meanwhile they carried the carcasses on a long pole back to the farm. Ingrid and I were near to tears for having taken part in the murder of these pooranimals.

There was a certain time in the morning when Uncle Fritz retired to his room and on no account was he to be disturbed. I

160

had borrowed a book from him and wanted to return it. I had forgotten that he was in his room at that time and did not knock. He was sitting bent over his radio and jumped up angrily when I came in. I knew at once that he was listening to Radio London. 'Don't worry,' I reassured him. 'My father listens to it too.' Relieved, he sat down again and we both listened. The situation in Italy had worsened. The fascist regime had broken down and Mussolini was a prisoner on Gran Sasso.

'A good-for-nothing race,' said Uncle Fritz. 'Always knew they couldn't fight,' and he switched off the radio, making sure he had turned it back to the Nord Deutsche Rundfunk position.

My four weeks in Domsuehl came to an end too quickly. I had put on some weight with all the good food, and looked well and brown.

Dimitri and I shook hands. *'Wiederkommen'*, [come back again] he said.

'I will, Dimitri, next year,' I promised.

How different the stations looked from four weeks ago. Homeless people from the cities sat on bulging suitcases, clinging on to bundles of bedding, waiting for the trains, which were mostly already too full to take on any more. So they waited for the next one. Red Cross nurses and Hitler Youth dished out cups of Maltcoffee and thin vegetable soup. Soldiers, lots of soldiers, mingled with the crowd. I had to change trains in Lueneburg. The loudspeaker announced: "The D-train to Hannover has been delayed for four hours due to a dive-bomber attack."

Sirens interrupted our waiting. Everybody pushed towards the large, sinister bunker on the station, large enough to take thousands, but everybody wanted to get there first, before it was too late. People fell, children cried but nobody took any notice. People kept on pushing, down the many flights of stairs.

It was the first time I had been in a bunker. I was terrified and thought I was going to be squashed to death. I wished I could have run home. I thought of Heinrich; he would have gone mad in this crowd.

'I am glad I am going back to the front,' a soldier next to me said. 'At least I can do some honest fighting out there. Give me the trenches any time!'

I got back to Lehrte at midnight, six hours late. As soon as I stepped out of the train the alarm sounded again. I left my suitcase at the station and ran until I reached our house. My parents had been very worried about me because telephoning had been impossible. It was so comforting to be reunited with them and Tante Krueger, and I swore to myself not to leave them again until the war was over.

During my absence some more people had moved into our house. Every night thousands were made homeless and the housing problem got more and more difficult. The whole of the ground floor was now occupied by three different families. We moved upstairs and my bedroom was turned into a kitchen. I moved into the small room in which the Jews used to hide. Through the open bedroom window I could hear Heinrich talking to his animals. More often lately I saw him running to and fro in the garden, always talking to himself, stopping in front of the well, and then running away from it, like a hunted animal. It was obvious that his condition had become worse. Herr Busch had heard the same rumours that Elizabeth had whispered into my ear, about the inmates of the mental homes, and he refused to send his son back to the asylum.

Food had become very scarce. Long queues waited outside every food shop. 'I almost can't remember what an orange looks like,' I heard somebody say one day in the queue. 'What is an orange, Mummy?' asked a little four year old girl.

Once a week I put an empty one-litre bottle at the bottom of a canvas bag, put my schoolbooks on top of it, and went to see Gabi. Tante, Gabi's aunt, filled it with milk and she took me by the arm and led me to a dark corner of the cowstall holding a pint measure of warm, foamy milk in front of me. 'Drink it,' she said. 'It will do you good, you are so skinny.' I drank it gratefully, holding my nose, because the sugar-beet silage left a nasty taste in the warm milk.

Once in a while Gabi's mother put a piece of ham or some eggs on top of the bottle for me to take home.

Farmers had plenty to eat throughout the war, but only very few were as generous as Gabi's family. People were quite right when they said that the farmers never had it so good; there was all the manual labour they could possibly wish for and exchanged goods of all description on the black market. People from the towns came into the country and brought with them articles which were dear and of sentimental value to them, but they were hungry and food was tempting. Not all farmers took advantage of these privileges, and quite a few helped wherever they could.

My brother and I had been keeping rabbits ever since we were old enough to look after them. We were very fond of our rabbits as they were the only pets we ever had. Since Gewi left to work on the farm, I had taken his into my care. There were plenty of dandelions and milk thistles in the garden, and in the winter I fed them on oats Heinrich had given me.

I was horrified when mother suggested one day that we should kill one of the rabbits for our Sunday lunch. The meat rations had become so small, we hadn't had a Sunday joint for quite some while. I refused to have our rabbits killed, but I weakened. I saw how thin my parents were getting. Tante Krueger, on the other hand, never lost any weight though her appetite was minute.

With tears in my eyes I put a rabbit into a basket and stroking it all the time, I took it to Opa Lieke, an old man in the neighbourhood who was an expert in killing and skinning rabbits. When he saw my tears, he said, 'They never feel a thing.' I asked him to wait a couple of minutes until I had run a certain distance away from his house, and with my hands over my ears, because once I had heard a rabbit scream with pain, I waited until he called me back. By then he had already slit its tummy open and was taking off the skin with his bloody pen-knife. He did not want to be paid, but kept the fur instead. Still crying, I carried back the skinned and, oh, so different-looking

163

rabbit. Never, ever have I eaten even the smallest bit of rabbit. I glared at my parents and Tante Krueger over the Sunday lunch, and if it had not been them, I should have wished they had choked on it.

Gabi and Anneliese had both become leaders in the Hitler Youth. They were the right material and took their duties seriously; whatever they did, they did it well. Inge and I were definitely not the right material and we had not the slightest wish to become too involved with the Hitler Youth. We had, however, become keen members of the *Sing-gruppe,* [choir] and now that art was no longer taught, we also joined the craft group. The Hitler Youth gave us plenty of chance to learn various crafts; the only drawback was that materials were difficult to get hold of by this time. Inge and I took up fret-saw work. Else, who had been our maid some years ago, and whose father-in-law was a carpenter, supplied me with plywood. Inge and I made keyboards, shelves, letter stands and little boxes, painted them in cheerful colours, and took them to the farmers' wives and exchanged them for food.

School started again in September. A lot of adjustments had to be made on the map. Offi soon put us in the picture. We knew perfectly well ourselves what was going on at the fronts, but Offi explained it in his own positive way. Did he still believe we would win the war? I am sure he did, and a lot of my classmates believed it as well.

'Badoglio, the Schweinehund, is a traitor,' he shouted.

Badoglio had sworn loyalty to Hitler but was secretly communicating with the Allies, who had landed a few days ago in Calabria. Italy and the Allies had agreed to an Armistice. American troops landed in Salerno, German troops retired to south of Naples, at the same time occupying parts of Greece which had been in Italian hands before. Some Italian divisions were taken prisoner when German troops took up position in northern Italy as far as the Brenner, and so yet another nationality was added to the P.O.W.s in Germany.

Offi had so much to tell us that the double German lesson turned into a two hour session on current affairs.

On the 12th of September a *Sondermeldung* [special announcement] informed us that Mussolini had been freed by German parachutists.

At the beginning of October we removed the pins from Corsica and Sardinia, and our troops withdrew from south of Naples to Monte Casino.

'We shall defeat our enemies from here,' said Offi and stuck the little swastika firmly onto Monte Casino.

A few weeks before Christmas we had a wonderful surprise. The whole family each received a small bag of three pounds of green coffee beans via Switzerland from Father's brother in Shanghai and a parcel with chocolates and cocoa from his sister in New York. Chocolates and real coffee for Christmas, what a treat! Mother never took more than six coffee beans at a time when, as a special treat, she made real coffee, and at the end of 1945 she still had some beans left.

I am afraid the chocolates and cocoa did not last nearly as long. From now on, when grandfather came to Lehrte he carried a small paper bag with coffee beans in his overcoat pocket and took back some ham or butter instead.

My father and his brother decided that my grandparents should leave Hannover and live on the Estate on the east bank of the river Elbe. The air attacks got worse daily; life in the country was definitely safer. Grandfather was delighted, but grandmother left Hannover with a heavy heart. Fortunately father's brother, who had "connections", managed to get extra petrol coupons, and a large lorry was hired to take the grand piano and clavichord, as well as the silver, most of the pictures, and some other valuable belongings, to the small Dower house which stood next to the manor house in the park. This was going to be their home for the next four years.

165

CHAPTER 18

1944 was definitely the worst year of the war. There was so much misery, hunger, cold and despair. The first refugees from East Silesia arrived when the ground was still frozen and covered in snow and ice.

We thought that the gipsies had returned when we first saw the slow-moving waggons with the snow-covered tarpaulined roofs from which pale-faced children peeped out at us. No young men came with them, only women, children, old men and shaggy little ponies which were thin and exhausted. Like tinkers' vans, pots and pans clattered underneath the waggons. The sacks, which had stored grain for the ponies, now hung limp and empty from their hooks.

One of the treks stayed in the village and many more followed until every farm had accommodated a family from Silesia. Other refugees from the east came by train. Our small town was full to the brim.

Frau Barufke and her prostitute daughter had moved back to Hannover. Their rooms were taken by a family from Breslau, a mother, grandmother and three children. They were nice people and stayed in our house for five years, after which a new house was built for them.

The smallest child, Diddi, was two years old and dangerously ill when they arrived. All we could see of her on that day were two large brown eyes looking at us sadly through the gap in the blanket in which she was wrapped. Our house was full.

We were now sixteen people in our small cellar and during air-raids we sat cramped like sardines. In the winter the cellar was full of underground water. Suitcases and feet were put on bricks, and we sat wrapped in blankets and eiderdowns, taking great care that nothing touched the water. My violin lay on my lap; there was now no more room for my bicycle.

Just before his 19th birthday in 1944 my brother had to join the army. After two months' training he was sent to France without first coming home on leave. We comforted ourselves with the thought that he had been sent to France and not to Russia.

Our swastikas on the map kept on retreating from the eastern front. Kiev was back in Russian hands, and the Red Army was in Estonia, close to the Polish frontier. Hitler transferred troops from the west to the east. Trains rolled day and night: transport trains, long and sinister ammunition trains and Red Cross trains. The last came from the east, driving slowly towards the west. Was there anywhere safe for them to go with the constant air attacks on German towns, we asked ourselves? Sometimes a Red Cross train stopped at our station and the wounded were taken to the military hospital in our old school.

Twice a week the Hitler Youth had "Station Duty". We dished out cold and hot drinks to the homeless who crowded the platforms, and when a Red Cross train stopped, we took large jugs with malt-coffee or hot soup into the trains, and handed them to the soldiers in their bunk beds. Their blood-stained bandages and the stench made us feel sick, but their sad, haggard faces made us forget our nausea. We tried to cheer them up. The response was varied; some still had some humour left, some eyed us silently but gratefully for the food or drink we had given them, some could not bear the sight of us in the Hitler Youth uniform.

The school we shared since our own school had been taken over by the Red Cross received several direct hits one night. Unless we found a room where we could have lessons, our schooldays were over. We were determined to carry on and found accommodation in a skittle alley behind a bar. There were no tables so we balanced our books on our knees. The map of Europe and Asia lay under the ruins of the school building, but Offi found a new one and fixed it on top of the score-board in the skittle alley.

Gewi just before he joined the Army

169

There were only ten of us left now, four girls and six boys. We were now the oldest age group; the boys older than us were soldiers and the girls were serving in the *Arbeitsdienst* [labour-force].

Offi was as confident as ever. He now talked to us about a secret weapon which was going to be put to use any minute now. Meanwhile the Allies marched into Rome and the Red Army into Rumania.

The air raids on German towns became worse and worse. Quite a few of my own relations were made homeless, but we could not take them in as our own house was already too crowded. All through the summer we sent baskets of fruit and vegetables to them to ease the food situation.

Uncle Claus, father's brother in Berlin, lost his lovely flat in which we had stayed, that summer of 1939, but he was lucky as he still had his house in Sakrow.

Everything was changing rapidly, even in our small and unimportant town. We met with unfamiliar faces in the streets and shops, people with foreign, East German accents. We were also beginning to wear peculiar garments, clothes were almost unobtainable, even on coupons. Inge appeared one morning wearing old-fashioned high laced boots she had found in her grandmother's attic. We all laughed, but at least hers were leather boots, whilst ours were made of canvas, with thick, uncomfortable wooden soles.

There was a large camp of Nissen huts surrounded by a high fence of barbed wire on the outskirts of our town. To start with, it had housed Russian P.O.W.s but these were now billeted on farms, and refugees from Latvia and Estonia occupied the camp. The conditions in the overcrowded huts were appalling and many people died of dysentery.

One day, an old white-haired man, dressed in a black coat with a wide collar of astrakhan, carrying a violin case under his arm, came to see my father. He had recently arrived at the camp in one of the transports from Latvia. He had been a professor in Riga and felt desperately unhappy in the camp. He came to borrow something to read and to talk to somebody of his own intellect. The violin he was carrying was a Stradivarius. It was not his own, but it was the only thing he had been able to take with him when they were all herded into the cattle train which took them, without any warning, to Germany. It belonged to a Jewish friend of his, a concert violinist, who had asked him to keep it safe for him, before he had been taken to a concentration camp.

Professor von Kurnatowsky asked if he could leave the violin with us for safe keeping, and from then on I had two violins on my lap in the cellar.

After a while, father managed to get a small unfurnished room for the Professor. On the day he moved into the small, dark room which he called his "heaven", he and I pulled a hand-cart to his new lodgings loaded with a bed, a table and two chairs. The Stradivarius was never returned to its former owner because he perished in the concentration camp, and the Professor took it back. I played on it several times, hoping that my playing would be transformed to heavenly notes, but apart from the thrill of playing on such a valuable instrument, the noise I produced was the same. The Professor became our good friend and after the war he taught father Russian, which of course he spoke fluently.

During one attack on Lehrte, the major part of the *Siedlung* was destroyed. The *Siedlung* was a new part of the town of about a hundred houses, built in 1935 for Hitler's workers. They were delightful one-family houses, with steep red-tiled roofs and fair sized gardens. Every family kept a pig and rabbits, and some people owned a Volkswagen as well. Hitler had looked after his workers well, but now most of them were homeless.

On the 6th June, for the first time, Offi's face looked worried. The Allies had landed in Normandy. Within six days 300,000 soldiers had landed on the north coast of France, and at the same time we lost Minsk, the last Russian city in our hands.

The invasion frightened everybody. Had Hitler left enough troops at the Western Front? Were we able to continue a war on three fronts after all the heavy losses we had incurred in Russia? My parents and I were horribly aware that my brother was in the north of France.

The 20th July, 1944, was a day I shall not forget. I was having a violin lesson with Fraulein Pook, when suddenly her maid, Emma, burst into the room without her usual timid knocking and stammered, 'There has been an attempt on the Führer's life!'

Fraulein Pook shrieked, 'Is he alive?'

Emma did not know. Like a mad person, Fraulein Pook ran out of the room into the street shouting, 'The Führer, is our dear Führer alive?' She was assured that he was. She came running back into the room. 'Thank God he is alive,' she said. 'Let's play *Deutschland, Deutschland ueber alles.*'

I had already put my violin back into its case and said I would like to go home. 'But don't you think it's wonderful that the Führer is alive?' she asked.

'Oh, yes,' I lied. 'It's terrific.' Fraulein Pook was a devout Nazi and I had to be careful what I said.

My parents were shocked and disappointed that the assassination on Hitler had not worked, and worried because they knew what lay ahead for those who had been involved. All our friends were disappointed, as were many more Germans, but nobody dared to express their opinions.

The Fuehrer was only slightly hurt and spoke to his people that same night. We did not turn on the radio, because we could not bear to hear his voice any more. Stauffenberg, who had put his briefcase containing the explosives next to Hitler, was shot on the spot, together with three other officers. 200 others were hanged within days and Hitler had their gruesome executions filmed. The persecution of those involved lasted until the final days of the war, and by then the number of victims had reached nearly five thousand.

Not only Generals and officers had been involved in the attempted murder, but the participants stretched into every class of the German people. Special instructions were given to all the clergy to give thanks for Hitler's survival, but at the same time father prayed for the relations of the victims. This he should not have done.

Offi had not been well lately and a young S.S. man, new to the district, had been sent to help him with his official duties. This young fanatic had heard that father had prayed for the victims' relatives. This presented an opportunity to imprison father at last. He arrived at our house with Offi and two Gestapo officials. Offi completely ignored me when I opened the door. They asked me if my father was in. I nodded my head and they pushed me aside and went straight to his room.

On the afternoon before this happened, I had taken father his afternoon tea, and found him with his head in his hands, sitting at his desk. He lifted his face when I entered, and looked at me. Never before had I seen his eyes quite so tired and sad, and he looked so thin and ill.

I had brought him three biscuits on a plate which a parishioner had dropped in on us the day before. 'For Herr Pastor only,' she had said. I am afraid I had taken a little bite out of one of them. They had looked so tempting and I had been so hungry. When I saw father's thin face I felt very guilty and confessed.

'I am afraid I have taken a bite out of one of the biscuits.'

'Take them all,' father said. 'I am not hungry.'

We shared the biscuits and left one for mother. I massaged his neck, which I often did lately when he had a headache, and put my cool hands over his aching forehead. Father had been offered a small parish in Westphalia a few weeks before, and I had been pleading with him to take it. It would be so lovely to go to the real country, away from the air raids.

'Can't we go, father?' I asked him. He drew me towards him. 'For your sake I should like to go,' he said, 'but a shepherd does not leave his flock. Can you understand that?' I understood and did not broach that subject again.

The same evening father was called to the hospital to give communion to a sick woman. On his way, he bought a small bunch of violets and put them into his pocket. Arriving at the hospital, the air alarm sounded, and immediately patients were wheeled into the cellar, the usual anxiety gripping everybody. Father helped with transporting the patients into the cellar but did not stay there himself, as a voice inside him told him that he

173

was needed upstairs. He walked along the long, deserted corridors; the doors to the wards were open and almost all the beds were empty. Only a few patients who were too ill to be moved had been left upstairs in charge of a nurse. An uneasy silence brooded over the empty rooms. His ear suddenly caught the sound of a nearly inaudible groan from a private ward. The door was ajar and cautiously he pushed it open and saw a young woman lying there alone, obviously dying. He went to her bedside and saw that she was a stranger, perhaps a refugee. He took her hand and asked if she would like him to pray with her. She nodded her head slightly.

The tense features of the dying woman relaxed and her eyes became more peaceful. Father remembered the violets in his pocket and gently he laid them in the hands of the dying woman. She clutched at the flowers as if she would never let go of them again. Her lips moved slightly, but he could not hear what she was saying. Her eyes looked at him gratefully and a weak but happy smile came over her face. She closed her eyes and died peacefully. Father sat beside her and waited until the "all clear" was given.

This had happened the evening before they came to take Father away for having prayed for those whom Hitler had condemned.

The young S.S. man said, 'I don't think you will be released this time. But you can always pray to your God for a miracle.'

He suddenly turned his back on father and, looking out of the window, he said in a quiet voice, 'Miracles do still happen. My wife died last night in hospital. Somebody put a bunch of violets into her hands, her favourite flowers. If only I knew who this kind person was who gave her this last pleasure!' He turned round and this arrogant, self-assured young S.S. man had tears in his eyes.

He and my father faced each other for a brief moment, then father said, 'I am ready.'

Mother and I had hurriedly packed a small suitcase for him, and in the presence of the four men we said goodbye to father. It was terrible. We were sure we would not see him again. I looked pleadingly at Offi who shook his head, but the S.S. man grinned. When father kissed mother and I, he, like us, had tears in his eyes, but with a firm voice he said, 'God will help us.'

We watched him go down the path towards the car, the Gestapo and the S.S. man on either side of him. Tante Krueger stood behind us and from every window facing the yard people watched him and prayers went with him.

An old parson from a neighbouring village stood in for father, but he was ill and the services had to be cut. Only funerals and weddings took place whilst father was absent. We had also been without any news from my brother for the last five weeks. He had always written to us once a week, and his silence made us fear the worst.

The next time I saw Offi at school he came up to me in break time when I was unwrapping my sandwiches. I did not look at him, for hatred was arising in me towards him. He put his hand on my shoulder and said, 'Let me see what you have on your sandwiches.' I made no move to show him but he took a sandwich and took it apart; he found a thin layer of jam on the slice of brown bread. 'Take my sandwiches,' he said, and put his in front of me. I could see thick slices of delicious ham between the bread.

'No, thank you,' I said, and pushed them away.

'Please take them,' he urged me, but I shook my head. 'I am sorry about your father, really I am sorry.' I looked up at him accusingly and saw that he did look sad. What should I believe? I was beginning to lose faith in Offi, my favourite teacher, who could be so kind and considerate, but yet he had helped to arrest my father, and at the same time he was offering me his sympathy.

A miracle did happen. My father returned after two weeks. Did Offi have anything to do with it? We never found out. No reason was given for his sudden and miraculous release. Oh, the joy when he stood in the doorway! This time we cried out with happiness and everybody in the house came and shook his hand again and again. If only we could get some news from my brother now. Every day we waited for a letter from him, and we

175

dreaded that there might be a letter from the government instead.

I began to realise that neither of my parents was well. Mother had always suffered from migraines, but recently they had become much more frequent and severe. Father had become so thin and often had pains in his stomach. One day they were so bad that he could not manage to cycle to the distant churchyard to conduct a funeral.

One of the six boys in my class had come with the treks from Silesia and was now billeted on a farm in the village. Once or twice I had been for a ride with him in a small trap pulled by two strong ponies, which had come with him all the way from his home. He offered to take father to the churchyard in his pony-trap, and it became a regular thing, several times a week. On the afternoons when I was free I went along too, and whilst father conducted the funeral, Wolfgang and I drove to the Autobahn Lake, close by. We got out and let the ponies graze. There were moments when we forgot all about the war. We lay back in the warm grass and shut our eyes and for a short while we, two sixteen year olds, dreamt of the days before the war when there had been no fear and no killing. Everything around us was peaceful, the skylarks trilled, the pigeons cooed from the wood; it was so quiet that we could hear the fish jump in the lake.

Wolfgang imagined himself back on his farm in Silesia. We both wanted to lead a life without murder, betrayal and fear; we longed for a carefree, promising youth. We wanted to listen to records, to dance, to be happy. Instead fear was constantly in our hearts, and a hate had grown in us, not only towards the Nazis, but towards other nations who destroyed our towns and our inheritance and brought misery and death to our people. We were aware that we also brought destruction and misery to other countries, but at that time we did not know the extent of the dreadful and unforgivable things our own nation inflicted on others. We wanted love to conquer our hate, but something had to happen soon to stop this cancerous seed from spreading.

Wolfgang's father had been killed in Poland at the beginning of the war. Wolfgang had been fifteen years old when he started

176

on the long six-week trek from Silesia with his sick mother and small brother. The responsibility during this journey had been entirely on his young shoulders. Those weeks of hunger, cold and fear he would never forget.

In the Autumn of 1944, Hitler declared total mobilization: total war. In his last desperate effort he sent 16-year-old boys to the front and commanded 60-year-old men to form the *Volkssturm* [resistance].

Wolfgang taught me to harness the ponies, so that from now on I could drive father to the churchyard.

For the last time we drove to the lake together. The next day Wolfgang had to join up. We sat in silence, both with a heavy heart. At last Wolfgang said, 'I wanted to become a doctor. Now I shall be cannon fodder.' He was so young, he had not even started to shave. I moved closer to him, he looked at me sadly and put his head into my lap. Softly I stroked his blond hair. Who else was there to comfort him?

The next day Wolfgang and the rest of the boys of our class joined up.

Three months later Wolfgang was killed in action.

CHAPTER 19

Now it was the Allies' turn to lead a *Blitzkrieg*. At the end of July, American troops broke through the German lines at Avranches. Paris was in de Gaulle's hands, and we lost Brussels and Antwerp by September. A bitter battle was fought over Arnhem and Nymwegen on 17th September, when our troops defeated the enemy, but in spite of this, by November, the first German city, Aachen, fell to the Americans.

At the same time the Russian army moved into East Prussia. From all sides the enemy moved in on Germany, and still Goebbels, the little man with the *Grossschnautze* [big mouth], tried to keep up the fast-sinking spirits of the German people and lied to us about the *"Wunderwaffe"* [wonder weapon] which would bring us victory. The majority did not believe him any more, and knew that the Nazis were making themselves ridiculous.

When Christmas came, the Hitler Youth Choir stood under the Christmas tree on the station platform and sang to cheer up the homeless and the many soldiers who passed through the station; not the nice old Christmas carols, but the new and meaningless Hitler Youth songs. We sang:

> *Heilig Vaterland . . .* and
> *Wir werden weiter marschieren wenn alles in Scherben faellt,*
> *denn heute gehoert uns Deutschland und Morgen die ganze Welt*
> (We shall keep on marching, amongst the ruins;
> today Germany belongs to us,
> but tomorrow the whole world will be ours).

We hardly dared to sing it. A soldier on crutches came up to us

179

and shouted, 'Shut up singing those bloody stupid songs. *Es ist ja alles Scheisse.*' [It's all shit.]

Inge and I sang with the Hitler Youth as we were told, but on Sundays in contrast, we sang in the church choir:

Dona Nobis Pacem, Pacem.

More refugees piled into our small town from East Prussia and Silesia, and with them came hair-raising stories about brutal murder and rape by the Red Army. The confirmation of these terrible deeds lay in the faces of those who survived the ordeals of the Winter of 1944–1945. Many did not make it. The weak and the dying, mostly children and old people, were left to perish near the roadside in snow and ice; there was no other way. The constant stream of fleeing, terrified human beings pressed forward, and could not give in to sympathy or heartache; nothing was allowed to slow down the endless treks on the small, unsuitable roads. The main roads were occupied by the vehicles of the Red Army, who stopped the refugees in their exodus, took away their warm clothing and food and abused the women.

Christmas of 1944 was the saddest I can remember. A letter arrived a few weeks before to tell us that Gewi was reported missing near Avranches. It could mean that he had been killed, but it could also mean that he was still alive. A few days after we received the letter, mother and I went to visit a friend of ours who had lost two sons in the war. The third and last was reported missing. Before we went home she opened the door to her garden and pointed to a small viburnum tree. Its bare brown branches were covered with delicate pinkish-white blossoms and it stood bravely amidst the snow and cold wind, a sign of spring, a long, long way away at that moment.

'Look!' she said, 'this little tree gives me hope.'

There were hardly any presents that Christmas. It did not matter. The only thing everybody wanted was peace. All the

180

families in our house came to supper with us on Christmas Eve. Potato dumplings with stewed prunes and apples took the place of the usual peace-time Christmas supper of *Carp Bleu,* and the next day another of my pet rabbits appeared on the table for Christmas dinner.

After supper we stood beside the Christmas tree and crib and sang carols. The tree and the crib were as beautiful as ever. The candlelight made the children's eyes sparkle as they knelt beside the crib. The two eldest recited the Christmas story, and father gave a short address.

He finished with the words: 'Look at the Christ child in the manger; God has sent it to comfort and help us.'

A little voice piped: 'But Herr Pastor, it is too small.'

'No!' said father, and put his hand on the child's head. 'Jesus is so big that He can be in everybody's heart, if only we would let Him.' The small boy looked at him and could not quite understand.

The grown-ups fought back their tears. I counted myself as a grown-up now. Everybody in the room, except for my parents and me, had lost their home. The husbands of the two young mothers were in Russia, and as for Gewi, we did not know where he was, or if he was still alive. And why did Wolfgang have to die so young? The Professor sat by himself near the stove, and I was just going to join him when the front door bell rang. I went to see who it was.

A tall woman I did not know asked to see father. From her voice I could tell that she was a refugee. She looked cold and unwell, and I was sure that my parents would want me to bring her upstairs into the warm room, so I asked her to come in. Snowflakes hung from her hair and headscarf, and clumps of snow stuck to her boots. With trembling hands, swollen from the cold, she tried to unbutton her overcoat. I helped her and brushed the snow from her boots. All this time she never said a word. She was quite a young woman, but when we climbed the stairs she moved with great difficulty and I had to support her.

Father met us at the top of the stairs. She did not introduce herself. All she said was, 'I have lost my child,' but it sounded like a cry of pain and a cry for help. When she entered, silence fell upon the crowded room. Father led her to a chair near the stove, where she sat for a while with her face in her hands. Her body shook from her sobbing. In her hair the snowflakes started to melt and, like giant tears, fell onto the carpet. When she became more quiet, she told us her heartrending story.

A few weeks previously she had left her village in East Prussia with her 18 months old baby and the other villagers. The child was taken ill, and needed medical attention, so she broke the journey and stayed for a few days in a hospital until it was well enough to travel again. The train, like all the others, was cold and overcrowded. She got out at a station on the way to get some warm milk for her baby and left it in the care of a woman unknown to her. Whilst she was waiting in a long queue on a different platform, the train moved on. In desperation and almost out of her mind, she ran after the train until it was out of sight.

Telephone communications did not exist anymore. Nobody knew where the train was going to, or when the next train was coming. She had to wait two days before another train took her to the next big town. She enquired at all the Red Cross centres, but nobody had handed in her child. Two days before Christmas she had arrived at the transit camp outside our town.

'Please help me to find my baby,' she pleaded, and clung to mother's arm. We felt only her grief; we forgot our own. The children had stopped playing and stared at her. She suddenly noticed two year old Didi asleep on her mother's lap, the small wet thumb hanging limply from her half-open mouth. The woman got up and went over to the mother and child. She stroked Didi's hair with a trembling hand and with the other she wiped away her tears lest they might fall onto the sleeping child.

I could not get to sleep that night. The woman's story was too much on my mind and I could hear my parents and Tante Krueger talking to her in the next room. I thought of Gewi, of Wolfgang, and I thought of the flowering viburnum tree. Once again I heard the little boy saying, 'But, Herr Pastor, the Christ child is too small.'

My parents' faith was so strong and unshakeable, and because I loved them and believed in them, their faith transmitted itself to me. I was still not yet sure if the Child in the manger was really big enough to help us all.

The woman stayed with us overnight. On Christmas morning, we found her bed empty. She had left very early to continue the search for her child. We never heard from her again, and all our enquiries about her remained fruitless.

Soon after Christmas we received our best Christmas present ever. It was a letter from my brother telling us that he was a prisoner of war in Texas and that he was well. These moments of relief, like when the letter arrived, or each time father had been released by the Gestapo, made the love we felt for each other even greater. From then on we received a letter from my brother once a month.

Our schooldays finished at the end of January. In peacetime, we should have passed our O-levels by now, and would be preparing ourselves for the *Abitur*. We had learned next to nothing during the last five years. All the schools were closed, there was no coal to heat the makeshift classrooms and the temperature was about 15 degrees below freezing.

'We will resume teaching in the spring,' said Offi, who looked very ill. In fact schools did not start again until the autumn of 1946.

Keeping ourselves warm was a great problem. There was still plenty of coal and food in Germany, but the transport system had broken down as there was no petrol. The only form of transport was the railway, but as railway tracks and trains were continually bombed, a lot of the food and coal remained in large stores all over the country. Sometimes a wagon-load of coal arrived at the goods station. The word spread fast, and in no time at all people arrived, waiting in long queues for hours for a few brickettes.

The wooden handcarts were our most useful form of transport.

In the autumn, when the large chimneys of the sugar factory billowed out yellow steam, day and night, for three or four months and the sweet smell of beet pulp spread all over the town, horse-drawn farm waggons piled high with sugar beet queued up outside the factory, and our handcarts stood beside them on the pavements. We begged the P.O.W.s, who were in charge of the waggons, to throw down some sugar beet. They always obliged, and after a couple of hours the handcart might be full.

The beet was then scrubbed and cut up, and after hours and hours of boiling the pulp, we were rewarded with a couple of pounds of dark treacle. It was all done on our small range in the kitchen upstairs. We were only able to keep two fires burning. The kitchen range burnt wood, and, so that they should last longer, we put brickettes wrapped in damp newspaper onto the stove in father's study.

On sunless days the house was like an ice palace. All through the winter the frost never left the window-panes. Even when the sun shone it could not melt it, but then at least a golden light filtered through the pretty, icy patterns.

A few of us suffered from chilblains because of our inadequate footwear. One of our refugees told us of a very effective remedy, though it did not sound at all nice. All the same, we tried it and one evening all chilblain sufferers sat with their feet in buckets full of horse manure and hot water. The smell of ammonia was overpowering and the short bits of straw tickled our toes, but it cured the chilblains. Rubber hot-water bottles were unobtainable; instead we heated bricks on the stove and wrapped them in newspaper before we put them into our beds.

Though my schooldays had come to an end, I was never bored. There was so much to do. Tante Krueger and I did most of the shopping whilst mother cooked and did the housework. Shopping took all day. Buying a loaf of bread could take anything up to three or four hours. Very often, after we had queued for a couple of hours, the air raid warning sounded, and however quickly we got back to the shop after the all clear was given, another long queue had already formed, and once again we had to join the end of it. I also did the shopping for Oma Thiele, our neighbour,

184

who had become very frail, and as before, she rewarded me with a very thin slice of smoked sausage.

Dina and I cut down old apple trees in the garden for firewood. We pushed the saw backwards and forwards through the trunk and I chanted: *Ein volk, Ein Reich, Ein Führer, Goebbels ist ein Luegner* [One people, One nation, One leader, Goebbels is a liar]. Dina laughed and nodded her head. Dina was not stupid.

Several times a week I drove father to the churchyard. The organist was in the army, and the old man, who had until recently played the organ, had died. There was no one else to take his place, except on Sundays. Father now wanted me to play my violin at funerals. This I did, very reluctantly, because it made the funeral services even more mournful.

On one cold February afternoon, father conducted a funeral for a Russian soldier. The Russians always buried their own dead and I can't remember why they had asked father to do it this time. Nobody attended the service except the grave digger, my father and myself. We did not even know the name of the dead man, except that he was a young Russian soldier. I lit two tall white candles beside the coffin, and father conducted the service in the same way he did for everybody else. He prayed for those who missed him in Russia, and he prayed for peace.

Quietly I played a hymn on the violin whilst father and the grave digger knelt beside the coffin. Then we carried it to that part of the churchyard where plain wooden crosses marked other graves of foreign soldiers from the camp. Slowly and laboriously we walked towards the open grave with the coffin on our shoulders. The grave digger was old, my father was not well and it was the first time I had carried a coffin With great difficulty we lowered it into the grave. The heaped-up earth around it was frozen hard and the old man used a pickaxe before we could shovel it on top of the coffin. It started to snow and soon soft snow lay like a white blanket over the new grave. The grave digger stuck a wooden cross, which said, "An unknown Russian soldier" at its head. I was shivering, father put his arm around my shoulders and held me tight. 'You are my good comrade,' he said.

CHAPTER 20

I had become good friends with the P.O.W.s of our neighbour, Herr Thiele. They were housed in dark little rooms above the stables. Every Saturday I took them their "Sunday treat" as mother called it. I gave a soft whistle – their rooms faced our garden – and out of every window popped a smiling face. They were so bored in their spare time, that combing their hair was one way of spending it, and I could smell the brilliantine from below. I threw apples and pears up to them and they leant out of the windows in a most alarming way to catch them, shouting thank-you's and other things in three different languages. Communications between us and the P.O.W.s, at least in the farming community, had become much more relaxed. I knew them all by name now; there was Emil, Henry, Paul, Stanislaus, Joseph and Serge, and they called me Renatta.

The air attacks on North West German cities became less severe from March onwards. Most of the cities were severely damaged and Hannover was one of them. *Flach* [flat] was the expression for these cities.

East Prussia was now completely cut off from Germany and Breslau was in Russian hands. The sufferings of East German people fleeing from the Soviet troops were beyond any description. To names such as Belsen, Treblinka, Auschwitz, cruel words symbolising the degree of evil of which humanity is capable, should be added: Dresden.

Masses of refugees waited in this city for transportation to different parts of Germany, on the night of 13th to 14th February, 1945 when Allied bombers transformed it into a sea of fire, and 80,000 people lost their lives.

March 24th brought the last phase of the war on the east and west fronts. British and American troops crossed the Rhine at several places and Soviet troops marched into Hungary.

187

"Deutschland kaputt," the P.O.W.s told me. I had never seen their faces so pleased. Yes, Germany was *kaputt*. Hitler's last idiotic effort, 60- year-old men in the *volkssturm* [Home guard], and 15-year-old Hitler Youth, could not stop the advancing Allies, but tragically many of both the old and young gave their lives in the last days of the war.

On the first of April we heard artillery fire for the first time, but we did not know whether it came from the German or the English side.

The last air raid on a North West German city was on the beautiful mediaeval town of Hildesheim, 40 miles south of Lehrte. It happened four days before the Allies moved into our own town and the Hildesheim was completely destroyed. It was the only time I have ever seen my father cry – when he heard that this ancient town, with its many Romanesque and Gothic churches had become a victim of the R.A.F. Lancasters.

A large army supply depot in Sehnde, a village 20 kilometres from Lehrte, opened its doors to the population when the Allies stood in front of Hannover and the artillery fire had become more than a rumbling. The warehouse was full of cognac and bales of tobacco. An exodus started towards this small village. Some walked all the way pulling their handcarts, but most of them cycled furiously towards the tempting goods. I am afraid I was amongst them. I did not go for the cognac but I wanted to surprise father with the tobacco. I went secretly because my parents would never have given me permission to go that far at this critical time. I was not a bit concerned about the artillery fire; the only thing that frightened me was bombs.

Henry, the French P.O.W. from next door, cycled beside me. I think there were more P.O.W.s than Germans on the road. Though they had not been officially released, they refused to work any more and nobody made them do so.

The inside of the warehouse presented a sad and debauched sight. It seemed that nobody could wait to drink the cognac. Many people had already passed out and lay in a stupor on the floor. Others climbed over them and stuffed their bags with bottles. Drunkenness and fighting were well under way. The other side of the warehouse, which housed the tobacco seemed slightly more civilized, but even here fighting had broken out and I did not dare to get involved in it. To my horror I saw that only a few bales of tobacco were left, and I feared that I had come too late.

I saw two men arguing over a bale, their fists lashing out at each other. They fell onto the ground and continued their fighting. Quickly, I got hold of the bale they were fighting over. It was not heavy, just cumbersome. I put it across the handlebars of my bike and, steadying it with one hand, cycled away as quickly as I could. I was thrilled with my luck, and the thought of presenting the tobacco to my father made me light-headed. Just as well, because the return journey was rather hazardous.

I have never seen so many drunks in all my life as there were that morning in April, on the road between Lehrte and Sehnde. The Poles were definitely the worst. Some drank the cognac whilst they were cycling, and with uncontrolled steering they drove all over the road, upsetting other bikes. Even the sober ones had difficulty in steering, as a bale of tobacco did not make it easy, nor did the heavy bags full of bottles hanging from the handlebars. Some lay in ditches near the road, drinking and throwing the empty bottles amongst the passers-by, and some had passed out completely. The Poles and Russians definitely celebrated their imminent deliverance, whilst the French were slightly more controlled, and we Germans just wanted to be back home as quickly as possible.

Suddenly, two low flying aircraft came towards us. They were flying so low that we clearly saw the blue, red and white ring on their wings. Everybody took shelter in the roadside ditches, leaving the bicycles with their wheels still spinning, on the road. I had taken the tobacco into the ditch with me. I wasn't going to take the chance of having it pinched. The Tommies directed their machine-gun fire towards the goods train thirty yards away from us.

When I came home and presented my father with the bale, his face showed displeasure and so did mother's and Tante Krueger's. Rumours of the chaos in the warehouse had reached

189

them, and somebody had told them that they had seen me there. But in the end father was pleased. It was excellent tobacco. We cut the bales into sections and hid them in the loft. Quite a bit of it we traded-in for food.

Hannover capitulated to the 9th U.S. Army on 10th April, 1945, and on the following day the first Army trucks, packed with gum-chewing soldiers, most of them black, rolled into Lehrte. It was the first time I had seen black men, except for the elephant keeper at Hannover Zoo.

There was no resistance. We had lost the war, but we knew it was better this way than to have the Nazis win, ruling not only Germany but Europe.

All the nice large houses of the town and village were taken over by the Army. A lorry and a jeep drove into the yard and a Captain with six men took residence in our house. Everybody was told to move out within one hour. When the Captain realised that father was the only clergyman in the town, he relented, and let my parents and I stay. We smuggled Tante Krueger in and they never noticed. They allowed us to keep the kitchen and father's study.

We were surprised at the noise seven soldiers could make. They were fairly friendly, but most of the time they ignored us.

It was not quite so easy to ignore them. They had spread themselves all over the house and brought in large amounts of food. One of them started to iron his shirt on the shiny surface of the old mahogany table, making a large burn mark with the hot iron. Mother took him the stand for the iron and showed him how to use it. He called her "a cute little momma". Two soldiers never moved from the harmonium and played *Chopsticks* all day long. There did not seem to be any order or discipline, and they never stopped chewing gum. For days after they left we found small hard balls of it stuck in the most unlikely places.

They were completely foxed by the old fashioned range in the kitchen downstairs. Also, the temperamental bathroom boiler was not what they had expected. They came to "Momma" for help, and we were kept on our toes all day long with heating up food and bath water. Our store of wood and the precious

190

brickettes disappeared rapidly.

Our knowledge of the English language was not great, but their pronunciation beat us. It was definitely different from that which I had learned at school.

Later that day a group of four soldiers arrived with a metal detector, to search our garden for weapons. We had a clean conscience and, amused, we watched them from the window. All the same, something must have made the needle on the instrument move up to the danger mark. Suddenly they were digging like fury, only to unearth a rusty old garden hoe. All afternoon they practised baseball on the lawn, crushing the clumps of snowdrops and crocuses with their big army boots.

After a week they moved out and everybody else was allowed to move back in again. One more refugee couple were squeezed into the house. Herr Mueller, in his sixties, was a tall, quiet man, a bundle of nerves; his wife, small and much younger, looked like a china doll with her ginger hair and white complexion. She talked nonstop in a twittering, rather annoying voice. Frau Mueller told us she had been an opera singer in Breslau. When she gave us a demonstration of her singing we were quite sure we would not be able to stick her for very long. Her husband must have thought the same. He shot himself the next day in front of the town hall. His wife was desolate and for once she was quiet. She surprised us when, a week later, she appeared in a new outfit, her face beautifully made-up and her hair freshly styled. She had exchanged her husband's clothes on the black market for her new bright red suit and shoes. From then on she twittered and sang again all day long.

Heinrich was in a bad way. Ever since the Americans moved in, he had been hiding in a dark corner of the barn. He could not understand what was going on. He screamed every time anyone came near him; not even mother could help him. Herr Busch decided to send him to the asylum, but Heinrich drowned himself in the well in the garden the day before he was due to go. His poor tormented soul had found rest at last. For quite a while I kept the curtains of my bedroom window closed, because I could

191

not bear to look on to the well below.

Hitler's suicide on 30th April in Berlin only brought relief to us.

The war in Europe ceased on May 8th. Church bells rang in the peace and mother played *Now thank we all our God*, on the harmonium. We were all grateful that peace had come at last, that the killing was over, that justice and humanity would hopefully rule from now on.

Meanwhile, the Military Police were kept busy controlling the looting. Russian and Polish P.O.W.s took revenge on those who had not treated them well during the war. The population of the camp demanded better housing, and they were hungry. A curfew was instituted; nobody was allowed outside their house after 8 p.m. All weapons and knives of a certain size had to be delivered to the town hall. House searches took place and those who had kept weapons wished they hadn't.

Three armed soldiers marched into Oma Thiele's room and looked for weapons. Of course she didn't have any, but seeing the chickens in the farmyard, they demanded some eggs. She did not know a word of English but she thought she understood, and went to fetch a large axe, which was immediately confiscated. Oma Thiele had meant no harm, but eggs and axe do sound similar.

An American padre came to visit father. Half an hour after his arrival there was a commotion at our front door and a soldier pointing his rifle at us demanded entry.

'Where is the padre?' he wanted to know. I pointed upstairs and showed him the way. When I opened the study door I could only just see father for all the cigar smoke, and the padre, who, like my father, sat in an armchair with a big fat cigar in his mouth, had his legs on the table. He burst out laughing when he saw his driver with the rifle. He had come to check up if he had been murdered, as his visit had taken longer than he had said it would.

For one month after the surrender there were no telephone

communications, nor were we allowed to send any letters. We were worried about my maternal grandmother in Schleswig Holstein. Passenger trains had not yet been made available to the German population, but goods trains were at our disposal. Mother and I decided to travel north to see if grandmother was all right. The only goods train we could get to Hamburg was a coal train.

Beggars can't be choosers, and we climbed into the open wagon and sat on top of the coal. It was an exceptionally slow train; we spent ten hours on top of the coal, whereas normally a train to Hamburg took three hours. Stiff, tired, black and wet – because it had rained during the night – we arrived at my grandmother's. She was in better shape than we were. She had been well looked after by Dolly, her maid, but like everybody else she was very short of food. We had brought her some butter, coffee beans and my last rabbit.

During the first night I was woken up by a peculiar noise coming from the street outside my bedroom window. It sounded like lots of people walking by, only it was more like a shuffling of feet. I got up, and saw below me in the light of a pale half-moon, a long column of German soldiers walking slowly and silently along the road. Some supporting each other, some limping, some with bandages on their heads and arms. The line seemed endless. Their silence was unbearable. Above all, lay the heavy sweet scent of the flowering lime trees. I almost thought they must be phantoms.

Another long column came past the next day in the midday heat. Again the silence, and everybody else looking on was silent. Their faces told us that these soldiers came from the eastern front. We would have loved to have given them a cool drink and an encouraging word, but the Military Police did not allow such things. We had lost the war, we had to remember. Mothers and wives went up to them holding photographs of their sons and husbands in front of them, and their eyes asked, 'Have you seen him?' The soldiers shook their heads. They had seen too many dead, they could not and did not want to remember.

One of the largest *Auffangslagers* [collecting camps] for

German soldiers was near Segeberg and throughout the three days we stayed with grandmother, German soldiers kept passing by.

The military hospital in our town needed voluntary help. As mother had a young girl again to help her in the house, I volunteered. I still had a horror of hospitals but hoped I might overcome it. The overall administration of the military hospital lay in American hands. They had their "office" on the ground floor, and kept a strict eye on the inmates, mostly German wounded, but also Russians, Poles and Serbians. Food supplies for the entire hospital came from the Americans. For the first time I saw their white loaves and tasted real butter again. I wore the Red Cross nurses' uniform without the cap and worked in the hospital with ten other volunteers for three months. We had one day off a week and worked from 7 a.m. until 8 p.m.

It was odd to see my old classrooms as hospital ward. All in all there were about 400 wounded. Our jobs varied from rolling up bandages, dishing out food, spoon-feeding the very sick, fetching bedpans, holding someone's hand whilst his wounds were dressed, or just sweeping the floors.

Those who had come from the eastern front, and whose wounds had not been dressed for weeks, were in very bad shape on their arrival. I did not faint, as I had thought I would, at the sight of their wounds, or the nauseating stench: what I could not stand was the fright in their eyes as they waited on the stretchers outside the operating theatre for their turn, holding out a trembling hand for comfort. Drugs and ether were not in abundance and they knew it. Some of the soldiers who had been so brave in battle now completely lost their nerve. Nurses were too busy, but we could sit beside the stretchers, holding their hands and talking soothingly to them, as best we could.

After the first month, the pressure lifted and fewer and fewer wounded arrived. Recovered soldiers were taken away to the *Auffanglagers* to be discharged.

One day there was a small revolt in the Russian ward. Because there was a shortage of staff in the kitchen, potatoes were always boiled in their skins. The Russians demanded that they should be peeled, but when this wasn't done they took the hot potatoes and threw them at us. When they ran out of potatoes they took anything they could get hold of. The Military Police had to be called in with their rifles to restore order.

I was always pleased when it was my turn to sweep the officers' ward. There was a good-looking young officer amongst them, tall, blond and blue-eyed. One day I had a terrible disaster in this ward. I had overlooked a bottle of urine under one of the beds, and with my broom I sent it flying across the room, its contents spilling in all directions. I stood, bright red with embarrassement, not knowing where to begin clearing up the mess. Everybody thought it was very funny except for the handsome young officer, who walked toward me with a slight limp and led me out of the room. He asked me where he could find a bucket and mop, and insisted upon clearing it up himself.

Lieutenant Joachim Ude and I spent a lot of time together from then on. Although curfew was from 8 p.m., it did not affect the school grounds. It was not the most romantic of places, but we held hands and kissed and suddenly life was beginning to be wonderful again. Joachim never told me anything about his time in the army. Whenever I asked him, he shook his head. I guessed his experiences must have been so awful that he didn't want to talk about them, so I did not ask any more. Soon afterwards Joachim was taken, not by a truck, but by an M.P. jeep to be tried in Hamburg. I did not know that he had belonged to the Waffen S.S. I never heard from him again.

After Joachim went it wasn't nearly so nice. A few Italians from the camp who suffered from bullet holes in their behinds, had been admitted. They had been caught by the Military Police stealing plums in the many allotments outside the town. They were told to come out of the trees, but when they took no notice, they were "shot down", and now we laughed at their sore backsides.

More and more soldiers were being discharged and at the end

of September there was no more work for us. Before we volunteers left, we gave a small variety performance. I don't know how I had the nerve to perform as Marlene Dietrich, but there I was, sitting on a high bar stool, my legs crossed in precious nylon stockings – donated by the Americans and dyed black by one of the nurses – wearing father's black top hat and a dinner jacket which I had smuggled out of our house, and holding a long cigarette holder. I sang with pursed scarlet lips: *Unter der Laterne, vor dem grossen Tor,* in the deepest and huskiest voice I could manage, hoping that my parents would never hear of my performance.

CHAPTER 21

When I met up with my friends and classmates again, most of us were at a loss as to what to do next. It was obvious that school would not start for some time yet. All the boys, except for Wolfgang, had survived the war. We decided to look for temporary jobs. We also decided to take dancing lessons. It was time we had some fun.

Fear and hate were leaving our hearts, but something else took their place. It was guilt for something we personally had not done. Yet we belonged to that nation, from which a small group calling themselves Germans, had done unforgivable and inhuman deeds, for which the soldier and the ordinary German was not responsible. Until the evidence of Dachau, Buchenwald, Treblinka and others was discovered, millions of Germans did not know the extent of the horrors committed in the concentration camps. We discussed if it was right to enjoy ourselves when there was still so much misery around. I think all of us, through our own individual experiences throughout the war, were more mature than we would have been at 17 in ordinary times. We would never forget the heartaches the war had caused, and was still causing, through Hiroshima and Nagasaki. The future offered us plenty of chances to contribute towards a more understanding and civilized world, even if it was, for the time being, only clearing away the rubble from bomb sites in our towns.

In October the Americans left North-West Germany for the occupation of the western and southern regions and the British army took over. The 224th battery of the 94th Wessex Field Regiment moved into Lehrte and one part of the town became the army quarters.

My brother had been writing to us regularly once a month, but since the occupation we ourselves were stopped from sending letters abroad. The new English Town Commander had taken up residence in the house of a friend of ours. She told us that he was very nice indeed, the perfect gentleman, not like the American Commandant who had refused her entry to her own garden to pick fruit and vegetables. She suggested that he might help with sending a letter to my brother. As my English was better than that of my parents, I was the one elected to ask him.

I remember the afternoon well. I was terribly nervous when I reached the house with "Out of Bounds" written on its front door. I did not know what that meant, and walked in. A Sergeant immediately stopped me and said, 'Sorry, you are not allowed in here.' 'Could I see the Commandant? I asked him. He looked at me, amused, and asked if I had an appointment with the Major. I did not know what sort of an appointment he had in mind; I certainly looked innocent enough with my pigtails. Mostly I wore my hair in a ponytail now, but sometimes I still had my plaits. I told the Sergeant that I had no appointment but that I should like to see the Commandant. Reluctantly he went into the next room to find out if he would see me.

Meanwhile I tried to rehearse what I was going to say to him, but I was so nervous that I could not remember a word. The Sergeant came back and said I could go in. I had imagined the Commandant to be an elderly man, and was very surprised when I saw a youngish man get up from behind his desk at my entry. He offered me a chair and sat down again himself. He had such a nice face; what struck me most were his rosy cheeks and his kind eyes which looked inquisitively at me from behind his glasses. I fumbled for words and eventually told him, in my worst English, the reason for my visit. He seemed to get the gist of it and, smiling, he put out his hand for the letter we had written to my brother. He said he would send it to England and ask his mother to post it to the States. He really was a kind man. He asked me what my name was and where I lived. I told him that father was a parson. I got up to go and said, 'Thank you very much for your great kindness,' and after the German fashion held out my hand to him. He got up from his chair and shook it and said, 'I hope I shall see you again.'

The next time I saw the Commandant was when I was painting the newly-repaired wrought iron gates to our yard. A jeep drew up behind me and he stepped out. 'I am a painter, too,' he told me. So, he was an interior decorator. 'I paint pictures,' he explained, 'Mostly horses.' So, he was an artist.

He had come, he told me, to ask my father if his troops could use the church on Sundays. He stayed to tea and we liked him very much. He had told us his name, but we did not quite catch it, so we just called him "the Major".

The second time he came, Tante Krueger opened the door to him. When she saw the Khaki uniform she had a mental block and for a second, she thought he was an S.A. man in the Nazi uniform and saluted with a *Heil Hitler*. Seeing the surprised look on the Major's face, she suddenly realised what she had done. In her distress she said, '*Oh, bitte vergessen Sie es doc*' [Oh, please forget about it!]. I am sure, had it been anybody else but the Major, she would have been in deep trouble. His kind smile showed her that he had not taken it seriously. In fact, I know now that he thought it was very funny, and of course Tante Krueger thought the Major was wonderful.

CHAPTER 22

We had not dared to tell my grandparents that, because they had now been absent from their flat in Hannover for more than two years, it had been confiscated. We were sure that for the moment they were much better off on the Estate by the Elbe than in Hannover, especially as it was in American hands. My grandparents did not think so and without telling us, decided to come back. My uncle and aunt tried to persuade them to stay but they were determined to return to Hannover. Telephone communications at that time were only permitted in a thirty-mile radius. We could not even warn them that they would be refused permission to enter the British Zone. My uncle took them as far as the ferry across the Elbe and from there they struggled with their heavy suitcase as far as the next town, only to be told that they had to return. It must have been such a disappointment to them when they had to turn back into "exile". Worse times lay ahead for the old people. Of all the family, my grandparents suffered most.

In Berlin, Father's brother Claus had been taken away by the Russians, despite the fact that his wife was half Russian. They had brutally pulled him from his sick bed – he had pneumonia at the time – and all they allowed him to take was his toothbrush.

Tante Clarutschka was driven out of their house, not being permitted to take anything at all. She had great courage and soon afterwards started up a beauty parlour in West Berlin, which was under Allied occupation. Eventually she built up a new home, where for the next seven years she waited for her husband to return. In all this time she was without any news from my uncle. Finally, Adenauer went to Moscow to negotiate with Khrushchev about the 50,000 German prisoners still in Russian captivity, taking with him a list of the handful of German scientists who were missing, my uncle amongst them.

Thus, after seven years, my aunt was told that her husband had died from a heart attack soon after he had been captured.

Some more sad news came from my aunt and uncle in Mecklenburg. Annemarie and her baby had got away before the Soviet troops had reached their farm, but the old couple had stayed on. The Russian P.O.W.s were taken away and when the troops looted their farm, they tried to pull the diamond rings from my aunt's fingers. When she struggled they cut off her fingers and shot her husband, who tried to protect her. Aunt Pauline died soon afterwards. It was hard to imagine that this peaceful farm of two years ago, amidst the golden cornfields and the scented pines and all its lovely people, was now witness to such cruelties.

Through a friend of my parents, Lieselotte N., I got a job with a school for the British occupation forces in Hannover. Lieselotte, who spoke English perfectly, helped with the teaching of the six to nine-year-olds. My job was pretty boring, but at least I could practise my English when I escorted the children to and from school on the buses. It was not a paid job, but I got my meals, and that meant English army rations, which were so plentiful that I could take half of them home every evening.

Food rations remained inadequate for nearly two years after the war. On the black market anything was obtainable, even extra ration cards and clothing coupons. Small wooden huts popped up like mushrooms in towns, selling cheaply-made textiles and household goods. Everything was badly made and of the poorest material, but at least it was there again.

We enjoyed our dancing lessons, and every Saturday went to the 5 o'clock tea dance in the Parkhouse. On other days it was used by the British officers and was "out of bounds" to the inhabitants of Lehrte.

We danced the tango, the foxtrot and the waltz to a small orchestra. In between dances we sat at small tables, smoking the American cigarettes somebody had managed to get on the black market and eating foul-tasting cakes. One of the violin players came over to our table, and full of emotion, he played and sang:

202

Bitte, bitte lieber Geiger mach Musik fuer mich
Bitte, bitte lieber Geiger, dafuer lieb ich Dich
Gibt es auch viel schoene Frauen, wo Dein Mund fuer
lacht,
Bitte, bitte lieber Geiger, spiel fuer mich heut' Nacht.

Many of the discharged German soldiers came from East Germany and had no home to go back to; some did not even know if their families were still alive. In the last two years the population of West Germany had doubled, and because of all the chaos in the months immediately before and after the war, it was almost impossible to keep records of everybody who had sought refuge here.

The river Elbe now divided Germany in two. The Allies occupied, with a few exceptions on the east bank of the river, all the land west of the Elbe, and the Russians ruled over the rest of Germany, east of the river, which was eventually called the D.D.R. (Deutsche Demokratische Republik). Berlin, Germany's former capital, was divided into three sections, the American, British and Russian sectors.

All foreign P.O.W.s (with the exception of a few Russians who preferred to stay in Germany, but were later forced to return by their own people) had been repatriated within the first few weeks after the war. Released German soldiers went back to their former jobs, if they still existed. Some, whose homes had been in East Germany, chose to stay in the West and hoped that their families, if still in the Russian section, would soon be able to join them.

In this transitional stage of the post-war years, any soldier without a home and work took on any job that was offered, provided it gave him accommodation and food.

Ernst, Heinrich's brother, came back at the beginning of July. Three years of fighting at the Russian front had left their mark on him. He returned just in time for the harvest. His father had grown old, his mother and Heinrich were dead. Many ex-soldiers, still wearing army uniform, the only clothes they possessed, were helping in that first peace-time Summer to bring in the harvest.

I stayed at the school in Hannover for only two months. Liselotte gave up her job in November and not liking the daily journey to Hannover in the cold, overcrowded train, I stopped going too. Liselotte started to give private English lessons and I became one of her pupils. I enjoyed my private lessons more than I had ever enjoyed any lesson of the previous years. Liselotte was an excellent teacher and I caught up with some of the lost lessons of my schooldays.

Liselotte not only taught me English literature but also German literature. We had missed out on so much during the war that my ignorance was alarming.

The best help I had with my English homework was from the Major, who now came at least twice a week to see us. At last we had cottoned on to his name and knew that he was called Greenshields, but he had asked us to call him Tom. At first I found it rather difficult to call him by his Christian name. He was so much older than I was, and as a rule we Germans had to know somebody for quite a while before being on Christian name terms. I found myself looking foward to his visits, so that when, for some reason he could not come, I was disappointed and missed him.

On some afternoons Tom took me to the riding stables in Kolzhorn, a small village about 15 miles from Lehrte, where a dozen horses, mainly Hanoveraners, were stabled for the officers. I had not dared to tell him that I hardly knew how to ride, as I very much wanted to go with him. Rather timidly I asked for a very quiet horse, and Sergeant Thompson, who was in charge of the stable, gave me the most docile bay. Tom's horse was a grey thoroughbred called "Danny Boy". 'It's the Major's horse and only the Major rides him,' Sergeant Thompson explained to me.

Tom soon realized that I could not ride. Patiently he showed me how to hold the reins, how to sit correctly and how to rise to the trot. When on the way back to the stables the horses began to get too lively, he fastened a leading rein onto the bridle of my horse to keep it under control so that I could arrive back at the stables with dignity.

Whenever we went riding, Tom fetched me in his armoured scout car from the end of our garden. I sat hidden in the back of the car, which was most uncomfortable and dark. We had to take care that I was not seen fraternising with the British, and the same applied to Tom. Somebody, unfortunately, must have seen me climbing into the armoured scout car, because one day a note about me was fixed onto the large notice board outside the town hall. The notice board was the greatest source of information during this time, and hundreds of people gathered daily in front of it. This particular note read: "The daughter of Pastor Ungewitter is fraternizing with a British officer who has made the child pregnant. Cut off her hair and give her the punishment she deserves!"

As soon as I heard of the note I pushed my way through the crowd in front of it and tore off the ridiculous bit of paper. Nobody said a word, nobody stopped me, and I am sure that whoever put the note there wasn't worth knowing. All the same, it was better to be more careful from now on. It did not matter that Tom came to see us, but we thought it wiser that I did not go riding with him for a while. My parents and I, and of course Tante Krueger, had become very fond of Tom, and I think the homely atmosphere in our house made a nice change for him from the army quarters.

It was made compulsory for us Germans to carry our identity cards with us wherever we went. A couple of times Tom arranged spot checks in Lehrte. Everybody in the street was stopped and asked for their identity card, and those who failed to produce them were locked up for six hours in a large garage in the town. During one of these checks, a woman leading a billygoat to serve her neighbour's female goat was stopped. Of course, she had not thought of bringing her identity card along as well. She and her billygoat were locked in the garage. She was not very popular with her fellow inmates and when they were released, after six hours, every one of them smelled strongly of billygoat.

205

Tom leaving his office in Lehrte

Apart from these little incidents no hardship was put upon us by the British occupation. The curfew was extended to 10 p.m. and after a while abolished altogether.

Christmas came, the first in peacetime. Diddi's father returned from the war just before Christmas, but the other young wife in our house was still waiting for her husband. Father's colleague and the organist also returned. At last, we thought, Father could begin to relax. During the war the population of Lehrte had risen from 12,000 to 24,000 and Father was at the end of his strength. On Christmas Day he collapsed with severe stomach pains. The doctor diagnosed ulcers and Father had to stay in bed for nearly four months before they healed. He became even thinner during his illness, and at the beginning of the new year we feared for his life.

A frequent visitor to our house was the English *padre*, Captain Merton. A rumour had reached him one day that father had died. He came immediately to see us. When I opened the door to him, he embraced me with tears running down his cheeks, and said how very sorry he was that father had died. When he realised that he had not, he embraced me again, this time with tears of joy. He visited father almost every day and supplied him with food he was supposed to eat, but we were unable to get ourselves.

Father had constant visitors all through his illness. It was touching to see how devoted his parishioners were to him.

As soon as Tom's jeep pulled up beside the gates, I ran into my bedroom, brushed my hair once again, put on some scent and rouge, but no lipstick – he had told me he hated lipstick – and waited at the top of the stairs until he rang the bell. I realized that I was falling in love with him.

The first snowdrops were out in the garden. I picked a bunch for Tom. He was so pleased when he saw them, and said that of all the flowers these were his favourite. He told us of the wild primroses in the Devon lanes in the south of England where his home was, and of the bluebells along the roadsides and in the woods. He told us of his parents and brother and sisters, and of the farm he was going to work when he got released from the army.

'Do you like farm life?' he asked me. I said I did. It was true; I liked being with animals and the Summer in Mecklenburg the previous year on Aunt Pauline's farm had been wonderful.

At the beginning of March, Tom asked me to marry him. I loved him very much but I had not thought of marriage. I could not imagine myself leaving Germany, living in a foreign country, away from my parents and friends, bringing up my children in a language I had not mastered myself. And anyway, I was only seventeen and a half, much too young to get married. Tom laughed and said it would be much easier than I feared.

When he asked my parents' permission, my father gave him the same answer that my great-great-grandfather had given when his future son-in-law had asked for his daughter's hand. 'She is too young and unruly.' (My great-grandmother, Justine von Hinueber, was also only eighteen years old when she married and, like me, was thirteen years younger than her husband. She became a farmer's wife and, like me, had five children.)

My parents loved and trusted Tom and gave their consent. They suggested that I should spend a couple of years in Switzerland to complete my education, but Tom said he wanted to marry me as soon as possible of course. They left the decision to me.

I decided to carry on with my lessons with Liselotte in the evenings, go and work on a farm to gain some practical experience, especially in cooking, and to marry Tom as soon as permission from the British Government could be obtained.

The Spring of 1946 was the happiest of my life. Tom and I spent as much time together as his job allowed, until he was due to be demobbed at the end of May. We thought it wiser not to tell anybody about our engagement for the time being, but of course Tante Krueger and Liselotte knew and they were delighted.

I still hid in Tom's armoured scout car when we drove to the hills near Hildesheim and had picnics in the woods, with their budding leaves and carpets of anemones and wild violets. Tom offered to bring along the food for the picnics, but when after our first picnic I realised that four tins of oily sardines and a loaf of bread was going to be all, I saved up my butter rations and, with mother's help, because I was not very domesticated, made some little cakes and sandwiches for our next picnic.

The first time Tom took me sailing on the Steinhuder Meer, (a large lake near Hannover), he dropped me off in his car at the far end of the lake where I could not be seen from the Officers' Clubhouse, but when he came to pick me up with the sailing-boat, the water was too shallow for the boat to come close, so I waded out to it fully clothed and got soaked. We found a remote spot where we could take the boat right to the edge of the water, and lit a fire to dry my clothes. Tom never got worried about anything, and was always cheerful. I liked that.

Once, on the way back from one of our excursions, we found a large carton of 50 slightly damaged Persil packets. We shoved them into the car, Persil being a real rarity. As I had to sit on top of the packets, I sneezed all the way home for 40 miles.

At the beginning of May the 24th Field Regiment got transferred to Westphalia, and at the end of May Tom was demobbed and left for England.

We had applied for permission to get married and now it was a case of waiting. Quite a few German girls had got engaged to English and American soldiers, but in Lehrte, I was the first one.

Meanwhile I got myself a job on a farm together with my former schoolfriend, Anneliese. It was thanks to Anneliese that I stuck to the job. Had I been on my own, I should have left after the first week.

The farm was a large modern one on the outskirts of Lehrte. Anneliese and I had applied for the job there because Frau B. trained young students in domestic science, and we hoped to get a good training in cookery. Instead, we spent most of our time milking cows and working in the fields. I got up at 5.30 every

Renate after capsizing on the Steinbuder Meer

day, including Sundays, and walked to the farm as I preferred to live at home. The only thing that cheered me up at that time in the mornings was my walk through a large cherry orchard where the grass, at the beginning of June, was covered with blossom from the trees, and the song of blackbirds, interrupted by the sound of the cuckoo, filled the early morning air.

Our first job was to milk three cows each, by hand. It nearly killed me to start with. Anneliese was so much better at it than I was. She had incredible patience, and she was also very funny. We had many good laughs which annoyed Frau B. She did not give us a minute's peace. As soon as we had washed-up the breakfast dishes, we set off with a horse and cart to the asparagus field, and for the next four hours we walked in between the raised asparagus beds, and dug the long, thick white stalks out of the warm sandy soil. By 10 o'clock it was boiling hot and we continued to work in our "bikinis" until noon. Half an hour's rest after lunch, then back to the fields, hoeing and thinning sugarbeet plants, hay-making, anything but cooking. I hoped that being a farmer's wife in England was not going to be like this. Thank God it came to an end after two months. Frau B., whom I had not told of my engagement to Tom, was told about it by somebody else. She said she disapproved and gave me the sack. I was only too glad to leave.

Everybody now knew that I was going to marry an Englishman, and all our friends were nice about it, except for Inge who had been my best friend for so long. She refused to see me any more and I have never been able to make contact with her again. I minded very much because I had been very fond of her.

The original inhabitants of Lehrte, my father's devout parishioners all wished me well, but the newcomers, the refugees, stayed away from the Sunday services. I minded for my father's sake. I knew that he was hurt, though he never said a word about it. What made me really sad was that once again it was as a result of my doings, just like at the beginning of the war, when I had joined the Hitler Youth orchestra. Neither of my

Renate working on the farm

212

parents ever said a word of reproach to me and they never even mentioned the half-empty church. Instead they let me feel their pleasure at my happiness.

By and by, the church filled again and gradually more and more people accepted the fact that the parson's daughter was going to marry an Englishman.

Tom's letters were illustrated with delightful pencil drawings of his dog and horses, of the farm and the house in which we were going to live. I had written to his parents and grandmother and they had sent welcoming letters back to me.

CHAPTER 23

The Estate on which my grandparents stayed had, at the beginning of the occupation, been in the hands of the British. This particular patch of country near the Elbe was given over to the Russians in exchange for another part of Germany at the end of the Summer. Conditions after the new take-over changed rapidly for the worse. My uncle was driven from the Estate by the Russians and my grandparents were also made to leave their house. They found refuge with the schoolmaster of the neighbouring village. Later the Estate was divided amongst Russian farm workers, and soon the land and buildings deteriorated.

When the Russian army moved in, the Russian P.O.W.s were still working on the farm. They had always been well fed and well treated by my uncle. The Russian soldiers gathered all inhabitants of the Estate into the farmyard and the officer in charge asked the P.O.W.s if they had anything to complain about during their stay with my uncle. Nobody complained except for one P.O.W. who had been a lazy so-and-so and had once, when my uncle had ticked him off for being too slow with the horses, given a disrespectful and objectionable answer, whereupon my uncle had boxed his ears. This he brought up in front of the officer. The officer took his pistol and gave it to the P.O.W. 'Shoot him!' he said. The P.O.W. shook his head and, handing back the pistol, asked permission to box my uncle's ears, which he did. He then shook hands with his former employer.

My uncle, his wife and two daughters did not feel that it was safe to stay on and escaped at night, across the Elbe to the western zone. My poor grandparents were now on their own, accommodated in a minute attic room in the schoolmaster's house. There was no food, no coal, no wood. The Russians had

215

confiscated everything, including their piano and most of their clothes and possessions, except for a small suitcase with some family silver and grandmother's jewellery, which the kind schoolmaster kept hidden for them in his loft. Grandmother wrote pitiful letters to us asking for food and warm clothes. We were not allowed to send anything, even our letters did not always reach them.

Grandmother pleaded in her letters that we should come and fetch them. She did not know that anybody trying to get into the Russian Zone from the west or the other way round, was shot on the spot by the Russians.

Eventually, towards the end of November, a hair-raising undertaking was planned between my uncle, who now lived in a village opposite his former farm on the west side of the Elbe, and my father. My uncle still had connections with the schoolmaster with whom my grandparents stayed. On a dark November night, a villager took my grandparents across the Elbe in his rowing-boat for a large sum of money. The suitcase with the silver and jewellery was all they had with them. My father and his brother waited on the other side of the river with a car. As soon as they had lifted my grandparents ashore, and before they had a chance to reach for the suitcase, the boat pushed off again: whoever had taken them across extracted a high price for his services. There was nothing they could do about it as everything had to be done in complete silence and in darkness. They were lucky not to be discovered and shot.

It was almost too much for the old couple. For the next two weeks they were compelled to stay in a transit camp without warmth or comfort. My father and his brother were not allowed to stay with them, and it was only when grandmother had a stroke a few days afterwards that they let my mother join them. Grandmother did not recover from her stroke and died in the camp.

Grandfather survived the ordeal and lived with my parents until he died four years later at the age of 92. (A few months before he died I flew to Germany with my one-year-old daughter, my first child, and his first great-grandchild. He put his trembling hand on her head and blessed her.)

On the tenth of December, on the same day that my parents came back from the transit camp near Lueneburg with my grandfather, I received the document which gave me permission to marry Tom. With it came the visa and the date of the crossing from Cuxhaven on 18th December.

Though I loved Tom and wanted to marry him, and I had been waiting for this document to arrive, suddenly everything seemed to be happening too soon. In just over a week, I had to leave.

Grandfather looked so sad and forlorn without grandmother, and my parents looked very tired, especially mother who had stayed with grandfather since grandmother died. It had been bitterly cold in the transit camp. Already we had a lot of snow and the temperature was well below freezing. It was going to be another severe winter. Dina and I had been busy cutting down more apple trees and the woodshed was well supplied with logs. Had it not been for the reassurance that Tante Krueger was there with her everlasting love and devotion to help my parents, I should have decided to stay until the Spring.

The last week before I left for England did not count as the happiest of my life. I was happy that soon I should be with Tom, but the circumstances of that particular time threw a great shadow upon my feelings and the old and dreaded homesickness was already creeping up inside me. Doubts, which I had tried to suppress up till now, came up anew; how would I cope with all the things expected of me? I was just 18 years old, but I was sure that for an 18-year-old girl I knew too little, and how could I explain to the English people that the war was partly to blame for my ignorance? Mother had tried to teach me to cook after I had left the farm, but it was all in theory; the materials had not been there for practice. Tom had told me that his mother and sisters were excellent cooks and very good at almost everything. I wished that I had more time to learn.

I said goodbye to my friends, to Gabi and Anneliese and all my other former classmates. They were back at school now – an extra two years had been tagged onto their school years, to catch

Copy of a letter dated 3 Aug 46 showing the
Regulations in force at that time.

"Subject:- German Women - Travel to UK for Marriage

There is no Directive at present but the following procedure is suggested:-

The applicant should forward the following documents:-

(a) Form 226 in triplicate
(b) Appx A to Form 226 in triplicate
(c) 3 Full and 2 side face photographs
(d) FSS Clearance
(e) A Statement from Mil Gov or other responsible British Authority that she is a suitable person
(f) An Invitation from the prospective husband
(g) A Witnessed statement from the prospective husband that:-
    (i) He is free to marry X
    (ii) He will marry her within two months
    (iii) He can support a wife (statement from Bank of Employer)
    (iv) he has accomodation for a wife.

Copy above made by:-

E. A. Bowden
Lt Col.
HQ 503 Mil Gov Det.

Burgdorf.
9 Aug 46.

Document for German brides marrying English soldiers,
(probably one of the first ones issued after the war)

218

up with all the lost teaching time. They would be twenty years old by the time they sat their *Abitur* (A-level).

I went to say goodbye to Offi. At the end of the war, he, like all other Nazi officials, was taken prisoner and sent for trial. He had been released a month previously on the grounds of ill-health. Offi had cancer and had only a few months to live. A smile came over his bony yellow face when he saw me; he held out his thin hand to me and said, 'I am sorry, Renate, for what I did to your father. We were made to do things we did not want to do.'

I took his hand and sat beside him. We knew we should not see each other again, and when I said goodbye, we parted as good friends.

There were so many people to say goodbye to. Liselotte, Oma Thiele, Herr Busch and Ernst, and the shoemaker and many others, and finally to Tante Krueger and my old grandfather.

On the morning of 17th December, just before my parents and I set off for Cuxhaven, the postman brought two letters. One was from Tom, saying that our wedding had been fixed for 6th January and that he would be waiting for me at Tilbury. The other was from my brother, telling me that he had been transported to England and was now a P.O.W. in North Wales near Ruthin and working on a farm. He was hoping I would come to see him soon, as he was not permitted to go further than three miles from his farm. It was a most comforting thought for my parents and me to know that my brother was in England. (My brother stayed in England for another 18 months before he was released, but he was given permission to work near us on a farm in Devon. My parents were allowed to visit us after two years.)

It was a beautiful winter's day when we left Lehrte for Cuxhaven. The flat landscape of North Germany was covered with a thick blanket of snow which sparkled in the brilliant sunshine and was almost too bright to look at.

We arrived at four o'clock. Cuxhaven itself was a dismal place. I had to report to block 501 at the army headquarters where I was given my boat ticket. The *Empire Halliday* was sailing to

Tilbury the next morning at 8 a.m. Meanwhile I was to go to barrack 68 to await further instructions. My parents were not permitted to come with me, nor was I allowed to leave the barracks until the next morning. There was no chance that my parents would be allowed near the boat to see me off. All we could do now was to say goodbye. I would rather not write about it, nor of their lonely journey home in the cold overnight train. I had been a lucky girl, with such loving parents.

Fifteen brides, all waiting to go to England the next day, huddled around the *Kanonen ofen* (the iron stove) in the barrack to keep warm. Before supper we were told to line up for a medical examination by a very brusque army doctor, whose main concern was to insure that we had neither lice nor V.D.

'I don't know what they think we are,' one of the group said, and we all thought the same.

We were given two army blankets each, and we shivered on our straw mattresses on the iron bedsteads throughout the night.

It was heaven on the boat the next day, so warm and comfortable, with plenty to eat.

All fifteen of us were accommodated in one large cabin. Erika, who talked so much about her fiancé, who was apparently absolutely *phantastisch* and owned a large factory, kept us entertained with all the new *Schlager* (hit) songs she knew: her favourite was an old one by Zarah Leander. *"Ich weiss, es wird einmal ein Wunder geschehn, und dann werden alle Maerchen wahr."* (I know a miracle will happen and all fairy tales will come true.) It was a very catching tune, and soon all of us were humming it.

Most of the group were going to live in towns, in Manchester, Liverpool, London. One went to Aberdeen. I was the only one going to live in the South of England. They were all over twenty years old; I was by far the youngest. *'Mein Gott,'* they said. 'Why do you want to get married so young?'

Towards the end of the evening we became rather quiet and Erika stopped singing *Schlagers*.

'Why don't you play a carol on your violin?' they asked me. I played and they sang. Halfway through *Silent Night* their voices petered out and I stopped playing. This song stirred too many memories; it was too close to Christmas, which we all wanted to spend in Germany.

Suddenly Erika, our cheerful companion, burst into tears. She did not want to go to England at all and confessed that her fiancé was a very small man of five foot five inches – Erika was five foot nine inches and very large. Besides he was not a factory owner but a vicar in Manchester. I must say, it was difficult to imagine Erika becoming a vicar's wife. We exchanged addresses and promised we would keep in touch with her.

When we were told by the steward the next morning that we were approaching Tilbury, a few of us went on deck.

It was a dark, grey morning. In front of us lay the coast of England, and the cranes of Tilbury Dock resembled inquisitive giraffes looking over a wall, as their tops emerged from a thick layer of fog. Faint lights, here and there, twinkled a welcome to us; all around the water was dark and unfriendly. An unfamiliar dampness, like a fine broken rain – I was soon to learn that it was called "drizzle" – descended on us. Suddenly I felt cold, frightened and very lonely. I went back to the cabin to pack.

An hour later I stepped ashore. My new and very different life had begun.